Fragments of Rainbows

STUDIES OF THE EAST ASIAN INSTITUTE
COLUMBIA UNIVERSITY

Fragments
of
Rainbows

The Life and Poetry of Saitō Mokichi,
1882–1953

Amy Vladeck Heinrich

New York Columbia University Press *1983*

The Japan Foundation, through a special grant,
has assisted the Press in publishing this volume.

Library of Congress Cataloging in Publication Data

Heinrich, Amy Vladeck.
Fragments of rainbows.

(Studies of the East Asian Institute)
Bibliography: p.
Includes index.
1. Saitō, Mokichi, 1882–1953.   2. Poets,
Japanese—20th century—Biography.   I. Title.
II. Series.
PL816.A5Z67   1983   895.6'14   82-12989
ISBN 0-231-05428-9

Columbia University Press
New York   Guildford, Surrey

Clothbound editions of Columbia University Press books are Smyth-sewn and
printed on permanent and durable acid-free paper.

For
Richard, Willy, and Danny

THE EAST ASIAN INSTITUTE OF
COLUMBIA UNIVERSITY

The East Asian Institute is Columbia University's center for research, education, and publication on modern East Asia.

The Studies of the East Asian Institute were inaugurated in 1962 to bring to a wider public the results of significant new research on modern and contemporary East Asia.

Contents

Preface

One of Saitō Mokichi's most famous poems is part of a sequence entitled "Shinitamau haha" (My mother is dying):

shi ni chikaki	As I lie beside my mother
haha ni soine no	who is close to death,
shinshin to	piercingly the call
tōta no kawazu	of frogs in distant fields
ten ni kikoyu	echoes in the heavens.

When I first read this poem, it moved me deeply—by the juxtaposition of the close stillness of death with the distant lushness of frogs in wet fields, by the slow pivot of the third line balancing the contrasting images, and by the immense pool of emotion implied beneath the surface ripples of the poem. It is a short work of great depth, which is even more powerful in its context within the sequence.

After reading a few of Mokichi's poems, I wanted to read more, at first for the experience—moving and unsettling and deeply satisfying—that such good poems provide, but later to try to understand how the poems were made that they are so effective, and to learn more about the materials with which they were formed. This study is a result of that exploration; in it I hope to illuminate some of the sources of Mokichi's poetry, explain the workings of various aspects of his art, and provide the English reader with a representative sampling of the poems.

In recent years, there has been a proliferation of books on Mokichi's life and work. One of his major disciples, Satō Satarō, noticed the increasing popularity of such studies and wrote:

> I suppose such things as whom he was in love with in what year, or the excavation of minute details, constitute research, but when I read that sort of thing I feel a kind of loneliness, an emptiness. Mokichi the man lives in his *tanka,* and it is impossible to think of Mokichi separated from *tanka.*[1]

Doubtless an intimate knowledge of the poetry is the best means toward an understanding of the poet. However, without some basic biographical information, some of Mokichi's poetry can be confusing or even, at times, misleading. For example, the following poem is from Mokichi's first published collection, *Shakkō* (Crimson light):

kyōjamori	The guardian of madmen
megane o kakete	puts on his glasses
asaborake	as the dawn breaks;
kyōin e yukazu	goes not to the asylum
Fuji no yama mi ori	but stands watching Mt. Fuji.

If a reader is unaware that the "guardian of madmen" is the poet himself, and that his choice of the terms for psychiatrist and mental hospital was guided not by a feeling of scorn but by a troubled assessment of the value of his own role, the tone of the poem is almost inaccessible. Mokichi was a physician specializing in mental illnesses throughout his adult life. The development of his medical career is reflected in his poetry, but not described; such information must come from elsewhere.

Mokichi was also a literary scholar and critic, a poetic theorist, and essayist, and these activities left a mark on his poetry. In addition, of course, he had ways and histories of relating to his parents, foster parents, wife, children, colleagues, and friends. He expected his readers to know something about his life, and indeed provided much of his biographical history in the form of memoirs and essays. While a great deal of the knowledge relevent to an understanding of the poetry can be drawn directly from the poems, many of the details cannot. With the appropriate information, the meaning of many poems, such as the following, can be expanded for the reader:

| akaaka to | Brightly, brightly |
| ippon no michi | the solitary road |

tōritari	passes through:
tamakiwaru waga	it has come to be
inochi narikeri	my own inviolable life.

Part one of this study, therefore, is a literary biography, in which I hope to provide the information that will enrich the reader's understanding of the poetry. Chapter 1 treats Mokichi's childhood in rural Japan; his move to Tokyo as a foster son, and eventually son-in-law, of a distant relative, his medical education and training; his marriage; and his early interest in poetry. Chapter 2 concerns the years spent in Nagasaki as doctor and professor, as well as the literary theories he developed there; his studies in neuropsychiatry in Vienna and Munich; and the difficult following years when he had to superintend the rebuilding of his hospital, which had been destroyed by fire. The final chapter in part one covers Mokichi's separation from his wife and later attachment to another woman, his war poetry, and the last years of his life when he returned to his native countryside.

Part two focuses on specific questions raised by his poetry, in the context of the biographical background. Chapter 4 analyzes Mokichi's choice of the *tanka* as his means of poetic expression with a detailed examination of his use of the form, its content in terms of sound and the quality of imagery, and his use of language, particularly the influence of the *Man'yōshū*. Chapter 5 concerns the *rensaku*, "a poetic form using more than two poems to treat a theme which cannot be exhaustively treated in one poem. Yet it is not simply a gathering together of single poems, but must arrange independent poems so as to compose a single, unified form."[2] The "Ohiro" sequence is examined in detail, with particular attention to its structure and imagery, and the nature of Mokichi's use in it of narrative techniques. The final chapter discusses two important subjects in Mokichi's poetry as a whole, his images of himself, especially in his role as "guardian of madmen," and his nature poetry. The last chapter discusses the response called forth by Mokichi's poetry: readers have had an unusual sense of intimacy with the poet, which derives from the structural and thematic unity of his body of work, his lifetime "rensaku."

Within the two parts of this study and the appendixes, 219 of Mokichi's poems are presented in translation. They are the fundamental material of this study, and if they do not seem in themselves worthy of the amount of discussion that surrounds them, the point of the study would be lost. Therefore the selection and translation of the poems that do appear is vitally important. Over the course of his career, Mokichi wrote about 17,600 poems, of which 14,200 were published in his seventeen volumes of poetry—over a poem a day, on the average, for the length of his career.[3] The selection of such a small percentage of his poetry for inclusion was a difficult process, and was based on three criteria: I chose first from among those poems that I thought both his best and most representative; second, in order to avoid an idiosyncratic collection based on my taste alone, I included many of the poems other critics have referred to most consistently; finally, I chose poems whose translations seemed to communicate most clearly a sense of the original work.

The translations were made with two goals in mind: that the poems, using Mokichi's conceptions, images, and tone, would read as poetry in English; and that they would be as faithful as possible to the originals, so that the discussion of the Japanese poems in the text would be comprehensible to the readers of the English versions alone. There are many obstacles in the way of achieving these goals. Good poems usually have implied meanings as well as immediately apparent ones, and the transition from a frequently nonspecific, ambiguous poetic language such as Japanese to the more specific and concrete English means that often one interpretation is offered at the expense of other, perhaps more subtle, ones.

Tanka, the form Mokichi used almost exclusively, are thirty-one syllable poems divided into five lines of 5–7–5–7–7 syllables respectively, although they are usually printed in one line. I have rarely been able to preserve the syllable count, but I have tried to have the linear structure of the English reflect the Japanese. I have also tried to retain the order in which images appear in the poems, although the demands of English syntax, often the reverse of the Japanese, occasionally made this impossible. With these and other difficulties facing the translator, clearly much of the poem is missing, but I have no doubt that it is better to have even a pale version of Mokichi's wonderfully powerful poems than no version at all.

Toward the end of his life, Mokichi wrote many poems on the beauties of the Mogami River. One in particular can be read not only as a depiction of scenic beauty but as an image of the poet himself, separated from us by time and language, as he appears in his poetry:

Mogamigawa no   Lingering there,
jōkū ni shite   in the skies above
nokoreru wa   Mogami River,
imada utsukushiki   still so lovely:
niji no danpen   fragments of rainbows.

Acknowledgments

Many teachers, colleagues, and friends have been kind enough to read my manuscript in its various forms. Although I might not always have had the sense to follow their advice, the book is the better for their help. Among them I am particularly indebted to Riva Danzig, Van C. Gessel, Earl Miner, James W. Morley, Edwin Seidensticker, and especially Marsha Wagner. While I was doing research in Japan, Haga Tōru, Kobori Keiichirō, and Kajiki Gō were generous with their time and advice. Takagi Kiyoko in particular, as well as other members of the Uchūfū Tankakai, taught me a great deal about the tanka form.

I am most grateful to the Japan Foundation for its support of the publication of this book. Dr. Saitō Shigeta has kindly given me much encouragement, as well as permission to translate his father's poetry and to reproduce the paintings for the frontispiece and jacket from photographs in Saitŏ Shigeta, eds., *Saitŏ Mokichi zengashŭ* (Chūō kōron bijutsu shuppan, 1969). *Monumenta Nipponica* has allowed me to include in appendix 2 the translations of "Shinitamau haha" (My mother is haha" (My mother is dying) which first appeared in that journal in winter 1978, vol. 33, no. 4.

Thanks are due to the following publishers for permission to quote excerpts from the poems of other authors: Farrar, Straus, & Giroux, Inc. for John Berryman's "Snow Line," 77 *Dream Songs,* copyright © 1959, 1962, 1963, 1964 by John Berryman; Little, Brown and Company for Emily Dickinson's "This was a Poet," *The Complete Poems of Emily Dickinson,* ed. by Thomas H. Johnson, copyright 1929 by Martha Dickinson Bianchi, copyright © renewed 1957 by Mary L. Hampson, and the Belknap Press of Harvard University Press and the Trustees of Amherst College for the same poem in the variorum edition, *The Poems of Emily Dickinson,* ed. by Thomas H. Johnson, copyright 1951, © 1955, 1979 by the President and Fellows of Harvard College; Random House, Inc., for W. H. Auden's "Musée des Beaux Arts," *W. H. Auden: Collected Poems,* ed. by Edward Mendelson, copyright 1940 by W. H. Auden; and Penguin Books Ltd. for Goethe's *Faust/Part Two,* trans. by Philip Wayne, copyright © 1959 by the Estate of Philip Wayne.

My husband, Richard A. Heinrich, and my parents, Dr. Abraham Klein and Mrs. Irene L. Vladeck Klein, have provided continuing support and encouragement, and my sons William and Daniel have provided me with an abiding source of a sense of proportion.

Finally, I am especially grateful to Professor Donald Keene, for introducing me to Mokichi's poetry and encouraging me to study it; for his careful and perceptive reading of my work over the years; and for convincing me to learn to write tanka, which has increased immeasurably my skill and pleasure in reading them.

Part One

A LITERARY BIOGRAPHY

CHAPTER ONE
Childhood, Marriage, and Medicine, 1882–1917

Early Years

THE small city of Kaminoyama in Yamagata prefecture incorporates the village of Kanakame, separated from the city proper by fields and woods and streams. It still looks very much as it must have looked in 1882, when a third son was born into the Moriya family. The house in which this birth took place has since been rebuilt from the foundations up, and the temple next door, Hōsenji, has a new main hall.[1] In its precincts is the gravestone commemorating the death of the Moriya son, seventy years later, after he had achieved great fame far from his village as the poet Saitō Mokichi.

The Moriya family farmed about eleven acres (4.5 hectares), and raised silkworms in the house. When Mokichi was born, the household consisted of seven other family members: his father Kumajirō, who had been adopted into his wife's family; his mother Iku; a maternal aunt and uncle who, as heads of the family, were treated as grandparents; his maternal grandmother; and two older brothers: Hirokichi, eight, and Tomotarō, six. Four years later the first daughter, Matsu, was born, but she died in infancy. The next year, another son, Naokichi, was born, and ten years after Mokichi's birth a final child, the daughter Nao, completed the family. This large household was one of the four or five interrelated, prosperous families of the village. It usually could afford two or three maids to help with the household work, principally to share the burdens of the silkworm cultivation with Iku. Mokichi himself never seems to have had to do farm work.[2]

But prosperity is relative, and the Moriyas worked hard for their position. Kumajirō was an active, energetic man, who sang and danced in all the village festivities, studied calligraphy and political speaking, and was a devoted Buddhist of the Jishū sect. But he developed a chronic asthmatic cough before Mokichi was born which lasted his whole life, and by his forties, "because he had worked terribly hard," was bent over from the hips like an old man.[3] He continued to work hard until his death at seventy-four, about which Mokichi later wrote: "In the heat of a midsummer day, he was weeding the fields; afterwards he developed a high fever and finally died of it."[4] Iku was, by contrast, a large, placid woman who preferred to spend her time at home. She was sensitive to weather changes, which caused her severe headaches. This union of contrasts between the skinny, active man and the large, passive woman seems to have been comfortable, however, and the family a happy one.

Mokichi is often said to have had a weak constitution as a child, which was explained in his family by the fact that he was born after his father had developed his chronic cough. In *Nenjushū* (Prayerbead collection), recollections of his childhood written after his father's death, Mokichi tells of playing near his mother in the kitchen while his father was occupied with his devotions at the household Buddhist altar. When Kumajirō was stricken by an attack of his asthmatic cough, Mokichi would mimic the odd sound of it. His mother would at first glare at him, but in the end the cleverness of his imitation would make her laugh.[5]

Mokichi's "weak constitution" seems to have been manifested primarily in bed-wetting problems, which continued into adolescence; and in unusually sensitive skin. Otherwise, he seems to have been a normal, active and mischievous child, involved in the same activities as the other village boys. The Sino-Japanese War of 1894–1895 inspired a generation of little boys with a passion for war games. The boys from Kanakame formed an army and, with Mokichi as general, charged the neighboring village. His leadership in such games may have reflected his family's standing in the community, or his own scholastic success, but it would not have been possible if his own constitution were so frail that he could not join the other children in their "wars." When these war games took place on the riverbank behind Hōsenji, and the boys got wet, they would make a fire using the wooden grave tablets as fuel in order to dry their kimonos.[6]

Hōsenji was, in fact, almost a second home to Mokichi. He and his younger brother Naokichi were in and out of the temple all day. The influence of its priest Sawara Ryūō remained with Mokichi for the rest of his life, in the way he would close his eyes to think, or write characters in the air. Hōsenji had for its basic tenets the three Amida sutras, and the efficacy of reciting the name of Amida, the *nenbutsu,* as the means of achieving rebirth in the Pure Land, or paradise. Kumajirō was especially devout, but all the villagers of Kanakame memorized at least parts of the Amida sutras. Mokichi was later to draw from a description of paradise in one of these sutras the title of his first volume of poetry, *Shakkō* (Crimson light). The word *shakkō* itself was part of a phrase he often heard a young apprentice priest chant while he did his chores, *shakushiki shakkō byakushiki byakkō* ("from the red-colored [lotuses], red light; from the white-colored [lotuses], white light"); not until he reached high school in Tokyo did he learn the meaning of the phrase, and realize that *shakkō* meant crimson light.[7]

There are Buddhist undercurrents in his poetry, notably in the famous poem from "Shinitamau haha" (My mother is dying), which is now carved on a stone by the main hall of Hōsenji:

nodo akaki	Two red-throated swallows
tsubakurame futatsu	are perched
hari ni ite	on a crossbeam;
tarachine no haha wa	my cherishing mother
shinitamau nari	is dying.
	(*Shakkō*)

Mokichi sensed a religious tie between the dying mother and the living birds, recalling the tradition that the animals of creation all gathered in mourning when Buddha died.[8] Occasionally there are specific Buddhist references, such as:

tsuki ochite	The moon sinks, and
sayo honokuraku	the night is dim and dark—
imada kamo	but still not yet!

Miroku wa idezu   Miroku* does not appear—
mushi nakeru kamo   and how the insects cry!

(*Shakkō*)

Mokichi was never a devout believer, but he did draw upon those themes and aspects of the Buddhism of his childhood which corresponded to his present perceptions and responses to use in his poems.[9] Ryūō's influence extended beyond Mokichi's religious life. Mokichi studied calligraphy and composition with Ryūō, and together they read *Nihon gaishi,* a history of Japan written in *kanbun* (Chinese) in 1827 by the scholar Rai San'yō. Ryūō's high opinion of Mokichi's talents, formed during these lessons, was to influence the course of his life.

When Mokichi was about ten, he learned how to make and paint kites, which he sold to other village children at one sen a sheet. He used the money he earned to buy books and magazines.[10] Mokichi enjoyed the artistic pleasure of making the kites, but more than that he prized the books he could buy. In *Nenjushū,* Mokichi recalled a visit with his father to the temple on Mt. Yudono at New Year. His father, in good humor, treated Mokichi to a fancy boxed lunch, but on their return, when they passed a bookstore in Yamagata city, Mokichi begged his father in vain to buy him a book of Japanese history. Mokichi wrote, "I walked behind my father thinking, 'why must he be so stingy?' "[11]

His father's refusal to buy the book probably stemmed less from stinginess than from his conception of relative importance: the Moriya family was neither scholarly nor literary. It is true that Mokichi's paternal grandfather Kanazawa Eikichi had written tanka; his maternal grandfather Moriya Denkichi had composed *haikai renga;* and Mokichi himself was taught the *Hyakunin Isshu* as a child; but he did not learn a great deal about poetry or scholarship from his family. In fact they evinced little interest in his own poetry even much later.[12] His intense concern with poetry began after he had left his parents. In the meantime, he led a stable, active, happy childhood. He liked to play, but also to paint, to practice calligraphy, and to read with Ryūō. He was a sensitive child, and his mind was frequently in the clouds. To his brother Mokichi seemed protective of a private, solitary world to which he often withdrew.[13]

---

*Miroku, or Maitreya, is the Buddha who is to appear in the distant future to explain the law and save mankind.

When Mokichi graduated at the age of fourteen from elementary school (which in those days included what is now called middle school), he still had no clear plans for the future. The Moriyas were a prosperous family, but not so prosperous as to justify educating a third or fourth son through middle school (the equivalent of a modern high school). Many years later, Mokichi described his thoughts during the spring of 1896 in these terms:

> As the time came for me to graduate from higher elementary school, I had all kinds of fantasies about the future. I was not going to be sent right away to middle school. On my way home from elementary school, I used to lie down in the woods when the spring weather got warm enough, and think, "Shall I study to be a painter, or would it be better to become a novice at Hōsenji? Or shall I start a farm by this new road, and raise silkworms?" I often passed the time in such reveries.[14]

So far his ambitions were limited to callings which were already part of his experience; the two professions—medicine and poetry—he would ultimately follow were part of an unknown world. That world was opened to him by a cousin, Dr. Saitō Kiichi. Kiichi at the time was the director of a flourishing general hospital in Asakusa, Tokyo, but he had as yet no sons to carry on his work. With the double motivation of providing for the education of a promising young man, and perhaps also of providing himself with an heir, he consulted the priest of his home temple, Hōsenji. Ryūō recommended Mokichi.[15]

Mokichi's father, pleased with the offer of an education for his third son that he himself could not provide, agreed to send Mokichi to the Saitō household in Tokyo. Even prosperous farmers could not afford to break up their holdings to provide for all their sons, and the Moriyas were following established practice in sending younger sons for adoption to other families.[16] The Moriyas' eldest son graduated from Miyazaki Prefecture School of Agriculture, but that alone was a special event to the villagers of Kanakame. The second son did not even graduate from primary school before working on the farm; eventually he obtained an education for himself after his military service, and became a doctor. Mokichi's younger brother Naokichi also was to become an adopted son.[17]

In late August 1886, then, Mokichi left Kanakame with his father and began the trip across Tōhoku, the northern provinces. The first night they stopped at a hot spring resort, and the following night reached the city of Sendai. On the third day of the trip, when Mokichi had already been intrigued by such unfamiliar sights as uniformed soldiers on maneuvers, and had eaten various citified foods for the first time in his life, he and his father took the train from Sendai to Tokyo. Mokichi recalled: "Just at dusk, we reached Ueno Station in Tokyo. And I thought, can anywhere in the world be so brightly lit at night?"[18]

During the fourteen years from Mokichi's birth to his move to Tokyo, the changes brought about by the rapid modernization of Japan, including the new constitution, the convening of a national Diet, and the Sino-Japanese War, had made themselves felt even in the small village of Kanakame at the foot of Mt. Zaō: new administrative districts led to the combination of small village schools, new roads had been built, new vistas opened to the minds of people who had previously known little but their own villages. Mokichi in Tokyo felt as if the pictures he had seen of the new culture had come to life.[19] But an even more dramatic change in his own life was the switch from a village to a metropolis, from a farmer's family to a doctor's. He treasured memories of his childhood: the landscape of his first home, especially Mt. Zaō; his family ties, especially those with his parents and his younger brother; and his early religious environment appeared in and influenced his poetry throughout his life. But in most ways he had been uprooted from his native soil, and he had to find his way in a new world.

Early Education

This new world opened to Mokichi at Kiichi's house in Misujimachi, in the Asakusa district of Tokyo. At the time, Kiichi had several apprentice medical students living with him who seemed completely at ease with city life: they enjoyed telling each other about the Yoshiwara district, going on outings to eat horsemeat—an unusual delicacy at the time—and doubtless boasting about their occasional brawls. Mokichi was impressed by their apparent sophistication. In "Misujimachi kaiwai" (The neighborhood of Misujimachi), recollections of his early years in Kiichi's house, Mokichi wrote:

As soon as I came to Tokyo, even before my father who had brought me returned home, I learned several Tokyo words. *Shōyu* [soy sauce] was *murasaki*. *Mochi* [rice cake] was *okachin*. *Settchin* [toilet] was *habaraki*. I accepted these new words without resistance, and endeavored to speak Tokyo language from then on.[20]

This endeavor was not long-lived; he retained his provincial speech patterns throughout his life. He seems to have felt in the end that his Yamagata accent was an integral part of his personality, and he never adopted standard Tokyo speech. Similarly, despite Kiichi's prominence as a popular doctor and his concern for keeping up with the times, a provincial atmosphere lingered even in his modern household: he took in primarily students from the northern provinces; even the maid who taught Mokichi the "Tokyo words" was from Yamagata prefecture, and in fact she was teaching him a feminine, rather than urban, vocabulary.

Mokichi was enrolled in the Kaisei Middle School in Kanda, under the shadow of the Nicolai Russian Orthodox Church. It had already imparted to many scholars, literary figures, and politicians its liberal educational policies and emphasis on language studies; the school pin, showing a cross formed by a pen and a sword, was said to derive from Bulwer-Lytton's line "the pen is mightier than the sword."[21] Mokichi was apprehensive about his entrance, impressed by what he perceived as the superiority of everyone and everything he encountered in Tokyo, but was relieved to discover that he could hold his own academically. English was the only subject that gave him trouble, since he had not studied it previously. On the other hand, he was surprised that his fellow students had difficulty understanding Rai San'yō's *Nihon gaishi,* which Mokichi had read with Ryūō in Kanakame. But when his turn came to recite, although he read fluently, everyone, including the teacher, laughed at his odd provincial accent. Some of his classmates remember Mokichi as a pleasant, if somewhat amusing, student, but he did not impress anyone as being likely to achieve greatness. Nevertheless, his grades were quite high, especially in Japanese language, composition, and history. Mokichi was intent on doing well in his studies, particularly German, which would be necessary if he entered medical school.[22]

The middle school was in the area of Kanda which is still lined with second-hand bookstores, and from his middle-school days, Mokichi en-

joyed browsing through science magazines, history books, and literature. He bought and read *Seishin keibi* (Neurophysiology) by Kure
Shūzō, the psychiatrist who had pioneered the development in Japan of
modern treatment for the mentally ill, and who later became his teacher;
but he also read Sasaki Nobutsuna's *Uta no shiori* (A guide to poetry)
and parts of his *Nihon kagaku zensho* (Complete writings on the study
of Japanese poetry), and he published a few poems in the school magazine.[23]

Mokichi seems to have made as mild an impression on his higher-
school classmates at Ichikō (Daiichi Kōtō Gakko) as he had in middle
school: they remembered him as a pleasant if provincial fellow with no
aura of future greatness. He was an adequate student but not more; he
took little or no part in extracurricular activities such as sports clubs or
literary groups; he was timid about the camaraderie of dormitory life—
he could scarcely get through the dormitory song—and avoided the
student roughhousing as well as he could. In later years he recalled his
own timidity, and also the awe he felt toward his surroundings: "The
teachers at Ichikō seemed to me at the time to be almost like gods, who
did not even eat common noodles." When he wrote about specific
teachers, it was of personal rather than intellectual qualities, although
he remembered gratefully Iwamoto Gen having made his reluctant German students, most of whom intended to study medicine, read G. E.
Lessing's *Laokoon*.[24]

It was during his last year at Ichikō that Mokichi became seriously
interested in tanka, but the stimulus was from outside the school environment. For example, here is a poem written during the Russo-Japanese War, in which both his older brothers fought:

hon yomite	"Read your books,
totōku nare to	and make yourself exalted!"
senjō no	from the battlefield
waga e wa zeni o	my brother has given me
kuretamai tari	these words and precious coins.
	(*Shakkō*)

Masaoka Shiki and Itō Sachio

The real impetus to Mokichi's intense interest in tanka occurred in his
final year of high school, when he accidentally came across *Take no sato*

uta (Bamboo village poems) by Masaoka Shiki, about New Year in 1905. Mokichi later wrote in "Omoidasu kotodomo" (Recollections):

> It was when people's nerves were strained to the breaking point over whether or not Port Arthur had fallen. One day I borrowed a slim volume of verse called *Bamboo Village Poems* from the Ishigaki rental library in Kanda. At the time I was living on the second floor of a storehouse at my father's [Kiichi's] hospital in Izumi-chō, where a space of about three mats had been cleared amid some worn-out old luggage. I had pasted on the glass window such things as the paper charm from the Narita Fudōsan for the success in battle of my older brother, who had just left for the front. Sitting in that room I read the volume of poems I had borrowed. From the very first page, I found both "sweet persimmons" and "tart persimmons." The tone was one of "ah, how tart! how delicious!" I was inexpressibly delighted.[25]

The references to persimmons are quotations from this tanka of Shiki's:

kaki no mi no	There was such sweetness
amaki mo arinu	encased in the persimmon—
kaki no mi no	there was such tartness
shibuki mo arinu	encased in the persimmon—
shibuki zo umaki	ah, how tart! how delicious!
	(*Take no sato uta*)

The poem could be about Shiki's tanka as well as about the lovely fruit: it was the freedom and ease with which the everyday real world was expressed to which Mokichi was drawn, an immediacy which could almost be tasted; and it was this quality that was so central to Shiki's achievements as a tanka theorist.[26]

Thanks to the interest of Watanabe Kōzō and other school friends in haiku, Mokichi was already familiar with Shiki's fame as a haiku poet and theorist, but his chance enounter with *Take no sato uta* provided his first glimpse of Shiki's accomplishments as a tanka poet and theorist. In his *Utayomi ni atauru sho* (Letters to tanka poets) Shiki was concerned with "the need to enrich tanka (in tone, subject and vocabulary) with elements from other genres and other cultures, and the demand for internal consistency within the poems."[27] The tone was to be strong and forceful, following the example of the *Man'yōshū* rather than the tradition of the *Kokinshū* and the *Shinkokinshū,* in which the limited poetic diction of tanka in turn limited its subject matter, thereby weakening the form. Shiki's ideas of *shasei*—"the depiction of life"—which he had applied to haiku, were applied to tanka as well, and insisted upon a realistic rather than a conventionalized view of the world. Finally, tanka, as well as haiku, were to be judged by the standards which are applied to all works of literature; the two forms were to take their place within the mainstream of Japanese literary development.

The fruit of this theory, the "sweet and tart persimmons," that is, the poems in the posthumous collection *Take no sato uta,* opened a new world of possibilities for Mokichi. He wrote later:

> It could be said that this kind of poem [*uta*] had never been made before, and it somehow gave an animated, fresh feeling; but it wasn't simply that. They did not seem difficult in the way poems had seemed difficult in the past; they persuaded me that even I could write this kind of poetry. At that point I began to feel that I would try to write poety, and I copied out poems from *Bamboo Village Poems* and read them over and over; I also frequently made my own imitations.[28]

Mokichi thought himself capable of writing such poems because he intuitively felt that he not only understood them but that their expression was congenial to his own nature.[29] Among the poems that Mokichi quoted in both "Omoidasu kotodomo" and "Bungaku no shi—igaku no shi" (Teachers of literature—teachers of medicine) is the following tanka by Shiki:

ki no moto ni	The place beneath the tree,
fuseru hotoke o	where, surrounding the form of the
uchikakomi	reclining Buddha,
zō hebi domo no	the elephants and snakes
nakiiru tokoro	are all there weeping.
	(Take no sato uta)

It is from a rensaku, based on paintings of the life of Buddha, called "E amata hiroge mite tsukureru" (Created after seeing pictures displayed in public). Mokichi began to write a similar sequence based on a scroll he had often seen as a child at Hōsenji, called "Jigoku gokuraku zu" (Map of heaven and hell).[30] In a letter to Watanabe Kōzō of May 10, 1905, he included, among others, the following poem from the sequence in progress:

kurenai no   The place beside
chieki no ike wa   the pond of crimson blood, where,
mahadaka no   in nakedness,
onna mōja no   a woman who has died
nakiiru tokoro   stands weeping.

Mokichi revised the sequence, and this poem appeared in *Shakkō* eight years later in the following form:

akaki ike ni   The place by the red
hitoribotchi no   pond where, entirely alone,
mahadaka no   in nakedness,
onna mōja no   a woman who has died
nakiiru tokoro   stands weeping.

The similarities between Shiki's tanka and Mokichi's are, of course, immediately apparent: each poem consists of an extended phrase, rather than a complete sentence, modifying *tokoro* (the place); and in both the subject matter is Buddhist—in Shiki's poem Buddha's death, and in Mokichi's a vision of hell. Other similarities can be traced through the sequences as a whole, in which the context gives weight to these and similar individual poems, none of which seems to me to be strong or complete enough to stand alone. But there are also, of course, differences. Shiki's sequence is more general and pictorial, Mokichi's more specific and dramatic.[31] Part of the difference derives from the pictures that provided the bases for the sequences. Mokichi's sequence progresses from hell to heaven, undoubtedly a dramatic progression. Yet Mokichi's revision of the first two lines of his poem demonstrates a sensitivity to the kind of specificity that creates drama. The "pond of crimson blood" becomes simply "the red pond," and the reader is allowed to realize the composition of that redness from the context and his own imagination; and the weeping dead woman becomes "entirely alone." The result is that her agony is not merely a response to her grotesque surroundings; it is an internalized punishment of spiritual isolation, and as such a much more intense and perceptive description of horror.

Mokichi sought advice about his poetic development, turning first to his old friend Watanabe Kōzō, who provided encouragement and criticism; by means of Kōzō's guidance, Mokichi wrote, his "eyes were gradually opened" to poetic teaching and the world of poetry. Mokichi learned of the journal *Ashibi*, published by Shiki's disciples of the Negishi school,★ and Kōzō helped him decipher the poems published there.[32] Mokichi also began to read the poetry column in the *Yomiuri shinbun*, edited by Ikeda Shūbin, a member of the Negishi school, and published poems in it from February through June of 1905. Kōzō also urged Mokichi to meet Shiki's tanka disciple Itō Sachio, but Mokichi, too timid and unsure of himself to take such a step, put it off. Early the following year, his struggle to master the Man'yō period language of the *Ashibi* poets led him to write to Sachio for advice.[33] Sachio's prompt and considered reply was encouraging, and Mokichi worked up the courage to send ten or so poems with his letter of thanks. Sachio responded by publishing five of them in *Ashibi,* and by asking Mokichi to visit him.

Mokichi was apprehensive about meeting such a formidable personage: he discussed with his foster mother what sort of gift to bring (deciding on Yamagata plum jam); he agonized during the trolley ride; and then he found, to his relief, that Sachio was not at all intimidating. Mokichi's first visit, in March of 1906, lasted for three hours, during which Sachio fed him cakes and tea, explained a *chōka* from the *Man'yōshū,* and gave him some back issues of *Ashibi*.[34] Sachio's praise and advice were invaluable. In "Bungaku no shi—igaku no shi" Mokichi wrote of his response to seeing his own poems published in the column Sachio edited for the *Nihon shinbun:* "It was an inexpressibly good feeling when five or ten of my own poems were printed in the newspaper. In addition to that, no one can know what a panacea it was to someone as timid as myself to be on occasion praised and encouraged."[35] Perhaps the most important advice he received from Sachio was to recognize his own talent and to stop imitating other people's poems as he had done in "Jigoku gokuraku zu." Mokichi then began to apply Shiki's theories of shasei to his own vision of the world, rather than Shiki's poetic techniques to his own poems. Mokichi's development of the theory of shasei was to come later (see chapters 2 and 4),

★The Negishi school (which takes its name from the section of Tokyo in which Shiki was living) was composed of poets who followed Shiki's honest depiction of scenes and emotions, following the style of the *Man'yō*. Mokichi had difficulty with the Man'yō diction they used; specifically, he borrowed their use of the particle *gamo,* only to be informed later that it did not exist.

but in this early period of his involvement with poetry, he was exploring some of its methods: he drew from life, as Shiki had, and also wrote from direct experience. In the spring of 1907 he sent Sachio a drawing and poem on a postcard. Sachio answered:

tennen ni	Although the colors
iro wa nizu tomo	are not like those in nature,
kimi ga e wa	your picture has
kimi ga iro nite	the colors of yourself;
ninakutomo yoshi	that they are unlike is a good thing.

Mokichi was further encouraged by this support of his own vision and the techniques he was developing to express it.[36]

One of the early, clear expressions of his view of tanka as "an expression of life" (*inochi no araware*), in which he was making his own Shiki's notions of shasei and the Negishi school concern with Man'yō studies, may be traced back to the poem sequence "Osana tsuma" (Child bride) from 1910. Among them, Kajiki Gō sees the following poem as symbolic of Mokichi's own leap toward poetic independence:[37]

hashi akaki	Even the tiny
kodori sae koso	red-beaked birds
tobu narame	must fly away:
harubaru tobaba	ah, how sad it is
kanashikiro kamo	to see them fly so far!
	(*Shakkō*)

But more typical of the kind of poetic juxtaposition, rather than direct statement, that would characterize many of his best early works is another, even more celebrated, poem in this series:

ki no moto ni	When I bit into
ume hameba sushi	a plum beneath the tree, how sour!
osana tsuma	the time has passed
hito ni sanizurau	for my child bride to blush
toki tachinikeri	when she confronts a man.
	(*Shakkō*)

The unexplained relation between his momentary experience of the sourness of the plum and the lengthy wait for his "child bride" to respond in an adult way; the commonplace language of the first two lines contrasted with the coined *osana tsuma* of the third and the unorthodox use of the Man'yō pillow word (*makurakotoba*) *sanitsurau* as a verb; and most important, the kind of intense work that reading such a poem demands of the reader, are all marks of Mokichi's most compelling poems of this early period.

Medicine, Marriage, and Poetic Independence

The "child bride" was Kiichi's second daughter, Teruko, thirteen years Mokichi's junior, to whom he was engaged in 1905 when he was twenty-four. It was the year he first read *Take no sato uta;* he was about to graduate from secondary school, and he had been living as a member of Saitō Kiichi's family for nearly ten years. Kiichi had decided definitely to make his adopted son a doctor, and Mokichi had been studying intensely for the entrance examination to Tokyo Imperial University Medical School. Years later he wrote about the tension of the period:

shiken nite	I saw myself
kurushimu sama o	afflicted by examinations—
ariari to	oh so vividly!—
toshi oite yume ni	in a dream as an old man,
miru wa kanashi mo	and how it saddened me.
	(*Sekisen*)

While there had been talk of making Mokichi heir to the Saitō family if he fulfilled his childhood promise, during the intervening years Kiichi's wife had borne a son, Seiyō. Therefore when Mokichi was finally officially entered into the Saitō family register, it was as the betrothed son-in-law of the then eleven-year-old Teruko. In later years he succeeded to the directorship of Kiichi's hospital, but his official status was brother-in-law to the family head. The formality of registration was apparently of little concern to Mokichi, but his relations with the family members and his position among them were of great importance.

Kiichi was a self-made man whose ambitions grew with his achievements, and his concerns and enthusiasms set the tone for the family. He had been born in the same village as Mokichi. The Saitō and Moriya families had been intermarrying for several generations, and there are indications that Kiichi's interest in Mokichi stemmed at least in part from a feeling of gratitude for the assistance he had received from Mokichi's grandfather Denkichi and a desire to offer some return.[38] In any event, by the time Mokichi joined the Saitō household, Kiichi's hospital in Asakusa was so prosperous that he established an additional facility in Izumi-chō in Kanda. Kiichi practiced everything from pediatrics to surgery in these hospitals. When he went abroad to study in 1900, however, he decided to specialize in psychiatry, and this choice was a response to contemporary changes in Japanese attitudes toward the mentally ill.[39]

The modern history of psychiatry in Japan had begun with the establishment of a mental hospital in Kyoto in 1875; a translation of a standard European text on mental illness—by the English psychiatrist Henry Maudsley—was published the following year. The German physician Erwin von Baelz began to lecture on mental diseases at Tokyo University in 1879, and it was not long before Japanese doctors went to study the field in Europe. Little was offered yet in the way of treatment, however, which remained a matter of controlling patients. Kure Shūzō was influential in opposing this policy of control rather than treatment. In practical terms, he pioneered in the release of patients from coercive physical restraints; in theoretical terms, he argued for the improvement of the vocabulary used for describing mental illness, and succeeded in eliminating from it characters such as *kyō,* meaning "lunacy, insanity," and substituting more neutral terms such as *seishinbyō,* "mental illness."[40] He eventually became a professor at Tokyo Imperial University Medical School and director of the Sugamo Mental Hospital; he was to be Mokichi's teacher at both institutions.

By the end of the nineteenth century, the treatment of the mentally ill had come to be considered important enough to warrant new governmental regulation. In 1900, the year Kiichi went abroad to study, a law providing for the custody of the mentally ill was enacted. It became illegal to confine a person on the grounds of mental illness—except in his own house, by his own family—without the approval of a doctor, the police, and governmental authorities. It also provided for a government subsidy to help pay for this hospitalization. Doubtless this provided an economic motive for Kiichi's choice of a new specialty; but it cannot be denied that he displayed a certain amount of courage at a time when psychiatrists were still considered "crazy doctors." He also seems to have been gifted in dealing with the mentally ill. In Europe he studied at Leipzig and Berlin, and received the degree of doctor of medicine in 1902. He also traveled to France and England to examine hospitals before returning to Japan.

Kiichi was proud of his accomplishments, and asked his subordinates to refer to him as "dokutoru mejichīne." He was also proud of his social acquirements, and introduced, along with his Kaiser Wilhelm mustache, European customs into his household: he and his wife slept in a double bed rather than on *futon,* for example, and they preferred Western soup and wine to their Japanese equivalents.[41] He changed his name from Kiichirō to Kiichi, with a different character for the Ki, which he thought looked and sounded more urbane, as he had required Mokichi to read the characters of his name as Shigeyoshi, since Mokichi had a "country-bumpkin smell" about it.* Kiichi even named his first son, who was born while Kiichi was in Europe, Seiyō, which means "the West," and his second son, who was born when Kiichi was in the United States, Yonekuni, "America."† His personality left strong imprints on every aspect of the lives of his children.[42]

Kiichi's daughter Teruko was an infant when Mokichi first entered the family. Sometimes he took care of her, and they played together. But she was brought up as though she were a daughter of the aristocracy, carried in a rickshaw to school at the upper-class Joshi Gakushūin, learned to speak an elegant language, and took no pains to conceal her pride in her position. When Mokichi was engaged to Teruko, she was only eleven, and the period of waiting until she was old enough to be married seems to have been trying for him. He wrote several lovely poems of yearning for her, but Teruko does not seem to have eagerly anticipated her marriage with such a provincial-seeming sort of man.

In any event, when Kiichi returned from Europe in 1902, he gave up his hospital in Misujimachi, changed the name of his hospital in Izumi-

---

* Mokichi used "Shigeyoshi" on all academic and medical documents until he resigned as head of Aoyama Hospital in 1933, but he used "Mokichi" when signing his poetry. His passport and his medical research in Europe were under the name of Shigeyoshi Saitō.
† Kiichi was in the United States and Europe from 1908 to 1910, examining methods of treatment and new equipment. Poor Yonekuni died before the end of World War II, when his name must have been a great trial to him.

chō from Kanda Tōtō Byōin (Kanda Tokyo Hospital) to Teikoku Nōbyōin (Imperial Mental Hospital); and began construction of his Aoyama Nōbyōin in Akasaka, which was finally completed in 1906. It was
an impressive-looking facility, with gardens, tennis courts, and a base-
ball field; there were both Western- and Japanese-style bedrooms; it had
an elegant European design, and Kiichi was particularly proud of its
clock tower.[43] Meanwhile Mokichi, who was studying medicine and
writing poetry, seemed to be more intent on perfecting his poetry. He
would bring poems for criticism to Sachio in the evening and sometimes stay up with him all night talking, and go directly to his classes
the next morning. It was during this period that he also was developing
close friendships with poets who were his contemporaries—among them
Nakamura Kenkichi, Tsuchiya Bunmei, Shimagi Akahiko, and Koizumi Chikashi. In addition, in early 1909 he began to attend meetings
of Mori Ōgai's Kanchōrō Kakai, whose purpose was to bring together
poets from diverse schools for a kind of cross-fertilization of literary
activity. There Mokichi met such important literary figures as Ueda
Bin, Kinoshita Mokutarō, Ishikawa Takuboku, Sasaki Nobutsuna, and
Kitahara Hakushū, and his literary world was indeed widened; he began
to experiment with strength of image and of expression.[44]

   Itō Sachio was also experimenting, but with prose. His work on the
novel *Nogiku no haka* (Wild chrysanthemum grave) left him little time
for the editing of *Ashibi,* and in 1908 he gave up this publication. He
soon afterward founded another magazine, *Akane,* but this was placed
under the editorship of Mitsui Kōshi. Disputes between Kōshi and the
group of poets around Mokichi led almost immediately to the creation
of still another magazine, *Araragi,* once again under the direct guidance
of Sachio. Mokichi published in the column of *Araragi* devoted to poetry selected by Sachio, until he all but stopped writing poetry between
late 1909 and the autumn of 1910. During this ten-month period, he
was suffering from the lengthy, recurring bout of typhoid fever that
delayed his graduation from medical school. When he did begin to publish again, he felt his style had changed, and he no longer submitted his
poems for Sachio's approval; he chose instead to publish poems of his
own selection in the columns of *Araragi* reserved for members of the
group. This marked the beginning of his rift with Sachio. In "Omoidasu kotodomo," Mokichi wrote about their estrangement:

However, before making the decision not to publish in [Sachio's] monthly selection, I pondered the matter at great length, and also asked for the opinion of a senior [at *Araragi*], Ishiwara Jun. He said that making one's own choices was a sign that one is taking responsibility for oneself, and also becomes a method of learning. After that I avoided Sachio's selection and published my own work. But my poems were no longer praised by Sachio. . . .

It was not only that my poems weren't praised. The poems of my friends which were not included in his columns were also not praised. Then, when I asked myself what kind of poems Sachio was likely to select and commend, they seemed to me to be no more than those which fitted comfortably inside the conventional, traditional monotony, faults, and odor of the style practiced by the Negishi school. . . .

Sachio and Mokichi argued about the styles of other poets, which sometimes led to harsh words. Sachio once complained, "What can a student like you, who knows nothing of suffering, understand?" Nonetheless, Sachio chose Mokichi to edit *Araragi* in 1911. Dissatisfied with what he believed to be a monotony of style, he solicited and published poetry by writers of other schools such as Abe Jirō and Kinoshita Mokutarō. Some readers of *Araragi,* including Sachio, were displeased. Mokichi and Sachio never severed relations: they took walks together, dined out together, and visited exhibits together, and held their monthly poetry meetings, but the discord remained. After one such meeting, marked by Sachio's particularly harsh criticisms of some poems by Akahiko, Mokichi lay awake all night troubled by it.[45]

Mokichi's admiration for Sachio had not entirely disappeared; in 1913, a manuscript he received from Sachio called "Horobi no hikari" (The light of destruction) moved him to tears, and he rushed to tell Sachio so.[46] Nonetheless, he spent more and more time with Kenkichi, Akahiko, and Chikashi. His life was also changing, and this was mirrored in his poetry.

Mokichi graduated from medical school, and in 1911 joined the staff of Sugamo Hospital under Kure Shūzō and Miyake Kōichi, and began to study his specialty of psychiatry. It was assumed as a matter of course that Mokichi would follow in Kiichi's footsteps; nonetheless psychiatry was, according to Kiichi, "a thankless specialty"—a warning Mokichi in turn was to give to his own son Shigeta years later. Mokichi's work at Sugamo included research into cell-dyeing and dissection techniques to study brain histology. He also had clinical chores not only within the hospital but outside, such as evaluating the mental health of prisoners scheduled to be released from Sugamo prison. He joined the Japan Psychiatric Society in 1911, and by 1915 began to lecture in the department of psychiatry at Tokyo University Medical School.[47] These experiences appear in such poems as:

kagamarite While bending over
nō no seppen o to stain a specimen
somenagara of brain cells,
akebi no hana o I found myself thinking
omou narikeri of akebia blossoms.
          (*Shakkō*)

The following two poems are from a sequence called "Kyōjinmori" (The guardian of madmen). Some of the strongest poems of the period reflect Mokichi's responses to the patients he was treating, and to his own role as their doctor.

kurenai no Crimson
sarusuberi wa the crape-myrtle
sakinuredo had bloomed
kono kyōjin wa and yet this madman
mono wa iwazukeri said not a word.

toshiwakaki The sadness of
kyōjinmori no the young guardian
kanashimi wa of madmen is
akebi no hana no the sadness of akebia
chirau kanashimi flowers falling, scattering.
          (*Shakkō*)

Transforming the experiences of his life as a doctor into poetry often infringed upon his duties in medicine. A colleague of his at Sugamo Hospital recalled, after Mokichi's death:

> Mokichi would often drop into a chair in the dispensary, close his eyes, furrow his brow, and silently meditate; these were the times he was thinking of poetry. During them, he would gradually seem to find inspiration, and begin writing characters in the air. The rest of us, not realizing that he

was in the process of becoming the illustrious poet he is now considered, would say things like "Saitō is catatonic again." In the trolley too he would often miss his stop, probably from thinking about poems; he was chronically late in reporting for work.[48]

He was also spending his evenings talking and drinking with his colleagues at *Araragi*, or with Hakushū, or Wakayama Bokusui and others. *Araragi* was not selling well, and all the young members, such as Chikashi and Akahiko, were poor; Bunmei and Nakamura Kenkichi were still students. Mokichi would check the bookstores, and one day he said, "I went to the bookstore today to have a look and they hadn't sold a single copy. It irritated me so much I bought three copies myself."[49]

Shakkō (Crimson light)

His third year at Sugamo, 1913, was an especially dramatic one in his personal life and in terms of his poetic output. In April he was separated from Ohiro, who was probably a maid in the Saitō household, and he wrote a moving rensaku on the pain of separation and the loss of love (see chapter 5). His mother died in May, and the grief was expressed in the great rensaku "Shinitamau haha" (My mother is dying).[50] Finally, Itō Sachio died in July. Mokichi's first volume of poetry, *Shakkō*, was published in October, and opened with a rensaku about the night of Sachio's death, "Hihōrai" (On receiving bad news). The first poem was:

hitahashiru	As I run desperately
waga michi kurashi	my way is dark,
shinshin to	it weighs on me
koraekanetaru	unendurably,
waga michi kurashi	my way is dark.

The loss of Sachio as a teacher to admire, learn from, and rebel against was responsible for some of the darkness. However, it was the elegaic quality of much of the best poetry in *Shakkō* that established his poetic voice, in such works as "Shinitamau haha," "Ohiro," and "Kinamida yoroku" (Record of yellow tears). Another of these works, "Okuni," about the death of a maid in the Saitō household, included the only poems Sachio praised after Mokichi's move toward independence.[51] Mokichi's use of these events illustrates his understanding of *inochi no araware*: "Tanka must be 'an expression of life' directly. It follows that a true tanka must be something that is one's self as one is. If someone composes a single poem, the self is born as that poem."[52]

The poem, then, is an individualized transformation of the particular experience of a specific being. Mokichi's ability to make universal his personal experiences with the pain of separation and death accounted in large part for the favorable reception *Shakkō* received.

The rensaku "Kinamida yoroku" was written in 1913 following the suicide of a patient at Aoyama Nōbyōin. The following poems are from part one, "Hōribi" (Funeral fire); they exhibit many of the characteristics of Mokichi's poetic voice of the period. In this section, the funeral cortege proceeds through the city to the cemetery; the body is cremated, even amid signs of ordinary daily life continuing as the ceremonies are performed; afterwards, the poet goes alone to the Ueno Zoo to compose himself.

2. jisatsu seshi
    kyōja no kan no
    ushiro yori
    memai shite yukeri
    michi ni irihi akaku

    Behind the coffin
    of the madman who has
    killed himself,
    I followed, feeling faint;
    the setting sun red on the road.

4. nakinagasu
    ware no namida no
    ki naritomo
    hito ni shirayu na
    kanashiki nareba

    The tears that flow
    as I stand weeping are
    bitter yellow, but
    let no one know of them—
    because there is such grief.

11. waga ashi yori
    ase idete yaya
    itami ari
    kutsu ni tamarishi
    tsuchi hokori kamo

    The sweat flows
    from my feet, and
    they hurt some—
    the dust of the earth
    has settled in my shoes.

13. shi wamo shi wamo
    kanashiki mono o
    narazaramu
    me no moto ni ki no mi
    otsu tawayasuki kamo

    Ah, death, death!
    maybe after all it is
    not such a sad thing:
    how easily before my eyes
    the fruit falls from the trees.

19.   Ueno naru   There were magpies
           dōbutsuen ni   at the zoo in Ueno
           kasasagi wa   that were eating
           niku kui itari   meat; it was
           kurenai no niku o   crimson meat. . . .

The relation between the development of tanka as an expression of life and the frequent appearance of death in Mokichi's early work is made clear in this sequence: the consciousness of life is the central motif; that consciousness is deepened by the pain of death.[53] The response of the poet is made more complex by this duality of perception. In the first poem, the speaker's faintness is at first seen solely as a response to the death of the patient, with the coffin as the concrete form of that death. But the last line then ties that response to the physical world, where the brilliance of the day's end is itself dazzling. The tie is emphasized by the staccato *i* sounds repeated six consecutive times in the last line, mi-chi ni irihi, and punctuated sharply by the final word *akaku* ("redly"), which lends further weight to the line by adding two extra syllables.

The next poem has a paradox parallel to the way in which death heightens consciousness of life: the grief is too deep to be made public, yet it cannot be contained—tears flow; and it must be spoken—the poem is written. The poet seems to be addressing himself in the imperative, *hito ni shirayu na* (let no one know); yet he cannot respect even his own need for solitary mourning. Reluctantly the grief is shared. The explanatory last line sounds almost like an apology for both the intensity of his emotion and his failure to honor his own instincts by hiding that depth of feeling. The next poem provides for a slackening of the emotional intensity of the sequence while recognizing that a heightened consciousness of life is not necessarily an exaltation; it is often a prosaic awareness of normality. Even as the emotions are engaged to the utmost, the body lives in the world. The poem is reminiscent of W. H. Auden's "Musée des Beaux Arts," which begins:

About suffering they were never wrong,
The Old Masters: how well they understood
Its human position; how it takes place
While someone else is eating or opening a window or just walking dully
    along . . .[54]

But it takes that perception one step further to realize, and to demonstrate, that suffering also takes place while the sufferer himself may be "just walking dully along" with sore feet. Kobori Keiichirō has called this touch of slight self-deprecation Mokichi's "brown humor":[55] that is, it is not black humor, because it is neither funny nor gruesome, but it is a sort of humor because it is a gentle reminder that all aspects of experience are not equally serious. Here it serves as a poignant demonstration that the world intrudes even when one would prefer to surrender oneself to grief; it restores a sense of perspective, which is reflected in the next selection.

In poem 13, the obvious realization that death is part of the natural cycle of life is strengthened by the fluid euphonic link in line 4 between the fruit and the speaker, *me no moto ni ki no mi* (the fruit of the tree beneath my eyes), which personalizes a universal truth into an individual momentary realization. Finally, this perception is enlarged in the last poem to include more of the natural world. That death is the natural end of life not only diffuses some of the pain in response to it; it also infuses ordinary processes of life with an ever-present reminder of death: the blood-red meat the birds eat to sustain life once had a life of its own.

Shakkō as a whole is characterized by the word and the emotion *kanashimi*, sadness, grieving. Mokichi's next collection, *Aratama*, is represented by *sabishisa*, loneliness.[56]

Aratama (Uncut gems)

In April 1913, before the deaths of his mother and Sachio, Mokichi had presented a paper at the twelfth meeting of the Japan Psychiatric Association entitled "Mahisei chihō to Wasserman-shi hannō" (Paralytic dementia and the Wasserman Response Test), which was a report of studies done under Kure at the Tokyo Psychiatric Institute. The Wasserman test, which was developed in 1906, was being refined to become a basic diagnostic tool in clinical examinations; it was especially useful in diagnosing paralytic dementia in patients with no history of mental disorders. That was the only bit of medical research Mokichi was involved with while training and working at Sugamo. His absorption in poetry precluded serious medical research; furthermore, Mokichi felt that he would have to study in Europe to make any progress in academic medicine.[57]

One year later, in April 1914, Mokichi and Teruko were married: he was thirty-three, and she was not quite nineteen, still a "child bride." Kiichi was apparently disturbed by Mokichi's involvement with the woman who was the model for "Ohiro," but he was also anxious for the marriage to take place before Mokichi went abroad to study. However, World War I broke out, and study in Europe became impossible.

Mokichi was dissatisfied with his inability to proceed with medical research, but he was prolific poetically. His second volume of poems, *Aratama* (Uncut gems), contained poetry written from 1913 through 1917 (although it was not published until 1920). There was a turn toward recording experiences of normal, everyday life:

machikage no	I tramp across
hara ni kōreru	the night's snow, frozen
yoru no yuki	in the fields within
fumiyuku ware no	the city shadows, and
seki hibikikeri	my cough reverberates.
	(*Aratama*)

His normal, everyday life, however, was not a happy one: within a year of his marriage he was yearning to escape from it. His uneasy relations with his new wife put a strain on his dealings with the rest of the family; his role as husband seemed to isolate him rather than integrate him more completely into the family. He spent a great deal of time with Nakamura Kenkichi, drank too much, and was often ill. There is tension, though, rather than grief, in the sequence "Teinen" (Resignation):

kono yoru wa	Tonight, may all
chōjō gyokai wa	the creatures of land and sea
shizuka nare	rest tranquil—
miren mochite ka yuki	myself as well: embracing my regrets,
kaku yuku ware mo	turning this way, then that way—

Above all, there is a sense of isolation and loneliness. In "Shigure" (Early winter rains):

yū sareba	As evening drew on,
daikon no ha ni	on radish leaves fell the
furu shigure	early winter rain;
itaku sabishiku	in pain, in loneliness,
furinikeru kamo	how it was raining!

In "Shunkō" (Spring light):

haru no hi wa	The springtime sun
sora yori wataru	crosses the wide sky;
hitori ite	because I am alone
kokoro sabishimeba	in heart-felt loneliness,
kuraki no gotoki	it is the same as darkness.

His professional life continued to appear in his work, but with a similar sense of isolation and dissatisfaction.

taku no shita ni	While beneath my desk
kayari no kō o	fragrant incense to repel
takinagara	mosquitoes burns,
hito nemurasemu	I am writing out prescriptions
shohō kakitari	to help other people sleep.

(*Aratama*)

His married life gradually achieved some stability, and his first son Shigeta was born in 1916. *Araragi,* now under the editorship of Koizumi Chikashi, often appeared late; the other members worried about its continued viability, and worried too about Mokichi's gradual withdrawal from it, as he published more and more work in other magazines.[58] Mokichi's poetic activity was creating problems elsewhere as well, as it interfered with his professional life. On the one hand, Kiichi had been very tolerant and rather proud of Mokichi's writing. He would say "medicine is old after a year; poetry is eternal." On the other hand, Kiichi's wife worried that Mokichi would be unfit to succeed Kiichi at Aoyama Hospital, and spoke to Kure about it.[59] Gradually Kiichi also became concerned. He wanted Mokichi under his own supervision, and he needed the young doctor's help, because in 1917 Kiichi was elected to the Diet, and could not handle the directorship of his hospital alone. He asked Kure to let Mokichi resign from the staff at Sugamo and return full-time to Aoyama Hospital.

When Mokichi left Sugamo in October 1917, however, it was to leave Tokyo entirely. Professor Ishida Noboru of Nagasaki Medical School had asked Kure to help find his replacement for the few years he was to be in America studying. Kure selected Mokichi, who thought it would be a useful change for both his poetry and his standing in the medical profession; Nagasaki retained the status of being in the forefront of medical studies it had enjoyed since the introduction of Dutch medicine in the Tokugawa period. Kiichi was also pleased about the professorial rank Mokichi would have, and agreed to let him go.[60] Mokichi reached Nagasaki on December 18, 1917. The last poem in *Aratama* concerns his arrival in Nagasaki harbor:

asa akete	At daybreak
fune yori nareru	the great steam horn
futobue no	sounds from the ship,
kodama wa nagashi	its echo lingering:
namiyorou yama	the mountains arrayed.

CHAPTER TWO
Nagasaki, Europe, and Reconstruction, 1918–1927

Nagasaki

MOKICHI arrived in Nagasaki in December 1917 to assume the positions Ishida Noboru would vacate in January 1918. Mokichi became chairman of the Department of Psychiatry at the Nagasaki School of Medicine, where he lectured on psychiatry and forensic medicine to fourth-year medical students. He was also chief of the psychiatric division of Nagasaki Prefectural Hospital, and counseling physician to the Nagasaki City First Aid Station.[1] He expected to hold these positions for two years while Ishida was at the Johns Hopkins Hospital in Baltimore. However, before Ishida could return to Japan, he developed symptoms of schizophrenia, and eventually shot and killed a colleague.* Mokichi therefore remained in Nagasaki longer than he had expected, for a total of three years and three months.[2]

---

*Ishida Noboru graduated from Tokyo University Medical School three years ahead of Mokichi. He was a promising young psychiatrist who had written a textbook on psychiatric disorders, as well as several novels under a pen name. He was studying the treatment of schizophrenia with Adolf Meyer (1866–1950) when he developed schizophrenic symptoms himself, and suffered from delusions and auditory hallucinations. He believed himself to be involved in a love triangle with a nurse and a German doctor, who supposedly was plotting against him. In the end he shot and killed Dr. Wolf. Conflicting expert opinions about his sanity led to his incarceration in a Baltimore prison. He was finally extradited to Japan through the efforts of the Japanese Psychiatric Association in 1925, and placed in Matsuzawa Hospital (formerly Sugamo Hospital). Mokichi visited him there in 1929. (Saitō Shigeta, *Seishinkai sandai,* pp. 87, 95–96.)

Mokichi's first lecture at the medical school was on January 8, 1918. He took his duties as a teacher seriously; according to students of his at the time, both the content of his lectures and the demands of his examinations were on a very high level. He earned the respect and friendship of his students.[3] Nonetheless, he was far from enthusiastic about this work. The following autumn, for example, he wrote to Nakamura Kenkichi, "Lecturing is unbearable, but I think that somehow or other I will try to get through it." As before, he was disturbed by his inability to find time for research.[4] Shortly thereafter, he began the experiments for his first paper, completed in February 1921, entitled "Kinchō byōsha no erugoguramu ni tsukite" (Concerning the muscular function of catatonic patients); a continuation of this research was completed in April 1921. The research used patients in Nagasaki Hospital as subjects, and himself and other doctors as controls, to measure the muscular activity in catatonic patients. His other research, influenced by prevalent trends in psychiatric research at the time, consisted of a paper on the functioning of the vegetative nervous system in relation to dementia praecox, which he presented to a conference in the spring of 1919.[5] He was also appointed to the board of the Japan Psychiatric Society, headed by Kure, which studied policies on mental illness with a view toward the development of effective hospitals and the reform of medical treatment of the mentally ill.[6] On the whole, however, his achievements in medicine failed to satisfy him, and he continued to feel the need to study in Europe.

His personal life was equally frustrating. He had gone to Nagasaki alone in December; Teruko and their son Shigeta joined him in June, but their home life was not ideal. Teruko moved back and forth between Tokyo and Nagasaki, and was with Mokichi for only about half the time he was there. During her stays in Nagasaki, she became involved with a fashionable set, including some members of Nagasaki's foreign community, who had formed a small orchestra. She went out often, dressed less like a staid married woman than her neighbors thought proper, and annoyed them by playing her piano and violin at odd hours. She and Mokichi quarreled a great deal, and there are even indications that she may have been involved with another man. For his part, Mokichi was busy with his medical work and his literary activities, and occasionally, in his loneliness, he sought solace in brothels in

Nagasaki's Maruyama district. Such diversions failed to comfort him.[7]
The discord between Mokichi and Teruko seems to have been a fundamental clash of personalities. Teruko was particularly close to her
father Kiichi, who would often say, "Ah, Teruko! If only you were a
man!" Her father seemed to embody an ideal which Mokichi could not
fulfill. According to Shigeta, Mokichi and Kiichi were like oil and water;
the same seems to have been true of Mokichi and Teruko. Their attitudes and aspirations were basically different: Mokichi's aesthetic sense
preferred bare wood; Kiichi and Teruko preferred painted surfaces.[8] A
character in Kita Morio's *Nireke no hitobito* (The people of the Nire
family) named Ryūko, who is modeled after Teruko, argues as follows
with a younger sister who wants to marry for love:

> "Do you think it made me happy to become Tetsukichi's [Mokichi's]
> wife? Just between us, I was miserable. But I became his wife without a
> murmur. . . . And if you want to know why, it was because it had been
> decided from the start that I would be Tetsukichi's wife: it was my duty
> to accept as my husband the heir to the Nire Hospital. If only Ōshū [Seiyō]
> had been born sooner . . . no, that wouldn't have helped much—since
> Ōshū just keeps failing his exams. But I got married and never said one
> word of complaint. Do you understand why? Because Father always told
> me to. . . ."[9]

If we can accept this passage from a novel as reflecting the facts, it is
difficult to blame Teruko for trying to live more in accordance with
her own tastes and desires; but her acquiescence to her father's dictates
did not lead to an agreeable family life for Mokichi.

Mokichi's life—with its demanding medical duties and disturbed
marriage—was disrupted when he fell victim to the worldwide epi-
demic of influenza in January 1920, and suffered lung complications in
June. He had a long convalescence, not returning to full duties until
October, but he was relatively lucky: two of his colleagues died of the
same illness. While recuperating, he spent time on literary activity: he
revised *Shakkō,* finished preparing the manuscript of *Aratama,* and began publishing in *Araragi* the series of essays known as *Tanka ni okeru
shasei no setsu* (A theory of shasei in regard to tanka). He makes specific
mention of his illness in the essays, and his weakness during his convalescence affected the tone of the work; one biographer finds a quality
in the style of the essays that suggests a final testament.[10]

Nonetheless, these essays form the core of his theory and practice of shasei. The refinement of the term into a literary theory cannot be credited to Mokichi alone: indeed, in his essays, he traces the use of the term to its origins in criticism of oriental painting, and shows how it developed in the writings of Shiki, Sachio, and other members of the Araragi group, as well as in the criticisms of the term and its implications by writers belonging to other schools. However, Mokichi's understanding of shasei is most germane to a reading of his poems, and this discussion will concentrate on his own refinements and explanations. The opening paragraph of the essay " 'Tanka to shasei' ikkagen" (Tanka and shasei: a personal view) is a description of how the concept of shasei had become indispensable to Mokichi in writing poetry. It was not that he created the theory for himself and then tried to write accordingly: "My theory of shasei emerged from the act of writing poetry, and so it is unthinkable to sever the theory of shasei from my works. . . ."[11]

The term *shasei* itself derives from the visual arts, and means sketching from life. One of Masaoka Shiki's definitions of the meaning of shasei, "to depict reality (*jissai*) as it is," seems to reflect this visual orientation. Shiki admired Western painters for their insistence on working from observed nature, rather than from imagination alone or from their knowledge of conventions for representing reality.[12] But the difficulty remained in defining "reality." In Mokichi's definition of shasei, he chose a Buddhist word for "reality," *jissō,* which broadened the implication from the concrete, tangible world to a more inclusive world of all realms of existence and perception. The writer's relation to that world he expressed with a word of his own creation, *kannyū,* "to see into, to penetrate". His famous definition is: "to penetrate reality and depict life as the unity of nature and self; this is shasei in terms of tanka." Nature is not merely landscape; it includes within it all human life as well.[13] It is interesting to note that Mokichi first used the term *jissō kannyū,* "to penetrate reality," in relation to the paintings of his friend Hirafuku Hyakusui, whose art he saw as the product of the difficult, solitary task of "penetrating reality."[14]

Mokichi recognized that this definition could be seen not as a specific literary theory but as a general theory equally applicable to all art. The specific requirements and implications of his theory emerged as he refuted criticism, frequently by the use of illustrations from visual art. The use of such examples and the origin of the term in the visual arts led some critics to suppose that shasei was purely descriptive, but Mokichi energetically denied the inference. He also denied that temporal or physical movement was excluded from art based on shasei, citing the work of such visual artists as Courbet, Cezanne, and such schools of painting as cubism and expressionism. To believe that shasei was merely a depiction of an external, static realism was a misunderstanding of the term. "Reality" included emotions as well as objects: "the expression of a natural outpouring of emotion becomes the depiction of one's own existence, the penetration into reality; it becomes shasei."

Mokichi chose several tanka by Shiki as examples of shasei; one was the poem cited in chapter 1:

ki no moto ni	The place beneath the tree,
fuseru hotoke o	where, surrounding the form of the
uchikakomi	reclining Buddha,
zō hebi domo no	the elephants and snakes
nakiiru tokoro	are all there weeping.

The first three lines, Mokichi felt, were not remarkable, but the selection of "elephants and snakes" (*zō hebi domo*) as the expression of all animals of creation, and especially the direct movement to their activity, was a special characteristic of shasei; a form of expression derived from a true penetration into the reality of the experience.[15]

Even apparently static, descriptive poems, if they are true examples of shasei, contain within them a kind of understanding of the essence of experience which transcends the merely descriptive. An example, also drawn from Shiki's *Take no sato uta,* is the following famous poem:

kame ni sasu	Because the clusters
fuji no hanabusa	of wisteria gathered
mijikakareba	in the vase are short,
tatami no ue ni	they do not even reach
todokazarikeri	as far as the tatami.

Mokichi insisted that the last line, *todokazarikeri,* "they do not even reach," contained feeling as well as fact, and expressed the importance of the simple action of perceiving the flowers in the life of the bed-ridden poet; there is emotion in expressing an objective fact in negative terms.[16] Mokichi insisted that no secondary concerns, no formal contrivances, intervene between the objective reality and the natural revelation of the poet's internal response. Nature is not the only subject of shasei; the beholder's response as well can be the central concern.[17]

Antecedents of shasei in the visual arts lead some critics—Yosano Akiko, for example—to suppose that writing a poem according to the theory of shasei resembled an artist taking a sketchbook to the country-side to draw landscapes: a poem was to be written on the spot. Mokichi vehemently denied this. ". . . Such opinions," he said,

> are really idiotic; there is no need to say that because something or other is shasei, one must follow a specific superficial method. It is perfectly fine to depict life on the spot; or to let time pass and then depict life; or to write from a distance; or to write later; or to write while walking; to write lying down is also fine. The point is that one must depict life by means of penetrating reality; this is what is shasei.[18]

Penetration, or discernment, is an internal process. Again turning to the visual arts, Mokichi cites Rodin on sketching: "I look at this [the object] as it is, without drawing. Then my spirit is satisfied and becomes permeated with the impression of it. In my head I continue to do sketches of this model. I memorize these moving lines. I repeat it a hundred times. Like a caress, I endlessly repeat this sketch." Mokichi believed that the most salient points were the memorizing and the repetitions in one's head. This internalization is, in shasei as well, part of the process of penetrating reality.[19]

A final definition of shasei is the following passage from Mokichi's essay: "By following the impetus of poetic feeling, freely, directly, profoundly, and with certainty—without mixing in secondary, worldly thoughts, without becoming carelessly distracted along the way—to express that which is to be expressed, is shasei."[20] Mokichi believed that from the *Man'yōshū* on through Genroku period haiku poetry, as well as in European painting and sculpture, a variety of artists in various times and cultures were unconsciously practicing shasei. Perhaps the clearest expression of a poetic ideal is best expressed in poetry, however, and a poem from American literary history which seems to do so is the following by Emily Dickinson. It could well be describing Mokichi's response on first reading Shiki's *Take no sato uta;* or the response of any reader to a poem that catches the essence of shasei:

> This was a Poet—It is That
> Distills amazing sense
> From ordinary meanings—
> And Attar so immense
>
> From the familiar species
> That perished by the door—
> We wonder it was not Ourselves
> Arrested it—before—[21]
> . . . .

During his more than three years in Nagasaki, Mokichi rarely published his own poetry; there was a "halt in the upward curve of his poetic development."[22] He was of course aware of this, and included in *Tsuyujimo* (Dew and frost), the volume of poetry containing his work from this period, a poem lamenting this slump in his career as a poet:

> Nagasaki ni   Do not question me
> kite yori awarenaru   about this piteous lack
> uta naki o   of poetry since
> ware ni na toi so   I came to Nagasaki:
> sabishiki mono o   there has been such loneliness!

Nonetheless, *Tsuyujimo* contains 706 poems written in Nagasaki; Mokichi did not compile the manuscript from his notebooks of the Nagasaki period until the summer of 1940, and it was not published until 1946; other notebooks were lost in the fire of 1924.[23] Evidently, he continued writing poetry, even if it was not among his best, during this period; in fact, Mokichi attended a poetry meeting in Nagasaki before he gave his first lecture. His home before long became a meeting place for aspiring poets who, until his arrival, had been associated with various other groups. He influenced some of these poets profoundly. The group became known as the *Yakiimo Tankakai* (The Baked Yam Poetry Group), because of the yams they enjoyed at their meetings. Following the practice of Shiki and Sachio, Mokichi would light a stick of incense and ask all present to compose a poem during the time it took the stick to burn. If, even after it burned out, Mokichi had not yet finished his poem, he would pick through the ashes to find the stub, announce that there was still a little incense left, and go on thinking about his poem. He was active in a publication devoted to poetry and the arts called *Orandabune* (Dutch boats), put out by medical students, and ran a column in *Araragi* in which he published the poetry written by his new disciples.

He rarely published his own poetry, however: despite his involvement with literary affairs, he was dissatisfied with his own creative efforts. He was definitely in a poetic "slump." [24] Mokichi described his state in strong language: "I feel like a madman fallen into dementia, who, without even speaking any last words, goes silently to his death." [25] Nevertheless, he was not quite silent: he continued writing, even experimenting with the *bussokuseki* (Buddha's footprint stone), a thirty-eight-syllable poetic form (see chapter 4). Some of the poems composed at this time merely relate to his interest in the exotic history of Nagasaki, and do not give the impression that he had penetrated any profound reality:

Hendoriku	The wife of
Dōfu no tsuma	Hendrik Doeff* was a woman
Nagasaki no	of Nagasaki;
omina nite sunawachi	that is to say, she bore
Dōfu Yōkichi umiki	the child Dōfu Yōkichi.

Others have greater poetic value:

yūgure no	The white blossoms
taizanboku no	of the magnolia trees
shirohana wa	in twilight:
ware no nageki o	as though enshrouding
ōu ga gotoshi	my lamentations.

In February 1921, Mokichi's dream of studying in Europe became a reality when he was appointed by the Ministry of Education to a position as a researcher abroad. On October 28, he set sail from Yoko-

---

*Hendrik Doeff was director of the Dutch factory on Deshima from 1799 to 1817, and worked at the compilation of a Dutch-Japanese dictionary, the Doeff Halma. (Donald Keene, *The Japanese Discovery of Europe, 1720–1830*, pp. 79, 125, 237n5.)

hama.[26] The last group of poems in *Tsuyujimo* were composed on the journey; this poem describes the Indian Ocean:

watatsumi no	Although the sky
sora wa tōkedo	above the broad sea
katamareru	is so remote,
kumo no naka yori	from within the clouds amassed
rai nari kikoyu	I can hear the peal of thunder.

Europe: Vienna

Mokichi was already thirty-nine when he went to Europe, and he felt as though time was gaining on him; before leaving Japan in the fall of 1921 he wrote to Akahiko, "Poetry I can do at any time, but somehow medical work gets more difficult as one gets older, and so I must do it now." His sense of self-respect demanded achievement and recognition in medical science; in the Japan of the 1920s study in Austria or Germany was the most respected path toward this end.[27]

Mokichi reached Berlin in mid-December, carrying letters of introduction from Kure Shūzō to various professors with whom Kure had studied twenty years earlier. In Berlin Mokichi met Maeda Mozaburō, a distant cousin from Yamagata prefecture, who held a League of Nations position within the Japanese Embassy related to the supervision of the German army after the First World War. Maeda, who was to offer considerable support and assistance to Mokichi during his European stay, was somewhat nonplussed at their first meeting. He was surprised by Mokichi's rather disheveled appearance, so different from the other Japanese students in Germany, who were younger and more cheerful; by his heavy provincial accent, so unexpected in a man who had received most of his education in Tokyo; and especially by Mokichi's uncertainty as to where he wanted to study. He was wavering between Hamburg and Vienna when his wallet, with the letters of introduction to professors in Hamburg, was stolen; this seems to have induced him to choose Vienna.[28]

In January 1922, he began to study at the Neurologischen Institute of Vienna University under the guidance of Heinrich Obersteiner (1847–1922), the founder of the Institute, who though retired retained an active interest, and his successor, Otto Marburg (1874–1948). Marburg assigned Mokichi his research topic, which concerned alterations in the histological organization of the brain cells of patients who had suffered from the progressive paralysis associated with the final stage of syphilis. Mokichi settled in to work with great diligence, feeling a responsibility to demonstrate his abilities now that his dream of study in Europe had come true; he also felt under pressure because of his own constant comparison of himself with the five younger Japanese doctors who were his colleagues. In a letter to Hirafuku Hyakusui written on February 2, 1922, he referred to the others, in their twenties and early thirties, as being in their prime, and then to himself as he approached forty as living and working like an ascetic recluse.[29] Unlike the younger doctors, study in Europe did not mark the beginning of his medical career; he had been practicing for ten years. Furthermore, he was obliged to return to a position which was not entirely of his own choice. The years in Europe formed a precious period in his life that seemed lifted out of its preordained course, when he could devote himself to his own medical research, and he was determined to make the most of them.

His first research topic formed the basis of his dissertation, "Die Hirnkarte des Paralytikers: Studien üben das Wesen und die Ausbreitung des paralytischen Prozesses in der Hirnrinde" (The Brain Patterns of Paralytics: Studies on the Forms and Distribution of the Paralytic Process in the Cerebral Cortex).[30] His findings were composed of the scholarly analyses of data obtained by the painstaking work of selecting, dyeing, and microscopically analysing fifty specimens from each of seven brains. The work required, if not conceptual originality, diligence, perseverence, and technical skill, a combination of qualities Mokichi possessed.[31] The manuscript was submitted as his doctoral thesis in Vienna in March 1923. It was accepted, and printed in April; together with his other work, it also earned him a doctorate in medicine from Tokyo Imperial University in September 1924. By the time Mokichi left Vienna, he had completed three other studies, covering physiology as well as neurology, and had studied some psychology as well.[32]

This intense work was made possible in part by the encouragement and respect of Obersteiner. Mokichi's teacher Kure had also studied under Obersteiner with Marburg, as well as under Kraft-Ebbing; in particular, Kure and Obersteiner remained on terms of mutual respect and affection for the rest of their lives. During the postwar economic turmoil in Austria, stipends sent by Kure to provide for Japanese students at Obersteiner's Institute were a tangible sign of his respect for the work of Obersteiner and his colleagues.[33] Mokichi met Obersteiner during his first weeks in Vienna, and although his daily contact was with Marburg, Obersteiner's interest and approval were of the greatest importance to him. In an essay about Obersteiner written in 1927, Mokichi recalled how he was working alone in the laboratory one day in March 1922 when Obersteiner came in, and in the silence watched him take specimens from a brain and carefully identify them. "Professor Obersteiner watched for a while, and then said, as if to himself, 'The Japanese are extremely skillful with their hands.' Then he said, 'That is a very demanding piece of work. But you can't expect to accomplish much in a single month, so you must be patient.' "[34] Mokichi wrote a poem about the incident:

omoimōkezu	Unexpectedly
rōsensei	the aged teacher came
soba ni tachi	and stood beside me;
kanketsu ni ware o	with great simplicity he
hagemashitamau	offered me encouragement.
	(*En'yū*)

Mokichi was heartened by Obersteiner's recognition of his technical skill and his diligence. Obersteiner frequently commented that nothing valuable could be accomplished quickly, and when he urged Mokichi to be patient and persevere, he touched a responsive chord.

Mokichi's first visit to Obersteiner's home increased their sense of mutual respect. Obersteiner inquired after Kure, and commented favorably on Mokichi's research, and on the fact that Mokichi was a poet. Obersteiner admired him for it because poetry, he said, emanated from "the interior of life." This was particularly gratifying to Mokichi, who wrote: "A year later I made my way to Germany, where I met many professors, but I was never again to hear words so filled with kindness as his."[35]

However, Mokichi's poetry during his eighteen months in Vienna was uninspired. *En'yū* (Distant travels), published in 1947, contains the poems written from January 1922 through July 1923. In the Afterword,

Mokichi wrote about his various research papers, and his travels through Austria, Germany, Hungary, and Italy: "This was the sort of busy life I had, but I thought that I would like, if possible, to leave some small remembrance of my time in Europe, and decided to note down poems in the margins of my record." With no time for deep thought or extensive revision, Mokichi treated the volume of poems that resulted from these jottings as "a poem diary."[36] As a result, the poems occasionally present a striking depiction of a specific circumstance, but rarely reach beyond to make universal a particular experience; they rarely permeate the realities depicted.

The completion of his dissertation was a great relief:

dare hitori	Since not a soul
koko ni izareba	is here beside me,
ronbun no	I close the pages
pēji o tojite	of my dissertation, and
namida gumitari	my eyes fill with tears.
	(*En'yū*)

He rewarded himself with a trip in June 1923 to Italy, which he recorded in a series of descriptive poems:

San Pietoro no	I stood close
maruki hashira ni	beside the rounded pillars
waga mi yose	of St. Peter's,
hekiga no gotoki	and watched a line of priests
sō no retsu miyu	as though peering at a fresco.
	(*En'yū*)

But it is through his essays and reminiscences, rather than through his poetry, that his experiences in Europe come most alive to readers. In narrative prose accounts such as "Seppun" (Kisses), or "Donau genryū yuki" (To the source of the Danube), Mokichi's reactions to the scenery and culture of Europe have an immediacy and drawing power that is lacking in the poems.[37]

Once his research had been completed, the restlessness Mokichi had been feeling in Vienna increased. He felt some dissatisfaction with the guidance of Marburg, especially after Obersteiner's death in November

1922.* Perhaps also he felt impelled by a need to take full advantage of the opportunities for research Europe offered. These circumstances persuaded him to continue his work in Munich.[38]

It is disappointing to discover that Mokichi seems to have evinced no interest at all in the work of Sigmund Freud, either in choosing Vienna as his first location in Europe, while he was there, or in the following years. However, at the time the work of neuropsychiatrists, who sought a physiological basis for mental illnesses, was most influential. Particularly important was the school of Emil Kraepelin (1856–1926), who in his career in both the clinical and neurophysiological aspects of psychiatry "succeeded in bringing into a chaotic accumulation of clinical observation a system of distinct disease entities that has stood up remarkably well into the present time," and whose "authority ruled supreme at the turn of the century and the following two decades."[39] Mokichi was therefore not out of the mainstream in taking this approach. Why the spheres of research and study were—and to some extent still are—considered mutually exclusive is unclear; however, there is no doubt that the exclusion of analytic theory from Mokichi's study was a profound loss to his work.

In September 1939, Mokichi wrote a brief obituary of Freud for the *Asahi shinbun,* in which he reviewed in somewhat deprecating terms Freud's career and achievements as the founder of psychoanalytic theory. The last line of the short obituary, which refers to the work of Freud's final years, is revealing: "This theory will probably make its mark in the world of the arts rather than in the sphere of medicine."[40] Mokichi's failure to see the implications of this judgment to his own life's works seems like deliberate blindness. Throughout his life, medicine and poetry were in opposition: either he devoted himself to one,

---

*Some of Mokichi's dissatisfaction with Marburg may have been because Marburg was a Jew. Mokichi had a particular interest in Jews, stemming from a visit to New Year's services in a Nagasaki synagogue during his stay in that city (see "Nagasaki tsuioku," *SMZ* 5:729–34), and increased by his association with Jews at the Institute and in the families with whom he boarded. However, his relief at discovering that Obersteiner was in fact not Jewish indicates that he had absorbed some of the anti-Semitism that was rife in Austria and Germany at the time. A Japanese colleague at the Institute suggests that Mokichi's difficulties with Marburg also derived from Mokichi's poor command of spoken German, which led to some tension and misunderstandings (Yamagami Jirō, *Saitō Mokichi no shōgai,* pp. 251–52).

to the neglect of the other, or he escaped from the rigors of one world into the satisfactions of the other. He seems to have avoided any attempt at integrating the two, and his rejection of Freudian theory, in his own words an apparently ideal means for approaching such an integration, is emblematic of that avoidance. So is his departure from Freud's Vienna on July 19, 1923, to go to study at Kraepelin's institute in Munich.

Munich

Mokichi moved to Germany with anticipations of a fruitful period of research, but his life in Munich was beset with difficulties. The inflation and social dislocation in the wake of the First World War had been severe in Austria, but it reached astounding proportions in Germany. One of Mokichi's diary-like poems on the subject has an arresting quality both because of its subject matter and because of the apparently artless skill with which the incident is recorded. It concerns a conversation overheard in September 1923:

gaijō o	Some young boys are
dōjira katami ni	talking to each other as
katari yuku	they walk down the street:
"pensaki hitotsu	"for one single penpoint
gojūman māruku suru yo"	I paid five hundred thousand marks!"
	(*Henreki*)

Mokichi's son Shigeta recalls a souvenir his father brought home with him: it was a bill issued in 1923 with a value of 2 million marks; the paper money had so little value it was printed only on one side.[41]

In "Nankinmushi nikki" (Bedbug diary), Mokichi chronicled his difficulties in finding suitable lodging. In room after rented room, he was afflicted by bedbugs, which were particularly tormenting because of his sensitive skin. With each new search, rents increased. Mokichi would spend the late summer days working in his laboratory, and the evenings examining or trying out new lodgings. He described one such evening as follows:

It followed a series of trying experiences, so I got my flashlight ready, undressed completely, and crawled into bed. Then I must have passed an hour or so in musings about my birthplace of Japan when, just as I reached the uncertain state between waking and sleeping, I was set upon by bedbugs. For a moment I felt terribly angry, but my feelings soon quieted down. So I hurriedly put on my clothes, opened the door, and went out into the street. People were still up and about. I stopped to drink a large glass of beer, then I fled back to [Marie Hillenbrand's]* place.[42]

Mokichi's difficulties in finding suitable lodgings were occasioned not only by the inflation and other financial problems that afflicted the whole city, but by his own extreme frugality: he considered only the cheapest rooms. Unlike many foreigners who came to enjoy themselves rather than to study, and who ended by paying someone else to write their dissertations, Mokichi studied diligently. He amused himself in his leisure hours by wandering through the city, strolling in cemeteries whose art he admired, sitting in cafes to read or watch passersby, ordering a cup of coffee every hour or so, and continuing the habit formed in middle school of browsing through second-hand bookstores. He scrimped on his lodging to have money for books, and asked Maeda to ship them to Japan to avoid export taxes. In a letter to Maeda of January 26, 1923, he had written that the medical books he bought were his "treasures."[43] They would enable him to continue doing research after he returned to Japan.

In late August 1923, in the midst of Mokichi's search for acceptable lodgings, he received word that his father had died the month before. It is an interesting comment on his poetic productivity during his stay in Europe that Mokichi wrote only two poems on his father's death, in marked contrast with the major fifty-nine-poem sequence on the death of his mother during the *Shakkō* period. Although it is possible to argue that the contrast results from differences in his relationships with his parents, and his own increased maturity in the intervening ten years, he

*Marie Hillenbrand was an Austrian woman of about sixty who was the subject of "Nihon ōba" (*SMZ* 5:778–83). She had been providing lodging and guidance to Japanese students since she was a young woman helping out in her mother's boarding house. She was known among the students as *Nihon bāsan* (Japanese grandma); her home was a refuge in times of trial. Willi Hillenbrand, her thirty-year-old son by a Japanese student who had long since disappeared, often assisted Mokichi during his search for a place to live. Mokichi lived in her house during his last seven months in Munich.

wrote prose with greater artistry and perception than he wrote poetry
during his years in Europe. Neither of the poems on his father's death
has great merit; one follows:

waga chichi ga	In this distant
oite mimakari	land of Germany, I am
yukishi koto	deeply lamenting
Doitsu no kuni ni	that my father, grown old,
hita ni nagekau	has gone to his death.
	(*Henreki*)

Instead, Mokichi's elegy was the collection of reminiscences, cited frequently in chapter 1, entitled *Nenjushū* (Prayerbead collection):

> When I learned that my father had died, I felt a terrible sense of loneli-
> ness. I was apt to find, then, that both during the day and when I lay down
> at night to sleep, mournful memories of my father from my childhood
> would float into my consciousness. Sometimes I would think that I would
> like to capture them in writing. . . . Should not memories such as these
> be told one by one, like the beads on a rosary? [44]

Less than a week after receiving the news of his father's death, on the
evening of September 3, 1923, Mokichi sat alone in a restaurant with a
half-liter of beer before him and began to read a newspaper. It contained an account of the Great Kantō Earthquake: 100,000 people dead
in Tokyo and Yokohama. Mokichi wrote: "For a while I held my breath
as I read those words, but somehow I was unable to feel that it was a
real event." Nonetheless, he could neither eat, sleep, nor work. He
spent time with other Japanese at Marie Hillenbrand's, waiting for the
next edition of the newspapers: each account was worse than the last.
The reports on the fires resulting from the earthquake described how
one could read at night by the light of the conflagration. German friends
expressed sympathy, and strangers stopped him in the street to condole
with him. [45]

> At night I did not sleep well, and as dawn approached, when I thought I
> was dozing, I frequently dreamt. In these dreams, a woman—who looked
> like my wife, but I don't know if she was my wife or not—and a child are
> sitting on the tatami. They are facing away from me, and no matter how

often I call to them, still they do not turn in my direction. I would wake up then from the dream. Some nights, I would come home drunk on beer, and sleep. When I did, I would dream of a scene filled with densely flickering flames. At other times I would become convinced that my family and friends in Tokyo were all lost.[46]

Among the poems Mokichi wrote in the agony of uncertainty is the following:

waga oya mo	When in my heart
meko mo tomora mo	I think that my parents, and
suginishi to	my wife and child, and
kokoro ni omoe	my friends as well, all are gone,
namida mo idezu	even my tears won't flow.

(Henreki)

But his prose seems to express better the unreal quality of this harsh trial of helpless waiting; it rises in emotional intensity as in the excerpt above, and ebbs with mundane details that show Mokichi's life in a foreign country creeping blankly forward as he clung to his Japanese friends, who shared his painful condition.

This limbo of uncertainty lasted until the evening of September 13, when a telegram* from Nakamura Kenkichi, sent from Kobe, finally reached Munich via Berlin: "YOUR FAMILY FRIENDS SAFE."[47]

There had been relatively little damage to the hospital in Aoyama: the brick wall surrounding the grounds had collapsed, and the roof had lost all its tiles, but there was no fire, and the hospital was intact. Kiichi had reached Odawara on his return from Hakone to Tokyo when the earthquake disrupted train service. He was walking along the tracks to Tokyo when fortunately he met a friend with a car, who drove him to Tokyo. It took him three days in all; Teruko had taken charge of all hospital affairs in the meantime. When Kiichi reached home, he collapsed at the door with exhaustion and relief that all were safe.[48]

---

*The day the telegraph office reopened in Tokyo, Akahiko sent word to Kenkichi, then working for the Osaka *Asahi shinbun* office. Kenkichi was able to send an overseas telegram (Katō Yoshiko, *Saitō Mokichi to igaku*, p. 94). It was among many received by the Japanese embassy in Berlin, but Maeda recognized the name and relayed it to Mokichi immediately (*SMZ* 5:802). Kenkichi sent the wire in English because it was shorter and therefore cheaper than romanized Japanese, which in any case is difficult to read (Saitō Shigeta, November 21, 1978, personal communication).

Shortly after the earthquake, Kiichi ordered Mokichi to come home: his help was needed. Mokichi had just begun to work in Munich and was reluctant to return, but he could expect no further support from home. He decided that he must stay, and sought advice from Maeda and financial help from friends at home. He eventually received money from Hyakusui,* who had solicited commissions and sent Mokichi the advances.[49]

A major reason for Mokichi's determination to remain in Europe was that when he moved to Munich in July 1923, he had arrived at the "mecca" of psychiatry of the time, the Deutschen Forschungsanstalt für Psychiatrie (Kaiser Wilhelm Institut), founded by Emil Kraepelin. Kure Shūzō had been the first Japanese to study under Kraepelin; he took back to Japan Kraepelin's *Lehrbuch der Psychiatrie* and used it in teaching. Kraepelin's theories had been familiar to Mokichi for years, and had dominated the world of Japanese psychiatry in which he had trained. Mokichi was eager to meet and learn from him. Kure had also studied, in Heidelberg, under Franz Nissl (1860–1919), and learned cell-dyeing techniques which he taught to his students.[50]

Mokichi was the first Japanese to study in postwar Munich; he had investigated the possibility the previous summer, and had corresponded with Walter Spielmeyer concerning possible research topics. His enthusiasm when he began his work was dampened on discovering that he was expected to relearn, from the beginning, techniques he had already learned at Sugamo Hospital under Kure.[51] His substantial medical experience and achievements were undervalued; he also found that he himself was not treated as a person of distinction by his Munich teachers as he had been by Obersteiner.

Mokichi's long-anticipated meeting with Kraepelin was a disaster. His first opportunity came in October, at the showing of a film on psychiatric disorders to be attended by the revered doctor and other medical dignitaries. In the auditorium before the film, a doctor from Hamburg University offered to introduce Mokichi to Kraepelin. Mokichi described what followed:

. . . we went up together to Kraepelin, and after introducing myself extremely politely, I said I was here doing research in the microscopy section

*Hyakusui was unable to complete all the paintings he committed himself to, and after his death in 1933 Mokichi handled the sale of his works in order to refund the advances.

now, and handed him my card. Kraepelin took the card, but did not even begin to read it. He did not utter a word to me. He immediately turned away and said, *"Bitte nehmen Sie Platz meine Herrschaften!"* Everyone took their seats. . . .

After the film Mokichi attempted again to introduce himself, and offered his hand. Kraepelin very pointedly refused to shake hands with him. Mokichi did not believe that it was a question of race, because Kraepelin was as polite toward two Javanese physicians as he was rude to Mokichi. But other Japanese scholars had had similar experiences. Mokichi eventually recovered a feeling of confidence and, when the occasion arose, could meet Kraepelin's eyes with assurance and perhaps a touch of defiance; but receiving this curt dismissal was a severe disappointment.[52]

This was Mokichi's most direct experience of the anti-Japanese feelings in Austria and Germany. Kraepelin's response is a puzzling one, since he had been hospitable to Kure when the latter visited Europe in 1920, and had accepted funds that Kure sent to Kraepelin's Institute from Japan. He seems to have been suspicious of Japanese with whom he was unacquainted. He was particularly angered by the fact that some Japanese students who fled Europe at the outbreak of the war later sought restitution for belongings they had left behind. His resentment over the exclusion of German and Austrian scholars from international organizations was directed against Japan in particular: perhaps he felt, as many Germans did, that Japan had been ungrateful and betrayed the country that had provided guidance for Japanese scientific progress during the Meiji period. Kraepelin himself had planned at the end of the Meiji period to visit Japan to carry out comparative research, but he never did so.[53]

Fortunately, Mokichi's immediate supervisor, Walter Spielmeyer, was warm toward Japanese students, and he and Mokichi spent off-hours, as well as working time, together. Mokichi's first research topic concerned obstructions in the human cerebellum. He had worked on it from his arrival in Munich in August, preparing specimens, consulting reference works, analyzing his findings, and considering his conclusions, until one December day when Spielmeyer came to check his progress and said: "You've been working hard for a long time; I think your research is fine. However, I do think you should stop here, and add more cases when you return to your own country. What do you think?" Spielmeyer went on to explain that he expected Mokichi, as an experienced physician, to draw original conclusions about the many interesting problems raised by the materials he had so painstakingly assembled, but thought that Mokichi had spent enough of his limited time in Munich collecting data. Additional samples could be prepared and the project completed later, in Japan; now it was time to begin work on a new topic. Mokichi, who did not expect to be able to continue his research in Japan, was disheartened. Spielmeyer's consolatory remarks describing his own experience with research that proved fruitless did not dispel Mokichi's impression that he had failed to live up to Spielmeyer's expectations. Mokichi put his materials in order, went alone to a cafe, and wept with disappointment; he had disobeyed Kiichi's orders to return home in order to continue the very research he had now been told to abandon.[54] His next research topic on the cerebral cortexes of domestic rabbits produced results which, according to one colleague, were of even greater interest than those of his Viennese dissertation, so Spielmeyer's advice proved to be sound.[55] Nonetheless, Mokichi's frustration was typical of his first six months in Munich.

He had been beset by the painful emotions stemming from events in Japan and by the distressing conditions of his daily life in Germany in the months since his move from Vienna; it was against this background that he received Spielmeyer's criticism of his research. The spring of 1924 passed less eventfully, and in May his report on his experiments with the cerebral cortexes of rabbits received Spielmeyer's approval. In July he met Teruko in Paris, and they traveled together to different parts of the continent and England, to return for a full month together in Paris.

Mokichi took the opportunity to immerse himself in Western art. He was so determined that he often tried Teruko's patience: sometimes he would stand for thirty or forty minutes in front of one painting. He was also single-minded in his behavior: when he found it difficult to look at the ceiling of the Sistine Chapel from a normal standing posture, he spread some newspapers on the floor and lay on his back to gaze at the frescoes more comfortably. His notebooks of the period are full of little pen drawings of paintings and sculpture, as well as the various landscapes and objects that caught his interest.

Mokichi's absorption in European art and art history is reflected in the sixty short essays he wrote, from January 1938 through December 1942, on the reproductions used as frontispieces in *Araragi*. He was especially drawn to the sculpture and paintings of the Italian Renaissance, but there is also a good representation of nineteenth-century French art, several Rembrandt paintings, and even a Picasso. The essays contain descriptions and impressions rather than analysis. As a rule, Mokichi identified the artist, the work, and its location, then described the work, providing details of background information such as the biblical story being depicted, for example, or the period in the artist's career when it was made. He frequently then describes when he saw it and how he responded. The essays display a firmly grounded general knowledge of European art history, but few insights. In such short articles, there is perhaps no room for analysis; they convey instead a sense of Mokichi's relationship with the specific works, such as a Donatello sculpture of Cupid he could not tear himself away from, or a Rembrandt painting he went to see whenever he was in Berlin.[56] He was apparently more interested in spiritual nourishment than intellectual engagement, but perhaps also there was insufficient time for him to integrate all he was absorbing.

There is a similar lack of synthesis in the poetry of the period. The work in *Henreki* (Pilgrimage), written during Mokichi's stay in Munich, is on the whole somewhat more successful than that in *En'yū,* but in general both collections are valuable only as source material in reconstructing Mokichi's activities in Europe. There are eulogies at the gravesides of great men which are saccharine in their worshipful tone; there are poems in praise of professors he met and landscapes he viewed; there are even poems chronicling current events such as Hitler's abortive Beer Hall coup. But there is seldom excellence. Mokichi's experiences in Munich, as in Vienna, are depicted in greater depth in the prose pieces written later than in the poetry written at the time.

One biographer believed that Mokichi's years in Europe were agreeable and left him enriched by many memories, but his son Shigeta agreed with Mokichi's disciple Satō Satarō that he constantly produced within himself new afflictions, as though he were made only to suffer.[57] Certainly the experience was enriching, and his medical achievements on the whole were gratifying, but his three years abroad were suffused with loneliness:

ii no naka no   In the moment
suna o kami taru   of biting a bit of sand
toki no ma o   in my bowl of rice,
ryūgakusei no   I feel such loneliness—
ware wa sabishimu   as a student overseas.

(*Henreki*)

Mokichi and Teruko sailed for home on November 30, 1924. The trip ended in indisputable sadness:

On receiving a wireless telegram, at 1:00 A.M.
on December 31, that the Aoyama Mental Hospital
had been totally destroyed by fire.

odoroki mo   Beyond the boundaries
kanashiki mo sakai   of bitter shock
sugitsuru ka   and deep grieving
koto taenikeri   words failed me
amatsuhi no mae   before the bright sun.

(*Henreki*)

Reconstruction

There was a sad irony in the fact that the Aoyama Mental Hospital survived the devastating earthquake and resulting fires of September 1923 only to be destroyed sixteen months later by a fire originating in the preparation of *mochi* (rice cakes) for the coming New Year's celebrations. The fire broke out in the kitchen after midnight on December 28, 1924, and spread through the main building. Within three hours, the imposing structure was gone; with it were lost the lives of twenty-three patients, a doctor, and a staff member. In addition to the tragic loss of life, there were associated minor tragedies that added to the burdens of the survivors. The first was that Kiichi had neglected to renew his fire insurance, which had expired on November 15. The other was that after the fire in the main building had been extinguished, and the firemen had left the hospital grounds, the storehouse caught fire; destroyed with it were nearly all the books Mokichi had sent home from Europe, still in their packing cases.[58] When Mokichi received the telegram informing him of the fire, he wrote in his diary, "I felt as though, with this, everything had ended."[59] When he and Teruko reached Tokyo on January 7, 1925, however, Mokichi found a great deal of work waiting for him.

For the sixty-five-year-old Kiichi the destruction of the hospital, which had been the culminating achievement of his medical career, and the economic difficulties compounded by the expenses of his political campaigns and the lack of fire insurance were overwhelming. He was unable to deal with the financial problems, with the opposition to reconstruction on the part of the hospital's neighbors, with the authorities who refused permission to rebuild on the site, and with the search for a new site. The entire burden fell to Mokichi.

To make the task easier, he traveled in Japan a great deal, combining fund-raising with relaxation, and used some of this time to write many of the essays about his life in Europe: he needed every bit of income he could get for the rebuilding, and accepted as many of the solicitations for his prose as possible. One well-known poem from the time is curiously reminiscent of the poem on German inflation; in both, the focus is on a specific sum of money:

utsusomi no	To deliver me
ware o sukuite	from this harsh reality—
aware aware	ah, how sad, how sad!—
jūmanen o	is there no one at all who
kasu hito naki ka	will lend me ten thousand yen?
	(*Tomoshibi*)

It was a painful period, exacerbated by Mokichi's lack of aptitude for the kind of administrative abilities required; he was characterized by what his sons referred to as having "zero capacity" for such matters.[60] Mokichi, reviewing the year 1925 in his diary entry for December 31, recalled the fire, the trials of rebuilding, illnesses in the family; he recalled as well some progress, some friends toward whom he felt gratitude. He concluded his diary for the year complaining of constant headaches and nervous prostration, and wrote: "I feel that I've aged ten years in this one year. However, I did my best. O gods, protect me, so small, so weak!"[61] Mokichi mentioned no medical research in this diary entry. To be sure, he had had no time for research since returning to Japan; but there was also little inclination. Trying to salvage a few books from the charred remains of the warehouse was a long and tedious process, it involved little hope: "One can say that at the same time that the reference books I had saved for and assembled burned up behind the red flames, my ambitions for the laboratory disappeared."[62] His scientific ambitions were never entirely lost, but he no longer believed he could achieve them. On the other hand, he began to write poetry again. His son wrote, ". . . The attitude with which he untiringly, painstakingly, faithfully peered at specimens through a microscope was embodied, in exactly the same form, in my father's poetry and poetic commentaries. . . ."[63]

But this observation comes with hindsight: it was not apparent to Mokichi himself. In April 1925, he published a collection of his poems called *Asa no hotaru* (Morning fireflies), an anthology of poems selected from *Shakkō* and *Aratama*. In the Afterword to that work he wrote that in the years since he left for Nagasaki and then Europe, the poetry circles of Japan had moved on, and it would not have mattered greatly had he died in 1917, when he finished writing *Aratama*.[64] Loneliness tinges this awareness of having been passed by, but there is also a hint that if *Shakkō* and *Aratama* were all he was to write, they alone would be a valuable contribution to Japanese poetry. However, he also wrote that during his years away from Tokyo he had few occasions to review his own past work, so that on his return, he reread his early poetry as though it were not his own.[65] He seems to have drawn some inspiration from this process: the volume *Tomoshibi* (Lamplight), which contains poems written from 1925 through 1928, is of far higher quality than anything he had written in those intervening years.

Tomoshibi shares with the first two volumes an elegaic quality, a sense of grieving. He wrote in the Afterword, "The fact that I named this volume of poems *Lamplight* suggests, perhaps, that in a life of affliction and darkness I have, with difficulty, lighted a lamp and walked on." It is also linked with the poems from his European stay: "In writing poetry there has been no great progress, because I have been devoting all my energy to my profession [of medicine], but like the poems I wrote in the West, some transcended the bounds of the diary."[66] These two comments reflect something of the nature of Mokichi's poetic composition: poetry was always a means of integrating experience, of imposing an order on the upheavals and experiences of his existence. During some periods of his life, he approached the process with less intensity of concentration, from either a reduced internal need or because of increased external demands on his time and attention, and so he created less compelling poems. The "diary-like" poems of the European period are among them: the words call forth a context of event and emotion in the mind of the writer, but not of the reader. Such poems are valuable at best as biographical sources, and even then not always reliable ones. These diary-like poems are to be distinguished from autobiographical poetry, in which real personal experience is transformed, in conception, by imagery, and by the use of language, into a work of art with wider meaning. Much of Mokichi's best work falls into this category, and is a result of his process of depicting his own life or, to use his term, by penetrating its reality and becoming at one with it. In other terms, he creates a poetic order with the disordered materials of his own experience, and makes it universally accessible.

However, many poems, including a fair number from *Tomoshibi,* fall somewhere in between these two extremes of diary-like and autobiographical poetry. For example:

yakeato ni	The books dug out
horidasu fumi wa	from the ruins of the fire
utsusomi no	are like the corpses
kabane no gotoshi	of the ordinary world—
waga me no moto ni	here before my very eyes—

The structure of the poem, in which the fourth line ends in a final form and the last line is a sentence fragment, provides its strength. The destruction is contained in a complete unit; the scorched books are compared to lost lives and their loss is experienced like a death. The poet is exiled to the last line, looking on the destruction—*waga me no moto ni,* here before my very eyes—but is unable to repair it, or salvage anything from it. Greater depth is apparent only with the biographical background in the reader's mind: those books were the foundation of future research, and with their loss is joined the loss of aspirations. The corpse image then is the additional ironic suggestion of those human corpses "of the ordinary world" on which his research would have been based. Even in partly diary-like poems such as this, then, the craft of the poet in structuring the poem is apparent; additional knowledge expands the poem's significance but is not the only support.

Shortly after his return to Japan, Mokichi wrote a short sequence, "Yakeato" (The ruins of the fire), which included the following poems:

yakeato ni I was standing
ware wa tachitari by the ruins of the fire:
hi wa kurete where night fell, and
inori mo taeshi even prayers failed me, at
munashisa no hate the limit of futility.

kaerikoshi At the house I have
ie ni akatsuki no come home to, at the table
chabudai ni as the day breaks,
honō no ka suru I am eating *takuan*
takuan o hamu that is redolent of flames.

ie idete When I left the house
ware wa koshi toki and came here,
Shibuyagawa ni I saw eggshells
tamago no kara ga floating, flowing with
nagare inikeri the Shibuya River.

There are several aspects to these poems to justify the feeling that Mokichi "directly confronted his life of affliction and darkness and went on to sing of it with a voice that flowed like gushing water." [67] In the first poem, the sense of hopelessness is made palpable by the debris, the darkness, and the sense of desperation. But it is an artfully constructed poem. It ends with nouns—*munashisa no hate,* the limit of futility—which create a verbal wall of finality, and in their lack of movement emphasize the totality of the destruction. Yet the poet, having confronted the abyss, moves on into a semblance of normality. The return to the poet's homeland of Japan is almost celebrated by the *takuan* (a pickle made of dried large white radish), a fundamentally Japanese food, and yet even that is flavored by the destructive force of the fire. The distinctively Japanese smell is overcome by the smell of fire. [68] The important point is that in familiar territory Mokichi was able to focus on the telling details, to see and use those images which in their apparent insignificance are most poetically significant. This kind of choice is clearest in the third poem, on the floating eggshells, which his colleague Koizumi

Chikashi praised for its grasp of mood, and in which his disciple Satō Satarō sees an intuitive grasp of a sense of inevitability.[69]

The choice of such details, whether conscious or not, becomes the means by which the reader is provided with an intimate awareness of the perceptions of the poet; the poems in turn become less diary-like and more self-contained. Mokichi in 1925 was again reaching a level of shared response in his poems, even when writing from a particular experience:

hitori komoreba	When I shut myself away
nani goto ni mo	I am resigned to
akiramete	almost anything,
agura o kakeri	and sit here with my legs crossed:
yoru fukenitsutsu	while the night is wearing on—

This poem is structurally similar to the poem in which the burnt books appeared as corpses, in that the fourth line ends with a final form, enclosing a situation in the first four lines. But it is done with an opposite intent: the poet is central to that situation. The incomplete sentence which is line 5 presents a world from which the speaker is excluded; the time passing highlights his chosen isolation rather than his helplessness. He is still, composed, and lonely, while the night passes to leave him behind, solitary. The poem is successful enough that whether or not one knows that Mokichi was to present a paper based on his Munich research at a conference in Fukuoka, but could not afford to go, is almost entirely irrelevant.[70]

During his travels in Japan, he wrote many fine nature poems:

mukō yori	I was standing there
se no shiranami no	by the Tenryū River
tagichi kuru	where white-capped waves
Tenryūgawa	of the river rapids
oritachinikeri	came cascading from beyond.

Again, the structure of the poem supports the imagery: the flow of the river is repeated in the rhythm of the language, which forms one uninterrupted unit throughout all five lines.

His activity in poetry circles resumed as well, in part because of Shimagi Akahiko's death in 1926: Mokichi resumed editing *Araragi,* until

Tsuchiya Bunmei took over in 1930. But his greatest exertions were still devoted to his career as a psychiatrist. A new hospital was eventually rebuilt in Matsubara, west of Tokyo, with a smaller branch hospital for the treatment of milder problems remaining in Aoyama. But the "open door system" adopted for the new hospital led to an increased number of runaway patients and patient suicides. In addition, the hospital was subjected to frequent inspections as a result of the tragic fire. In the end it was decided that Kiichi's supervision was no longer adequate, and in 1927 Mokichi succeeded him as head of the hospitals. (Kiichi died the following year, alone, during a visit to a hot springs resort in Atami.) [71] After the first few years following his return, Mokichi's life achieved an equilibrium, although his absorption in his medical responsibilities remained a source of pain at the frustrations and conflict between his two careers:

nariwai wa	In my calling
itoma sae nashi	there is not a single
monogurui no	moment of respite:
koto o zo omou	I think about insanity
nete mo samete mo	both waking and sleeping.

(Tomoshibi)

CHAPTER THREE

Separation, the War Years, and the Final Years, 1928–1953

The Public Poet

MOKICHI returned to the forefront of literary activity as the firmly established Araragi school and its major representatives were being attacked by younger poets. Ishikure Shigeru, a young Marxist poet who had been associated with *Araragi* for a short time, published an article in February 1928 entitled "The Progress of Tanka Reform: Araragi Reactionism." Mokichi had written an article on the Kamakura shogun poet Minamoto no Sanetomo, in which Shigeru discovered various reactionary sentiments, claiming that "when a snake crawling through a grassy field shows even an inch of his head, one may understand the size of its whole body." Mokichi's interpretation of Sanetomo suggested to Shigeru that he was feudalistic in spirit; even the modernism in *Shakkō* and *Aratama* was seen as a bourgeois response to social conditions of the Meiji and Taishō periods. Mokichi, who had read Marxist literature in Europe, carefully prepared his response, even requesting Maeda in Berlin to send him additional sources. He challenged Shigeru's use of Marxist terminology by citing original sources, and reversed the charge of bourgeois poetry by citing examples from Shigeru's own poems. The dispute continued for years, with no significant results other than to display Mokichi's determination to have the last word and his enjoyment of the process.

While the dispute was still in progress, Mokichi was attacked on another front. In the November 1929 issue of *Araragi*, he published the following poem, later included in the collection *Takahara* (High fields):

yoiyoi no	In this field where
tsuyu hiemasaru	night after night the dew
kono hara ni	grows ever colder,
yamukari ochite	*an ailing wild goose falls—*
shibashi dani iyo	rest here, for but a moment!
	(italics mine)

Several months later, Ota Mizuho dismissed the poem in a few words as an imitation of Bashō's symbolism in the well-known haiku:

yamukari no	*An ailing wild goose*
yosamu ni *ochite*	*Falls in the evening cold—*
tabine kana	A wanderer's resting place!
	(italics mine)

Mizuho later used this "imitation" as a good reason to call for dissolving the Araragi faction, which had outlived its usefulness. Mokichi, in reply, asserted that the image was not in any case original with Bashō: it first appeared in a poem by the Sung dynasty poet Yang Wan-li (1124–1206). The dispute trailed on with charges and countercharges, but reached no real resolution, because it never focused on the quality of the poem itself or the use Mokichi had made of the image and symbol.[1] Mokichi valued the poem enough to include it in his poetic memoirs, *Sakka yonjūnen* (Forty years a poet), written in 1944. At that time he wrote that the bird was a symbol of the poet, himself ailing, and alluded to the charges Mizuho had leveled at the poem.[2] The notoriety did indeed make the poem famous, but both the dispute and Mokichi's own reference failed to touch on several more interesting considerations. As Okai Takashi points out, in addition to echoing a line from Bashō's haiku, which Mokichi surely knew well, the poem repeats the two first lines of a poem he himself wrote twenty years earlier:[3]

yoiyoi no	Beneath the far skies
tsuyu hiemasaru	where *night after night the dew*
tōzora o	*grows ever colder,*
kōrogi no kora wa	all the young crickets must
shinite yuku ran	be moving toward their deaths.
	(*Shakkō*—italics mine)

In both tanka, the waning of the year, when "night after night the dew / grows ever colder," brings illness and even death to animals in the natural world. There is a difference, however, in the poet's relation to those animals. In the poem from *Shakkō,* the young crickets appear only in the poet's speculation about them; in the later poem, the ailing wild birds are aligned with the poet who addresses them, and who in fact saw them as symbols of himself. Bashō's haiku is both a picture of a sick migratory bird fallen to rest during his journey and a metaphorical depiction of the poet himself. Mokichi's later tanka and Bashō's haiku are similar in the conception of the shared experience of all the creatures in nature, man included; this similarity has greater significance in regard to Mokichi's work as a whole than a single shared, or even borrowed, image.

These literary disputes were carried on during a period of relative stability in Mokichi's life, and a corresponding lack of poetic intensity. The two volumes that follow *Takahara* chronologically, *Renzan* (Mountain range) and *Sekisen* (Stone spring), are filled with observant, competent, but for the most part uninspired poems. Even when written under painful circumstances, such as the grave illness of his brother, the poetry has a placid tone:[4]

urato idete	Going out by the
ware hatanaka ni	back door, I stand grieving
nageku nari	amid the fields:
hito no inochi wa	human life itself merely
kai no ue no tsuyu	dew upon the scallion leaves.
	(Sekisen)

Private Casualty

Mokichi's next volume of poems, however, represents another peak in his creative career: *Shiromomo* (White peaches), published in 1942, contains poems written in 1933 and 1934, and begins with several sequences written during trips throughout Japan. The poems from this period are characterized by a particular attention to sound, for example:

yōyaku ni   Gradually
yowai wa fukete   the years pass,
Hiei no yama no   and I cherish,
hitoakatsuki o   as I walk, a single
oshimiarukitsu   sunrise on Mt. Hiei.

The first three lines are filled with soft sounds: many of the syllables begin with *y* and *h,* a euphonic softness and fluidity suggestive of the natural world at dawn. The last two lines are connected to the first three by sound in the initial syllable *hi,* and by structure because the five lines together form a single sentence. It is the manipulation of sounds in the final two lines, however, that is particularly impressive. They are related to each other by a complex repetition of similar vowel and consonant sounds in altered sequence, with a technique Kenneth Burke calls "tonal chiasmus,"[5] so that the seven syllables of *hitoakatsuki o* (a single sunrise) are projected as if kaleidoscopically on those of *oshimiarukitsu* (I cherish, as I walk). The deliberation required to create this euphonic impression is apparent in the fact that Mokichi coined the word *hitoakatsuki,* presumably for this purpose.[6] The effect of the sound of the poem on its significance is to knit together the natural event of the sunrise with the activity and response of the beholder, so the two form an intricately connected unit. In poems such as this, Mokichi penetrated the reality of the natural world and became one with it.

Toward the end of 1933, however, a series of events ushered in a period Mokichi described as one of "spiritual wounds" (*seishinteki fushō*), and the grief which characterized his earliest work reappeared.[7] Hirafuku Hyakusui and Nakamura Kenkichi, two of his closest friends, died; and between the two deaths, his wife Teruko was involved in the "dance hall scandal" which led to their separation. Mokichi was at a memorial exhibition of Hyakusui's paintings on October 7, 1933, when he was informed that Teruko, along with other patrons and an instructor of a Ginza dance hall, had been arrested for illicit and immoral behavior. The patrons included upper-class women, both married and single, from prominent families, who shared an attraction for the lower-class young instructor. He was nicknamed Eddie Cantor, and earned his living as a paid dance partner. Teruko was known to have accompanied him to other places on ostensibly innocent outings. She denied any wrongdoing in an interview in the *Asahi shinbun,* claiming that she danced as a cure for her insomnia, with her husband's knowledge.

Mokichi was certainly aware of her frequent absences from home: he recorded her early departures and late returns in his diary. The couple had little in common in the best of times, and Mokichi's fierce temper coupled with Teruko's indomitable response led to increased friction. There is also some evidence of sexual incompatibility.[8] The scandal, then, did not destroy their marriage; it merely made its inadequacies public. The publicity devastated Mokichi, and he felt himself betrayed. They lived apart for the next twelve years.

> kanashikaru   There are those men
> tsuma ni shinareshi   who have lost beloved wives
> hito aredo   to death, and yet
> ware o omoeba   when I think of my own state
> hito sae ni nizu   I am unlike even them.

Mokichi had lost a wife who was not particularly beloved, and who had not died; nonetheless he felt abandoned, and his sense of unique misfortune led him to withdraw. He ceded as much administrative work at the hospital as he could to Teruko's uncle. He felt old and a stranger to his own family.

> kitazora ni   In the northern skies
> yūgumo tojite   the evening clouds close in;
> utsusemi no   in this real world
> ware ni semarikomu they weigh down and engulf me—
> yuki ka ame kamo   bringing snow perhaps, or rain—

In four lines a scene is opened on a great expanse—the northern skies—which immediately contracts as clouds appear in the deepening darkness, then closes in on the solitary poet, overwhelming him. The fifth line is appended almost as an afterthought, as if to show it mattered little what the clouds would bring along with their oppressive quality: either way, it would be more oppression. Satō Satarō recalled a remark made to him by the painter Nakagawa Kazumasa to the effect that "Mokichi's poems have a quality that is like the howling of an animal," and found it particularly apt in regard to this poem.[9] It has a sense of inexplicable suffering whose source is inseparable from the whole of the real world, which the poet confronts unprotected. The American poet John Berryman has a poem similar in conception, written in the voice of a domesticated animal, a sheep or cow, lost in a snowy wilderness. The final stanza is:

> I'm too alone. I see no end. If we could all
> run, even that would be better. I am hungry.
> The sun is not hot.
> It's not a good position I am in.
> If I had to do the whole thing over again
> I wouldn't.[10]

In both poems the speakers are without defenses in a world that provides no support. The scandal deprived Mokichi of more than a wife with whom he shared little; he also lost for a time the support of propriety and position. In response he not only withdrew from his professional administrative duties, but also immersed himself in research on the *Man'yōshū* poet Kakinomoto Hitomaro.

Mokichi had absorbed an interest in the *Man'yōshū* even as he learned poetic technique from Itō Sachio and the Araragi school, which saw in that great collection the unself-conscious practice of shasei, the outgrowth of a vital spirit. Mokichi thought Hitomaro was the most profound of the *Man'yōshū* poets. The immediate impetus for his study, however, was a request by the editor of the journal *Tanka kenkyū* for a response to two articles by the critic Hasegawa Nyozekan, who had maintained that Hitomaro was overvalued, and that lacking the social awareness of the best *Man'yōshū* poets, Hitomaro was no more than a petty official and court poetaster. Mokichi had begun the research for his reply to these charges before the scandal; afterwards, the research was the one area of his work that did not seem fruitless in the context of his own grief and anger; "in fact, Mokichi was saved by Hitomaro."[11]

The Love Poems

Mokichi was also saved by love: in 1934 he met Nagai Fusako at a poetry meeting commemorating Masaoka Shiki. Fusako's father was a childhood friend of Shiki's, and the families were distantly related. Fu-sako herself was deeply interested in poetry, and had joined the Araragi group the previous year.[12] She approached Mokichi with reverence for his poetry, and was elated when he read and praised her work. The master–disciple relationship gradually developed into love, bringing joy to Mokichi's lonely world. His life was stained with death and disillu-sionment, and she was young, beautiful, and intelligent. They met fre-quently, corresponded, even traveled together; but Mokichi felt it nec-essary to keep their ties secret. They would send love poems to each other in the archaic, difficult-to-read characters of the *Man'yōshū* to keep them safe from prying eyes.[13] The many love poems in *Gyōkō* (Crim-son dawn) appear with no indication of the object of that love. A se-quence of eight poems entitled "Kōbai" (Crimson plum blossoms) was occasioned by a gift of such blossoms from Fusako:

kozomenishi	These plum blossoms
sakinioitari	deeply dyed and flowering
ume no hana	in fragrance:
asa na yū na ni	in the mornings, in the evenings,
mi ni chikazukenu	I draw them close to me.
oiraku no	Although it is said
hito to iedomo	I am a man grown old,
otome saburu	I will never grow
akaki ume no hana	weary of these red plum blossoms,
ani akame yamo	so like a young maiden.

Even in these two poems, there are indications of the nature of the love shared by Mokichi and Fusako. In the first poem there is a constancy: "in the mornings, in the evenings," they seem to have been aware of each other. When they could not meet, they telephoned; when they could not speak, they wrote letters. In the second poem Mokichi pic-tures himself as an old man, responding warmly to the fresh brightness of the maiden-like flower. Fusako was twenty-eight years younger than Mokichi, and she lent him the sense of youth and freshness contained in the blossoms.

Fusako was, in a sense, Mokichi's first love: his early elegies for the shadowy figures who were models for "Okuni" and "Ohiro" con-cerned unrequited or failed love; his yearning poems as a young man toward his "child-bride" were filled with the anticipation of love. With Fusako, Mokichi could bare his spirit, sharing even his love for poetry with her. Once he sent her the opening three lines of a poem and asked her to supply the final two.[14] They agreed on a completed version:*

hikarihanatsu	Cared for by
kami ni mamorare	the light-granting gods,
morotomo ni	together—
aware hitotsu no	such empathy! with a single
iki o ikitsuku	breath we breathe a sigh.

They could not agree, however, on the course their love should take. Fusako, still single at twenty-seven, was pressured by her family to find a husband. Mokichi, well-established at fifty-five with four children, did not offer himself as her husband, although his ties to his wife were nearly all broken, and he was plagued by jealousy at the thought of Fusako in connection with any other man.[15]

Mokichi in the end was very much tied to the world and his position in it as a prominent doctor and a major poet. This position had real meaning for him, and he seemed incapable of living in the world without such supports. The most painful aspect of Teruko's dance hall scandal was the disgrace of public knowledge and disapproval. Even for the love of Fusako he could not bring down the similar notoriety of divorce on himself. He thought about a life beyond this world; it was during this period he began to plan for his own death by selecting a posthumous name and writing out the characters that were to appear on his tombstone.

ka no kishi ni	After we have reached
itarishi nochi wa	that other, distant shore, all
madokanite	will be tranquil;
otoko omina no	the divisions between men
kejime mo nakemu	and women all will disappear!
	(*Gyōkō*)

It was Fusako who finally found the situation intolerable. She broke off an engagement she had formed at her family's insistence, and left

---

* Mokichi found Fusako's first response a little weak, and wrote again to request another try. His love apparently did not interfere with his poetic judgment.

Tokyo to return home to Matsuyama. When her father died, she felt it to be retribution, and stopped corresponding with Mokichi. She also stopped writing poetry, and never did marry. She learned of Mokichi's death fifteen years later while watching the news on television.[16]

The social conditions of the 1930s may have played a part in separating Mokichi and Fusako as well:

> As the war progressed, Mokichi became timid in love. He feared the notice of the militarists, who thought of the raptures of love as a crime, and his feelings of hesitation before the world grew stronger. Mokichi was taken in by this, and wrote and published many poems in praise of war. This activity and love did not go well together. . . .[17]

The War Poems

Mokichi's son Kita Morio has said that the family should thank Nagai Fusako for appearing as she did in Mokichi's life during a time of loneliness and grief. He has also said that although he has love and admiration for his father, he finds it difficult to forgive the effect of his nationalism on his critical judgment and poetic creativity.[18]

As *Shiromomo* was characterized by poems on the destruction of an unhappy marriage, and *Gyōkō* by hidden love, Mokichi's next volume, *Kan'un* (Cold clouds) was characterized by poems glorifying war. In it Mokichi progressed from a poet of love to a poet of patriotism.[19] He also changed from a private to a public poet. The war in China intensified following the Marco Polo Bridge Incident, and the home front responded: five patriotic poems of Mokichi's were nationally broadcast on radio on October 9, 1937, among them the following:

kurogane no	Let us put on
kabuto kamurite	our helmets of steel
idetatamu	and go forth!
ōkimi no tame	in the cause of our sovereign,
oya no kuni no tame	in the cause of our fatherland!
	(*Kan'un*)

The poem is not without craft. There is a strong rhythmic progression in the first three lines, and there is strength in the final two lines with their parallel structure and noun endings. Still it lacks the poet's own voice: it is all art and no emotion.[20] It can be classed with those poems Mokichi referred to as "uniform poems": the "uniform" is a military one, and since "thousands of poets, tens of thousands of poets" have chosen that uniform as their subject, there is bound to be monotony. However, since the subject is a national one and not an individual one, they cannot be judged by ordinary literary standards.[21] Mokichi consoled himself with this notion, but many of his war poems are indeed individual, and still not very good. In the same year, he wrote the following two poems on the war with China:

Shanhaisen no	When I think of the corps
butai omoeba	at the battleground at Shanghai,
honōdatsu	my heart is ablaze
kokoro to narite	with rising flames, and
koyoi nemurezu	tonight I cannot sleep.
obitadashiki	Looking on as
gunba jōriku no	the legion of chargers
sama o mite	is going ashore,
watakushi no atsuki	my own hot tears
namida sekiaezu	flow unrestrained.

(Kan'un)

Mokichi wrote poems such as these after watching newsreels in movie theaters. From the evidence of his diaries as well as his poems, there is no doubt that the emotions expressed were genuine, but the sentiments can also be interpreted as those of an older man watching younger men go to battle, and in this sense as vicarious feelings. Neither of these poems is particularly well crafted, although Mokichi's euphonic sensitivity is apparent in, for example, the transfer of sounds within line 4 of the second poem, *watakushi no atsuki,* softened in line 5 with *namida sekiaezu.* The extra syllables in all but the third line serve no apparent internal purpose.

His support of the war was especially conspicuous because of his literary fame and productivity, and for this reason he was singled out as an object of censure after the war; but he was by no means alone. In reply to a question regarding the current national situation in the October 1937 issue of *Tanka shinbun,* Mokichi wrote, "poets are also citizens of the nation, so I will exert myself as a member of the general mobilization"; nearly all the other poets questioned replied in basically the same way.[22] As Donald Keene emphasizes in an article on literature of the war years, *"almost everyone was involved"* in the production of patriotic, inflammatory writings.[23] Kitahara Hakushū, for example, "saw no need to question the direction in which his country was going. Like most contemporary poets, he wrote his share of jingoist verse; poems on patriotic themes for children in particular enjoyed widespread popularity."[24] In Mokichi's case, his book of commentary, *Man'yō shūka* (The best poems of the *Man'yō*), was carried into battle by thousands of young soldiers.[25]

Mokichi's support was not merely a matter of course; it was enthusiastic: war stirred his blood. He was a patriot in the Meiji mold, and firmly believed it his duty to follow, and not to question, the Emperor and through him the nation. His responsibility was to serve, not to judge. The roots of this patriotism were firmly planted in his childhood, in his war games, and his prayers for his soldier brothers who fought in Manchuria. They were nurtured in his manhood as well, in his study of the *Man'yōshū* and his association of himself with Hitomaro. Mokichi viewed Hitomaro's reverence for the Emperor as an expression of a vital age, and he sought to transpose that vitality to modern times.[26] This was not simply a response to the increased militarism of the 1930s, but was an outgrowth of the respect he inherited from Shiki and Sachio for the spirit of the *Man'yōshū* age. He admired the following poem by Hitomaro:

> *Poem written by Kakinomoto Hitomaro at*
> *the time of the Empress' excursion to*
> *Ikazuchi Hill, "the hill of thunder"*

> Our Lord,
> a very god,
> builds her lodge
> above the thunder
> by the heavenly clouds.[27]

In *Tomoshibi,* a collection which had been predominantly concerned with Mokichi's own trials, there is a poem with the same two initial lines:

ōkimi wa	Our Lord,
kami nishi maseba	a very god,
atarashiki	eternally
chikara o tsune ni	favors us with the
tsukurase tamau	creation of new strength.[28]

This kind of celebration of the nation's source of strength as resting in the being of the Emperor guided his responses to the war. Mokichi was not ignorant of political theory, as we have seen; however, he was looking at the visible reality in the form of newsreels, and not at the underlying causes for the activities. After the war he wrote:

gunbatsu to	When I think that
iu koto sae mo	I did not even know
shirazarishi	of such a thing
ware o omoeba	as military cliques,
namida shi nagaru	my tears flow forth.
	(*Shirokiyama*)

Mokichi believed in the ideal: he had no political acumen and no interest in politics. In 1933, for example, he wrote poems and diary entries on his response to the Japanese incursion in northern China, but made no reference at all to the Japanese withdrawal from the League of Nations. His dispute with the Marxist Ishikure Shigeru, which involved studying Marxist theory in order to be able to respond effectively, strengthened his conservatism by forcing him to defend shasei as it was manifested in the *Man'yōshū*. He considered the *Man'yōshū* not only a poetic model but a spiritual one, and he valued the obedience to the imperial will expressed in the Frontier Guard poems.[29] For Mokichi, a sense of duty dictated his support of the national course. He had seen enough of the aftermath of defeat in Europe in the early 1920s to believe that victory must be attained no matter what the cost.[30]

His spirit, then, was wholly engaged, and the poor quality of his patriotic poems cannot be attributed simply to technical virtuosity without substance. It was difficult for him to compose his first public nationalistic poems: ". . . for the first poems for broadcast, I was completely in the dark as to the methods I should use to create poems for the public taste."[31] His difficulty was that his own strength as a poet was in *dokueika*, "poems recited alone," as he had recognized years before in "Dokueika to taieika" (Poems recited alone and poems recited to another), published in final form in 1919 but begun in 1910. The main point he had then made was that the poet must address either himself or a single other person directly, and not pay any attention to a third person. Only in this way can the poet be totally faithful to his own feelings.[32] By addressing himself to the entire Japanese population, Mokichi lost his own poetic voice. His nationalism, objectionable as it may be to modern readers, was at least a true expression of his background and beliefs. The literary product of that nationalism was an abandonment of his own poetic truths, and is also objectionable. "The prominence of the practical, patriotic Mokichi was, regrettably, the regression of the literary Mokichi."[33]

The Final Years

Mokichi remained in Tokyo during the early years of World War II, administering the two branches of the Aoyama Mental Hospital. His written instructions to his staff in 1941 cover all aspects of hospital routine, from patient care and staff procedures to the treatment of visitors; and they conclude with emergency procedures in the event of fire or air raids.[34] The ordinary tensions of the work were increased by the war, and Mokichi was growing tired. There was in fact a fire at the Matsubara Hospital in 1943; afterwards, Mokichi began to spend a great deal of his time in Hakone.

In March 1945 he evacuated Tokyo and returned to his home town of Kanakame. As the war intensified, the army was purchasing additional hospital space, and in early May 1945 Mokichi sold the Matsubara branch. Later that month the Aoyama branch and house were destroyed in the bombings; after forty-three years in operation Kiichi's legacy was gone.[35] This was the immediate cause of Mokichi's reunion with Teruko, who joined him in Kanakame.

Mokichi remained in Kanakame (after Teruko returned to Tokyo to live with Shigeta and his wife) with his younger sister Nao throughout 1945, although he was troubled by the additional burden he was placing on his family when times were difficult and food was so scarce. His sister recalled how he would offer to help with the farm work, get himself appropriately dressed, and join her at work in the fields, only to stop after a few short minutes and admit defeat.[36] Nonetheless, his return home after fifty years away brought a certain tranquility in spite of the difficulties of adjustment and the grief of Japan's defeat. In the following poem from *Shōen* (Small gardens), his depiction of himself, while tinged with sadness, is also colored by a gentle sense of proportion:

akagane no	The color of copper
iro ni naritaru	it has turned,
hageatama	my bald head—
kaku no gotoku ni	to become like this
ikinokorikeri	have I lived on.

In January 1946, Mokichi moved to the town of Ōishida, where food was less scarce, at the invitation of the poet Itagaki Kaneo. The poems he wrote during the two years he lived there are collected in *Shirokiyama* (White mountains), which is the fourth and final major peak of his poetic career.[37] While he regretted leaving the familiar landmarks of his childhood home, especially missing the daily sight of Mt. Zaō, the town of Ōishida amid a snow-covered landscape and beside the majestic Mogami River soon felt as much like home. Two poems in the first few pages of *Shirokiyama* reflect these responses:

asa na yū na	Mornings and evenings
kono yama mishi ga	I have gazed at that mountain,
amanohara	but now I have come
Zaō no mienu	to where Zaō in fields of
tokoro ni zo koshi	heaven cannot be seen.

shizukesa wa	Is this what
kaku no gotoki ka	quietude is like?
fuyu no yo no	on a winter night
ware o megureru	the sounds of the air
kūki no oto su	which surrounds me.

Mokichi had glimpses of quietude for perhaps the first time in his life, yet he was still troubled by his old companions of loneliness and grief. There is a progression in *Shirokiyama* which reflects, first, Mokichi's sorrow at the trials of the immediate postwar period, exacerbated by his own illness during his first spring in Ōishida; second, a repose which followed from the isolation of an old man in a new age and brought with it its own loneliness; and finally, an uneasiness which found its expression in longings for his family in Tokyo, especially for his new grandson Moichi, Shitega's first son, who was born in April 1946 while Mokichi was still in the north.[38] In this collection, however, Mokichi's poetic voice is strong; he had returned to the autobiographical poems which, though derived directly from his own experience, are self-contained, and rarely require knowledge of his biography. One that does require some background and information concerns a burdensome sense of responsibility for his collaboration with the war effort:

> michi no be ni   Beside the road
> hima no hana saki-   the flowers of the *hima* plant
> tarishi koto   were blossoming:
> nani ka tsumi fukaki   like my feeling of
> kanji no gotoku   some kind of heavy crime.
> (*Shirokiyama*)

The *hima,* or castor-oil plant, was cultivated for its oil, which was used in medicines and manufacturing.[39] Its contribution to the war effort was surely made in total innocence; the poet himself had believed in his own rectitude. Yet he cannot deny a sense of guilt, even though he is as yet unable to define his own crime.

This sense of the incomprehensibility of a reordered new world left him with an emptiness that was difficult to dispel:

> Mogamigawa no   Float on, upon
> nagare no ue ni   the current of
> ukabeyuke   Mogami River!
> yukue naki ware no   oh, destitution
> kokoro no hinkon   of my driftless heart!
> (*Shirokiyama*)

The contrast between the stately and graceful flow of the river and the heavy heart of the speaker is, as in all Mokichi's best work, created by both sound and structure. The first three lines flow with a predominance of *a* sounds and repeated soft *g*'s; the fluid lines are tied to the consciously directionless poet as the last word in line 3, *yuke* ("go on"), is repeated in slightly altered form and meaning in the first word of line 4, *yukue* (destination). The last word of the poem, the object of "Float on" (*ukabeyuke*), is *hinkon* (destitution): with its heavy syllables and double consonant endings, it falls like a stone in water.

The pain earned Mokichi a certain sense of resignation, if only to his own alienation and aging. The following poem was written after the promulgation of the new constitution in November 1946, which heralded a "new age" for Japan:

atarashiki   I try to live on,
tokiyo ni oite   growing aged in
ikimu to su   this new age,
yama ni ochitaru   like a chestnut
kuri no gotoku ni   fallen in the hills.
                                  (*Shirokiyama*)

The abstract quality of the effort in the first half of the poem is given a peaceful and homely concrete form in the second. The ripening and falling of the chestnut is unself-conscious and unnoticed, but natural and in keeping with the order of its world.[40]

In sickness as well, there was comfort in the continuing cycles of nature for the poet who was suffering from a sense of dissociation from the world as well as from illness:[41]

maboroshi no   As I pass my days
gotoku ni yamite   like an apparition
arifureba   lying ill here,
koko no yozora o   in the night sky above me
kari ga kaeriyuku   the wild geese return.

In these poems from *Shirokiyama,* Mokichi was again exploring the reality around him and the emotions within him, and selecting the details and language that would convey them most clearly: he was practicing shasei at its best. During his years in Tōhoku, he again took up painting, which he considered equal to poetry as a means of "penetrating reality."[42] Mokichi had been fond of drawing as a child, even to the point of imagining that he would be an artist when he grew up, and this fondness never left him. When he first became a disciple of Sachio, he had done some paintings, and throughout his life he filled his notebooks with sketches of scenes and objects he wanted to remember. One of his closest friends, Hirafuku Hyakusui, had been a painter; and one of his joys in Europe had been his study of Western art. But his talent was not fully realized until his stay in Ōishida.[43] While Mokichi was still in Kanakame, a poetry disciple named Katō Tōryō presented him with painting supplies in an effort to allay his sadness. Katō showed him some of the fundamental techniques, and recalls Mokichi's delight when he learned how to make grapes look round. Mokichi's intense involvement with painting did indeed bring him great joy. In Ōishida where he was warmly received and hospitably treated, the tranquility of his daily life and surroundings, in spite of his sorrows and loneliness, contributed to the development of his artistic talents.[44] From the second floor of his little detached house, he could look out at the view of the Mogami River, and it was here he did most of his paintings. He developed a warm friendship with the painter Kanayama Heizō, and together they would go out to sketch, until Mokichi's avid questions and comments prompted Kanayama to tell him to go away and write a poem. Mokichi's early efforts were clumsy: he tried to depict simple stones, but they looked, according to Itagaki's children, like beefsteaks.[45] But Mokichi applied himself to his task with characteristic tenacity, and acquired considerable skill in a comparatively short time. Katō and Itagaki were both so impressed they were convinced that if Mokichi had chosen to become a painter, he would have been a master. After his death they assembled his paintings and documented them, sure that once Mokichi's paintings became widely known, they would inspire the compliment of forgery.[46] Whether their fears were justified or not, the book they produced of his paintings is most impressive. The pictures of stones, it is true, are not successful, but they are bolstered by Mokichi's sure calligraphic hand in the accompanying poems. It did not take long for his paintings, almost all of them depicting fruits, vegetables, plants, and flowers, to become more confident. The focus in the beginning was on form and texture, with little obvious attention to composition, although in some of the earlier works the depictions of fruit—five small cherries or two or three plums—make fine use of the surrounding blank paper. As Mokichi gained control over the technique of painting, he turned his attention to pattern and composition. A series of paintings of single peony flowers emerging from a tangle of leaves, executed in May and June of 1947, shows a dazzling command of pattern and composition.[47] While it is idle to speculate on Mokichi's potential achievements as a professional painter, as an amateur he was able to achieve an unusual individuality of vision.

The development of Mokichi's painting was halted, however, by his deteriorating health and his return to Tokyo. In early 1947, he was stricken with a mild partial paralysis of his left side, which was followed by insomnia. Even when he managed to sleep he had nightmares, and his vision was disturbed by spots before his eyes.[48] New taxation laws made him worry about money, particularly with respect to his sons' ability to support themselves and their families. Mokichi wrote furious letters to Shigeta, who had opened a private practice in psychiatry at the end of the war: to be assured of patients and income, Shigeta should "treat anything"; psychiatry was too risky in hard times. Shigeta compromised and added internal medicine to his practice. In a similar mood, Mokichi insisted that his second son, known by his pen name Kita Morio, study medicine, because no one could be sure of earning a living as a zoologist, Morio's first interest, let alone as a writer.[49] (Both sons have done admirably well in their chosen fields.) Mokichi finally returned to Tokyo in November 1947. He was by then an old man in health and attitudes, although only sixty-six in years: the pleurisy of the first spring in Ōishida and the paralysis of the next year had left their mark:

> kono karada   This body of mine
> furuku narishi   has become so old
> bakari ni   that when I go
> kutsu tsukiyukeba   to put on my shoes,
> tsumazuku mono o   I find myself stumbling—
>   (*Tsukikage*)

A freedom from convention was a compensation for this sort of trial of old age: he no longer cared what people thought of him. In fact he would embarrass his children with so complete a disregard for propriety as rinsing out his false teeth in public, or sitting down to rest on heavily trafficked stairways.[50] His grandson Moichi was his chief source of joy. In Shigeta's busy household, Mokichi was the child's most constant caretaker and playmate.[51]

Mokichi also worked on preparing manuscripts for publication, many consisting of works written years before. *Tomoshibi,* for example, was written during the years 1925 through 1928, but not published until 1950. The poetry written during these last years in Tokyo was published posthumously in *Tsukikage* (Moonlight). In 1951, Mokichi received a national award for cultural achievement, the *bunka kunshō.* From then on he grew continually weaker. In March 1952 he paid his final visit to Asakusa, the neighborhood where he had lived when he first came to Tokyo:

> Asakusa no   There were times
> Kannondō ni   when I would make my way
> tadori kite   to Kannon's temple
> ogamu koto ari   in Asakusa and pray:
> ware jishin no tame   prayers in my own behalf.
> (*Tsukikage*)

Mokichi died on February 25, 1953, of heart failure. His death was a peaceful end to a full life. Kita Morio, who had just completed medical school, has said that Mokichi's kidney, lung, and circulatory problems, and general weakening, suggested that he had worn himself out by having lived with such intensity.[52] It is difficult to sum up the life of a man who contributed so much in so many fields, spanned such drastic social changes during his lifetime, and lived in so many worlds. Much in his collected works has been outdated: in medicine, scholarship, and critical theory, even the most influential works lose their importance except to the historian. Mokichi's poetry, however, is a permanent contribution: the more one reads it, the more alive the poet seems, even in poems such as this which concern his own death:

> akatsuki no   In the faint light
> hakumei ni shi o   of early dawn, I have
> omou koto ari   thought of death—
> jogairetsu naki   that death which brooks
> shi to ieru mono   no exceptions.
> (*Tsukikage*)

Part Two

THE POETRY

CHAPTER FOUR
Tanka

SAITŌ MOKICHI, unlike many of his contemporaries who ex-
perimented with a variety of poetic forms, wrote and published tanka
almost exclusively. In his collected works there are 11 free-style poems
and 55 haiku drawn from his letters, notebooks, and occasional publications; but of the 14,200 or so poems published in his seventeen poetry
collections, all but one poem sequence are tanka.[1] This sequence consists of 25 poems in the thirty-eight syllable, six-line form known as
Buddha's-footprint-stone poems (bussokusekika). It was written in com-
memoration of Kure Shūzō's twenty-five years as a professor of medicine, and is included in the volume entitled Tsuyujimo (Dew and frost).
The sequence opens with the following poem:*

Nagasaki no	To the mountain range
minato o yorou	arrayed around the harbor
yamanami ni	of Nagasaki,
kimukau haru no	the approaching springtime comes,
hikari sashitari	its light shining brilliantly!
amatsuhikari wa	ah, its heaven-filling light!

In the Man'yōshū, the six-line form was used for religious and celebra-
tory poems. The sixth line often repeated the fifth in the same or slightly
altered form, and was a means of emphasis and of closure.[2] Mokichi
chose the form to honor Kure, and wrote one poem for each year of

---

*The opening poem is the only one of the twenty-five that does not specifically refer to
Kure; it is therefore the least "occasional" in character, and the most useful for purposes
of comparison.

Kure's career. As in the above poem, the last line frequently emphasizes the image of the preceding line. Here, the single word *hikari* (light) is repeated, and it occupies a different position within the seven-syllable line. In line 5, it is in the opening position, and is followed by an action (*hikari sashitari,* "the light shining"); in line 6, it is in the second half of the line, and is preceded by a modifier indicating the source of the light (*amatsuhikari wa,* "the heavenly light"). The action of line 5 brings the light to earth, to illumine the harbor and hills of Nagasaki. The modification in the next line widens the poem's sphere to include the heavens, exalting the scene. The last line is further integrated into the poem by the continuation of the many *a* sounds which dominate the poems. Nonetheless, the poem seems bottom-heavy; the functions of the sixth line do not justify its presence in poetic terms.

The images and language recall an earlier, famous tanka, the last poem in *Aratama* (Uncut gems):

asa akete	At daybreak,
fune yori nareru	the great steam horn
futobue no	sounds from the ship,
kodama wa nagashi	its echo lingering:
namiyorou yama	the mountains arrayed.

This poem, though shorter, seems more complete. The auditory image of the steam horn sharpens the visual image of the mountains as it passes through them, while the light of the longer poem almost obscures them. As readers of Mokichi's poems, we are more accustomed to the five-line form, and so the sixth line takes us by surprise. However, as a writer Mokichi too was more accustomed to the tanka, and the sixth line was treated with conscious intention and deliberate craft, but not with complete success.

Mokichi was above all a tanka poet; the form suited his voice so well that he rarely looked beyond it. The regulation was itself liberating: by acknowledging the requirements, he was able to control them and not be controlled by them.[3] Kitahara Hakushū's well-known description of a tanka as "a small, green, antique jewel . . . old but still valuable"[4] is a comfortable but misleading one, for in Mokichi's hands the tanka was certainly not an unchanged or unchanging form, receiving only surface luster as it passed from generation to generation. He dealt with the restrictions of the form because he believed in the intensity of the "texture" of the multilevel structure which the form provided.[5] Although one may speculate about why Mokichi never ventured beyond the tanka to create original forms for his creative energies, the central concern of this chapter is to explore the restrictions and possibilities inherent in the form and the use Mokichi made of them: to discover why he wrote tanka by examining how he wrote them.

The Form

In the most fundamental terms, the tanka is a poem of thirty-one syllables which are divided into five lines of, respectively, 5–7–5–7–7 syllables each. The sounds and meaning of the words that fill those lines must cohere to form a unified whole. Both elements, sound and sense, have equal importance.[6] The order of word groupings within each line must be considered, as well as the order of the lines. No line is independent; each is read with the memory of the preceding line or lines in mind.[7] For example:

yakeato ni	I was standing
ware wa tachitari	by the ruins of the fire:
hi wa kurete	where night fell, and
inori mo taeshi	even prayers failed me, at
munashisa no hate	the limit of futility.
	(*Tomoshibi*)

The first line presents a picture of burnt embers which fills the line and establishes the scene of the poem: *yakeato ni* (by the ruins of the fire). The next three lines expand on the scene with a sequence of noun subjects and descriptive verbs: line 2 places the speaker beside the ruins, *ware wa tachitari* (I was standing); the third line widens the image of the scene by enclosing it in natural darkness, *hi wa kurete* ("the sun fades away," night falls). Line 4 provides a brief hope with its first word, *inori* (prayers), which it extinguishes in the next, *taeshi* (failed). The final line then characterizes the entire small world created in the preceding four: *munashisa no hate* ("futility's limit"). The sound and sense units within the first four lines have been divided fairly equally, so they have a feeling of balance. The final line reinforces this balance, although it ends with a noun rather than a verb (*hate*, limit), modified by the fluid sounds of "emptiness" (*munashisa*). In effect, the smooth and rhythmic progression from line to line in the first four lines ends with a final rush toward an unalterable finality, an inescapably conclusive closure. This is one example of the ways in which the poet's use of the established five-line form can work to his advantage.

The relations among the five lines are not, of course, always cumulative:

yūyami no	Crossing the sky
sora o tōrite	filled with the dark of evening,
izube aru	it goes to the source
mizu ni kamo yuku	from which the water flows!
hitotsu hotaru wa	a solitary firefly—
	(*Gyōkō*)

Line 1, again, presents a single image: *yūyami* ("evening darkness"). The next line further defines the image, *sora* (sky), and adds movement, *tōrite* ("crossing through"). Line 3 presents a new location, a place which is a source for something not yet mentioned; line 4 provides that "something" with *mizu* (water), as well as an additional action, *yuku* (goes). Line 4 also adds an exclamation, *kamo*, indicating that this mysterious scene is moving to the poet, and breaking the line into four units *mizu.ni.kamo.yuku* ("to the water—ah!—[it] goes!"). The line thus has an unsettled tone, appropriate to the equally disconcerting fact that we do not yet know the subject of the verbs of action *tōru* and *yuku*. In the fifth line, *hitotsu hotaru wa* (a solitary firefly) the poem is completed; the actor is provided. But it is not a final culmination of the preceding lines; it is reflective. The scene of dark sky and water source is reconstructed with these two words to include a moving point of light. With the last line, the whole poem "reverberates" anew: this is the source of the poem's strength.[8] The grammatical inversion, in which the subjects of the verbs follow rather than precede them, functions in such a way that in effect the poem is read both forwards and backwards.

Grammatical inversion within the five-line framework of a tanka was used by Mokichi not only to provide retrospective significance to the images of a poem, but to provide contrast as well:

akibare no	The light has become
hikari to narite	imbued with autumn's brilliance;
tanoshiku mo	how joyfully
minori ni iramu	must they greet their ripening!
kuri mo kurumi mo	the chestnuts, and the walnuts—
	(Shōen)

The subject of the third and fourth lines is unstated until the final line, when "the chestnuts, and the walnuts" appear. However, unlike the previous poem in which the image of the dark night sky was altered by the addition of the firefly, in this poem the established image of the brilliant autumn light is intensified by the contrast with the small dark-brown nuts gleaming in it; the conjectured emotion is explained but not altered. The importance of the concise final images of nuts is emphasized by the great economy of sound in the two word clusters in line 5. Okai Takashi demonstrates this by using roman letters to analyze the component vowel and consonant sounds; here there are only three of each: *krm.krmm; uio.uuio.* In this poem as well as the preceding one, the use of inversion completes the poem and gives an added dimension.[9]

The prescribed five-line form, then, creates expectations in the reader's mind that influence his or her reading, and it allows for the manipulation of those expectations by the poet to strengthen the poem. The last line can both expand the poem's emotional content and allow for a strong conclusion, as in the following simple, declarative poem:

otōto to	My brother and I
aimukai ite	sit facing one another,
mono o iu	speaking of things;
katami no koe wa	our voices to each other's ears
chichi haha no koe	echoing our parents' voices . . .
	(Shiromomo)

The first four lines of the poem interrelate in several ways. Lines 1 and 3 have more vowels than consonants, for a softness of tone; in line 1 all five syllables are *o* sounds, and three of the five vowels in line 3 are also *o*. The speaker's younger brother, *otōto,* has been introduced in line 1; lines 2 and 4 then repeat the reciprocity of the relations between the two men: *aimukai ite* (facing one another), and *katami no koe* (each other's voices). The picture created so far is a simple, tranquil one of two brothers chatting together; line 5 adds a dimension of time and the impression of two more people present at the scene. From the date of the poem, as well as the impression it creates, we know that both father and mother had died many years before; their presence, hovering within the brothers' voices, is implied by the sentence fragment *chichi haha no koe* ("father's and mother's voices").* The fifth line projects an added function back onto line 4; it not only emphasizes the focus of the brothers on each other; it also provides a structure for line 5 to follow. The echoes of the parents' voices in the brothers' memories reach the reader because line 5 parallels line 4 in form and content. They are nearly the same: *chichi haha no* ("father's/mother's"; "parents") replaces *katami no* (each other's) and the particle *wa* ("as for") provides the connection; the word *koe* follows in each case. The brothers, themselves adults, find the reflection of their parents in themselves comforting, for they retain something of those they love even when they have lost them.

Parallel structure such as this exploits the fact that the tanka form requires certain lines to be the same length. Mokichi used that restriction to good advantage, even on occasion repeating whole lines intact, as in the following poem written on the death of his teacher Itō Sachio. It is the first poem of a ten-poem sequence "Hihōrai" (On receiving bad news), in which Mokichi learns of Sachio's death and runs through the dark night to inform his friend and colleague Shimagi Akahiko:†

hitahashiru	As I run desperately
waga michi kurashi	my way is dark;
shinshin to	it weighs on me
koraekanetaru	unendurably;
waga michi kurashi	my way is dark.
	(Shakkō)

Lines 2 and 5 are identical, yet the meaning is altered by means of its context within the poem. Line 1 is an action, *hitahashiru* ("running desperately"); line 2 fills in the scene of the action and, since line 1 modi-

---

*The poem was written in 1934; their mother had died in 1913, their father in 1923. The verb "echoing" is added to the translation because English is not as comfortable with sentence fragments and their implied conclusions as is Japanese.

†Mokichi added a short description of the event in prose to the sequence; he also described it in greater detail in *Sakka yonjūnen* (*SMZ* 10:409–11).

fied line 2, the identity of the actor, *waga michi kurashi* (my way [where I am running] is dark). It has a physical, concrete connotation. Lines 3 and 4 concern the emotional response of the actor, in which the situation described in the earlier lines is perceived as unbearable. Therefore when line 2 is repeated as line 5, it has a figurative connotation: "my progress through life is in darkness." The worlds of objective reality and subjective emotion merge, and the darkness of one is intensified by the darkness of the other.

Mokichi manipulated the five short lines of the tanka to serve various poetic purposes. However a tanka, like a sonnet, cannot adequately be defined merely by the number of lines it contains. The way the contents are organized in relation to the structure of the form is also important. In the sonnet, the fourteen lines may be divided into an octave and a sestet, or into three quatrains with a final couplet, depending on the meaning of the poem and its development, so that form and sense are unified. The five lines of the tanka may also be organized in various ways to suit different poetic conceptions, but the form is often spoken of as having two parts: *kami no ku,* "the upper lines," that is, the first three lines, and *shimo no ku,* "the lower lines," that is, the final two seven-syllable lines. While this division is occasionally no more than a customary manner of speaking about a poem, it often has real meaning: there is frequently a break between the two in both the sense and the rhythm.

shi wamo shi wamo	Ah, death, death!
kanashiki mono	maybe after all it is
narazaramu	not such a sad thing:
me no moto ni ki no mi	how easily before my eyes
otsutawayasuki kamo	the fruit falls from the trees.
	(*Shakkō*)

The poem begins with the word death (*shi*) followed by the exclamatory particles *wamo;* this pair of words is repeated to form line 1. It states the topic of the poem, and lines 2 and 3 form a hypothesis. The three lines are a clear unit thematically, and since line 3 ends with the final form of the conjectural ending *ramu,* they are a clear unit grammatically as well. Together they form the *kami no ku.* The *shimo no ku,* lines 4 and 5, present a concrete observation in support of the hypothesis.

The thematic contrast between these two parts of the whole is strengthened by the formal composition of lines within the five-line unit. Line 3, for example, is a single unit grammatically and euphonically, *narazaramu;* line 4 is a string of seven short words, four nouns linked together by three connectives; *me.no.moto.ni.ki.no.mi* ("before my eyes the tree's fruit"). The contrast between the elements within lines 3 and 4 emphasizes the two-part structure of the poem; the relation between these two parts is the essence of its meaning. The reader must participate in the association which makes the thematic unity of the poem apparent.

The five individual line units are clearly intact as well, although the requisite syllable count is not. The poem has thirty-four syllables in lines of 6–6–5–8–9 syllables respectively. It is a *hachō,* "broken meter," poem. Mokichi wrote many such poems. Lines characterized as *jiamari* (too many "letters") or *jitarazu* (too few "letters") are acceptable in the conventions of the form if they satisfy a particular poetic requirement.[10] At least one admirer of Mokichi's work, the poet Tsukamoto Kunio, finds the broken meter in this poem totally unacceptable. The poem, he believes, is "a flood of unregulated sentimentality"; not a heart overflowing and bursting the dam of words, but a stuttering, faltering clumsiness as though the poet were unable to control his own language.[11] It is important to realize here that the poetic justification for altering the established, and expected, form must be strong enough to propitiate a reader whose sense of norms is violated: the poem must have a sense of inevitability.

Certainly this poem's conception is a truism: death is part of the natural cycle of life. In its position in the sequence "Kinamida yoroku" (Record of yellow tears), where the poet's response to death is surrounded by his observations of the minor details of life, the poem's association of natural life cycles with human life and death seems appropriate. The preceding poem concerns the activities of life within the very province of death, the crematorium:

> kasōba ni   The narrow brook here
> hosomizu shiroku   by the crematorium
> nigori ku mo   flows whitely clouded—
> mukō ni hito ga   upstream someone must have
> kome o togi tareba   rinsed off the daily rice.

The *kami no ku* presents a condition; the *shimo no ku* the conclusion the poet draws from it. Line 5 is *jiamari*: it has eight syllables. The poem following "Ah, death, death!" is also concerned with minor detail; it also states a condition in the *kami no ku,* and comments upon it in the *shimo no ku;* lines 2, 4, and 5 each have an extra syllable:

ryōte oba	There I was with
zubon no kakushi ni	both hands thrust into my
ire itari	pants pockets:
ono ga mi o hashi to	I don't think of myself
omowanedo sabishi	as pitiable, yet I felt desolate.

The two-part structure and the extra syllables, then, are part of the context of the sequence as a whole as well as of the poem. All three poems are concerned with the contrast between the trivial details of normal life and the overpowering pain of human death, and the juxtaposition of the two seems to overflow the form. The apparent irreconcilability of those two elements of existence is reflected in the two-part structure; the intense effort being made to reconcile them is reflected in the way the lines exceed the conventional limits of the form.

Furthermore, since the poem "Ah, death, death!" was unaltered in the revised version of *Shakkō,* we must assume that Mokichi used the *hachō* qualities deliberately, and we may speculate about his reasons.[12] In lines 1 (*shi wamo shi wamo,* Ah, death, death!) and 5 (*otsutawayasuki kamo,* "how easily it falls!"), the extra syllables are tied to exclamations, which alter statements of obvious fact into momentary, individual perceptions. The short (*jitarazu*) second line (*kanashiki mono,* a sad thing) is emphatic because each syllable must carry a little extra weight; and the long line 4 has a progressing staccato rhythm (*me no moto ni ki no mi*). Such justifications by hindsight, however, are not always sufficient. In this case I believe that the context supports the sense of the poem, in which common, unregulated details of life give rise to a perception that, however true, takes a trauma to be believed; and also justifies the form, in which limits are expanded to contain the seemingly incompatible worlds of normal daily life and of painful bereavement.

The poem is, however, a relatively mild form of broken meter, in which the poet relied upon the five-line units and the two-part division for support. Mokichi's departures from the convention were occasionally more extreme, and often successful. Mokichi believed the *hachō* in the following poem to be justified because of its "artlessness" and as an exercise in shasei; he even chose it as a representative work from *Tsu-yujimo* to include in *Sakka yonjūnen* (Forty years a poet):[13]

yuizuru yama no	The light of the moon beyond
tsuki no hikari wa	the mountain where hot springs flow
kumanakute	is everywhere,
makurabe ni okishi	shedding its light upon the
shirogane no tokei o terasu★	silver watch that I had placed beside my pillow.

The two parts of the poem are reasonably clear, but there are more syllables, thirty-nine in all, in this tanka than in a *bussokuseki* poem, and the division of the words into five lines, especially in the *shimo no ku,* seems arbitrary. However, the profuse quality of the poem reflects the pervasiveness of the moonlight; balanced on the third line, *kumanakute* ("with no corner [untouched]"), of standard length, the breadth of the exterior vista and the rich detail of the interior scene compensate for the radical departure from the norm.

Another broken-meter poem which seems successful despite the even greater disregard of convention is one which Mokichi wrote on the occasion of his first ride in an airplane in January 1929.† The poem is in part one of a five-part, fifty-six poem sequence entitled "Kokū shō-gin" (Songs of the sky) that opens with the roar of a plane called Comet 102:[14]

aradani no	As I pass through
jōkū o sugite	the skies above the wild gorges,
shinjū ni ukabu	it floats to my mind:
"Des Chaos Töchter	"Des Chaos Töchter
sind wir unbestritten"	sind wir unbestritten."

(Takahara)

This is the sort of poem Mokichi had in mind when he referred, in the Afterword, to having altered tanka expression; nonetheless, he did con-

★Tanka are normally printed in one line; I have followed Satō's interpretation of the five-line units (Satō Satarō, *Mokichi shūka,* 1:72–73).
†The ride was part of a series of such opportunities offered by the *Asahi shinbun* company; Kitahara Hakushū, for example, took a similar ride earlier, in 1928.

sider it a tanka.[15] The skeletal structure of the form is present in the suggestion of five-line units, as indicated above, although the poem was printed in a single line as was usual. It is also apparent in the obvious two-part division. Moreover, there is the tanka-like quality of a single conceptual flow, which Satō Satarō finds in this poem, and in an earlier, similar poem from the same sequence:[16]

> sugu me no shita no sangaku yori
> semarikuru *Chaos* / kibishiki sabishisa
>
> From the mountain peaks right below my eyes
> rises Chaos imminent, of bitter loneliness.

The presence of a single foreign word, *Chaos,* in even such a radically altered form, however, is not as mystifying as two entire untranslated lines in the previous poem. The line in German in the poem "As I pass through" is from Goethe's *Faust*. In a section of part two, II. iii., subtitled "Again on the Upper Peneus," Mephistopheles borrows the appearance of the incomparably ugly Phorkyad sisters, and is delighted with himself, as "Chaos' well-loved son." The Phorkyads respond, "we are the daughters of Chaos, indisputably."

Mephistopheles had been, earlier in the scene, disconcerted by the strangeness of his surroundings:

> Though Northern witches I command with ease,
> I'm not so sure of foreign sprites like these.
> Around the Blocksberg I prefer to roam,
> A place where I can feel myself at home.
> . . . .
> But here you step a step and never know
> Whether the ground will bulge up from below.[17]

Mephistopheles is pleased by his temporary new form as a child of Chaos. It is perhaps possible that Mokichi was comparing himself in this sense with Mephistopheles, disconcerted, intrigued, and at moments frightened by the new experience of flying and the new appearance of the world from above. A translation of *Faust* by Mori Ōgai was available, in which the line above read *sore wa watashitachi ga konton no musume da to iu koto wa tashika desu* ("And it is certain that we are the daughters of Chaos"); however, it seems improbable that Mokichi assumed his readers would be familiar with this relatively obscure reference.[18]

It is more likely that Mokichi used the line for its sound rather than its meaning, to communicate the strangeness of the experience and the wildness of the scene below; and that the sense of chaos is contained, in terms of the poem itself, in the unfamiliar German sounds. Mokichi had been using German words in his tanka since his years of study in Europe. Foreign words, Chinese loan words, and modern terms enlarged the vocabulary of tanka, and were one of the ways in which Mokichi, following Shiki's example, enriched the received form. Although Mokichi had insisted on the equality of sound and sense, for many readers the euphonic message of his poems has been a primary form of access to its significance, with sense following in second place. Sound is a major element in the content of his tanka.

The Content

Akutagawa Ryūnosuke, in a famous commentary on Mokichi's poetry in "Hekiken" (Biased views), wrote that Mokichi's work opened his eyes to the beauties of poetry and artistic form; then he added that it "opened his ears" as well.[19] Mokichi used sound as well as sight for imagery, and sound as well as sense to convey meaning. Kajiko Gō writes of his first encounter, as a middle-school student, with a tanka by Mokichi. He read it through silently, then he read it aloud; before he had any idea of the meaning he was moved to tears by the flow of sounds.[20] The poem is from *Aratama,* the first of the sequence called "Ippon michi" (A solitary road):

akaaka to	Brightly, brightly
ippon no michi	the solitary road
tōritari	passes through:
tamakiwaru waga	it has come to be
inochi narikeri	my own inviolable life.

Mokichi would have approved of Kajiki's process through the poem: to understand the "voice" of a poem, he believed, it must be read

aloud.[21] Kajiki, in retrospect, analyzed the tempo of the poem to discover why it so moved him. The pause provided by the adverbial particle *to* at the end of line 1 is followed by the slow, constricted double
consonant and final *n* sounds of *ippon* ("a single length [of road]"); the
tempo is then increased by the repeated *i* sounds of *michi* (road), and
relaxed in the long vowel sound of *tōritari* (passes through) and by the
parallel structure of its components *tōri* and *tari*. The heightened tone
created by the almost indefinable *makurakotoba* (pillow word) *tamakiwaru* (inviolable) is again relaxed in the fluidity of line 5, *inochi narikeri*
("it has come to be [my own] life"). The component sounds of *narikeri*
echo those of *tōritari* in line 3, thus linking the image with the poet's
interpretation of it.[22] The last line also recalls a famous poem by the
priest Saigyō:

toshi takete	Did I ever dream
mata koyubeshi to	I should pass this way again
omoiki ya	As an old man?
inochi narikeri	I have lived such a long time—
Sayo no Nakayama	Nakayama of the Night.[23]
	(*Shinkokinshū* X:987)

Mokichi himself recognized the suggestion of Saigyō's poem in his own,
although he said that the meaning of the line differed in their respective
poems. In Saigyō's usage, it means "because of my [continuing] existence (I have again passed this way as an old man)." In his own poem,
the line means that his life has become identified with the single long
road.[24] However, the allusion adds the implication that his life will also
be long; the road as the poet's fate is projected forward in time.

The poem is in many other ways a difficult one, relying on the cumulative effect of the sequence as a whole and Mokichi's commentary
to provide the context within which to understand it. It refers again to
Mokichi's progress without the guidance of Itō Sachio; the road is shining yet isolated and unalterable, and the poet follows it with a complex
mixture of feelings of resignation and determination.[25] Nonetheless, it
works on the most fundamental level, reaching the reader's emotions
directly as the sounds provide a shape with which to communicate experience. Mokichi was deeply concerned with the sounds of his poems;
this interest influenced his choice of words and diction belonging to an

older, oral tradition, and is clearly demonstrated in the way he "sang" rather than spoke his own poems.*

A less ambiguous experience is shared in the following:

aki fukeshi	Autumn deepens
yama no yūbe ni	and in the mountain evening
waga takishi	even the low-burning flames
hikuki honō mo	that I have kindled here
kōshiki mono zo	seem such beloved things!
	(*Shiromomo*)

By means of the repetition of sounds, the natural context and the speaker's activity are united: the objective reality is merged with the subjective response. In the gentle natural setting depicted by the soft sounds of the words *yama no yūbe ni* (in the mountain evening), the movement of the season and the action of the poet, lines 1 and 3, coincide. The lines are parallel in structure in several ways. Both five-syllable lines are composed of two clusters of two and three syllables respectively. The first cluster in both cases is a noun (*aki*, autumn; *waga*, I), and the second is a verb (*fukeshi*, deepened; *takishi*, kindled). The verbs have the same past ending in attributive form, *shi;* and the sounds of the first word of the section, *aki*, are embedded in the last, *taki*shi. A similar parallelism is apparent in the second section as well; in both cases, an adjective (*hikuki*, low; *kōshiki*, beloved) modifies a noun (*honō*, flames; *mono*, thing). The altered repetition of similar sounds, more clearly seen by following Okai's method and isolating the vowels and consonants (*hkk.hnm/kshk.mnz; iui.oōo/ōii.ooo*), unifies the concrete subject, the low-burning flame, with the poet's perception, its beloved quality. By means of the sounds in which the images are couched, Mokichi indeed seems to have penetrated the reality of the natural world and become one with it; the result is a deeply felt sense of peace.

The following poem uses a similar technique in its arrangement of sounds for a different effect:

sugi kodachi	The grove of cedars
tachite kuraki ni	standing; in the darkness
tachimachi ni	suddenly

---

*See pp. 97–102. Mokichi recorded nine poems in 1938; the recording can be heard at the Saitō Mokichi Kinenkan in Kaminoyama, Yamagata Prefecture.

                chi wa furuite   the earth shudders, and
                rai nariwatari   thunder reverberates.
                                                    (*Takahara*)

The solidity and apparent invulnerability of the scene is constructed by
the heavy repetition of *dachi, tachi,* and *tachimachi;* the fifth time the *chi*
sound appears, however, at the beginning of line 4, it forebodes change.
The sounds in the first section of the poem might be described as ver-
tical sounds—strong, firm, immovable, expressive of the standing trees;
and those in the last lines (. . . *furuite/ rai nariwataru*) as horizontal—
fluid, melodic, expressive of the movement of approaching thunder.
The alteration from one to the other is disturbing. Mokichi creates a
strong impression of a natural occurrence in the poem by means of
visual and euphonic images.

   In addition to sound, Mokichi also depended heavily upon trivial detail, *saji,* as a means of expressing reality. He believed, as I have mentioned, that a tanka is ideally an "expression of life"; that "life" is the
poet's own. He therefore excluded the realms of fantasy from his work,
and relied on details as the component parts which best communicated
the subjective perceptions of his life.[26] Mokichi's shasei relied on the
depiction of a reality (*jissō*) formed of such details as having sand in
one's shoes, or noticing the light play off a flower. There is no impo-
sition of meaning; there are no didactic intentions; and symbolic implications, when they appear, arise almost organically from the perceived
world.[27] Mokichi considered the next poem the kind of successful shasei
he had been trying to write ever since he had read Masaoka Shiki's *Take
no sato uta* (Bamboo village poems) thirty years earlier, and he was delighted with the achievement even though the poem could be accused
of "trivialism."[28]

                oki no ue ni   From the grains
                ware wa sutenaru   of rice I have discarded
                iitsubu yori   atop the embers,
                kemuri wa idete   smoke is emerging, and
                kuroki yakeyuku   it goes on blackly burning.
                                                    (*Gyōkō*)

The images of burning encase the poem, which opens with *oki,* embers,
and closes with *yakeyuku,* goes on burning. At the center, line 3, are

the grains of rice, *iitsubu,* from which the subsequent smoke and fire come; while perhaps no symbolism was intended, in effect an item of no intrinsic significance is the source of the poem's activity. It literally provides the fuel for the poetic fire. Mokichi's attainment of an ideal he had visualized many years before by means of a trivial detail speaks for the value in his work as a whole of such apparently unimportant observations. It is possible to see the poem as a metaphor for Mokichi's process of shasei: the rice burning upon the charcoal is the reality (*jissō*); his own act of placing it there is the process of penetrating that reality (*kannyū*).

Penetrating reality is a deliberate act; shasei is an active, questioning process aimed at unifying the perceived world and the self. Mokichi, especially in his early work, made much use of the first-person speaker acting volitionally. This is the case in the next poem, the second in the sequence "Hihōrai":

honobono to	Faintly, faintly
onore hikarite	its own light shining on
nagaretaru	its wandering,
hotaru o korosu	I kill the firefly:
waga michi kurashi	my way is dark.
	(*Shakkō*)

As is usually the case with Mokichi's poems, the sounds are intimately related across lines: *honobono to* (faintly, faintly) of line 1 is carried over into line 2 in *onore* ("itself"). Three of the four consonants, h.k.r.t, within *hikarite* (shining) are embedded in *nagaretaru,* the *k* replaced by its cognate *g,* and appear again in line 4 in altered sequence in *hotaru o korosu* (I kill the firefly). The faint flicker of light is destroyed, to be replaced in the last line by a darkness, *kurashi,* whose consonants are a slightly altered version of those in *korosu,* to kill. The action of the speaker and the context of the act are thus seen as part of a continuum by means of the sounds of the words.

The sense of the words supports this: the literal and figurative meanings of line 5, "my way is dark," have made even the tentative self-produced light of the insect intolerable; the perceiver acts to alter the reality. The contrasts within the poem become not merely the result of the opposition between light and dark, but also between the speaker and the natural world in which both light and dark appear.[29] In addition, the poem can be read in two ways grammatically. Lines 1 through 3 all modify "firefly"; that is, "the firefly which wanders, shining its own light faintly." The verb *korosu* can be read as a final form, so that line 5 stands alone. In this way the speaker's dark road is set against the scene of action in the previous four lines. On the other hand, the verb *korosu* can also be read as an attributive form modifying *waga michi* (my way), so that the darkness of the road is seen as a direct result of the previous action: "My way, where I kill the firefly which wanders, shining its own light faintly, is dark."

The complexity engendered in this short and apparently simple poem arises from the interplay of sounds, the shifting relationships among the lines, and the active role of the poetic voice. It is a clear demonstration of the wealth of opportunity Mokichi found in the tanka form, a wealth often employed most successfully in autobiographical poems such as this when the speaker of the poem has a strong presence.

Mokichi occasionally used, in conjunction with this active speaker, a device that provided distance in time, thereby creating two levels of experience: the momentary response, and the memory of it. It is another way in which Mokichi created depth of feeling, as in the following poem from *Shiromomo:*

aware aware	How sad, how sad!
den no gotoku	Like a bolt of lightning
hiramekite	flashing through me
waga kora sura o	I have found myself hating
nikumu koto ari	even my own children.

The crux of the poem is the momentary psychological response of feeling hatred where one should, and normally does, feel love; it is sharpened by the six-syllable, exclamatory line 1.[30] The objects of this emotion, the children, *kora,* are accentuated as well by the emphatic word *sura* (even): the two words are the same length, with the same final syllable, and the effect is the euphonic equivalent of the visual devices of italics or capital letters in English. Mokichi believed the poet had to choose carefully among synonyms: among words to express the color red, for example, the poet must chose from among *aka, ake, kurenai, seki, shaku, beni,* and *kō* the one whose rhythms, syllables, and connotations are most appropriate.[31] The word *sura* has an effect that *demo* or *sae* would not have had, even though the meanings are equivalent. The emotion is undoubtedly a piercing one; it has a more suffused meaning, however, because of the use in the last line of *koto ari* ("I have had the experience of"). The poet is speaking from a time when the emotion is past, and he has returned to a more conventional response. Thus the shocking quality is heightened by contrast, and expanded by the residue of feeling. The poet exclaims *aware aware* not only at the flash of feeling, but at the lingering after-image of perception remembered. The *koto ari* creates a distance between the poet and the primary experience, but that space is employed to create a wider context for the experience.

Mokichi used distance in the above poem to place a specific experience alongside its own consequences; in a later poem he used it to place a specific experience in a universal context:

akatsuki no	In the faint light
hakumei ni shi o	of early dawn I have
omou koto ari	thought of death—
jogairei naki	that death which brooks
shi to ieru mono	no exceptions.

(Tsukikage)

The only natural imagery appears early, in the four-syllable words that begin both lines 1 and 2. The faint light of early dawn represents the beginning of a new day, of course; but crowned as it is by the word death (*shi*), it is also seen as an ending, to a long night spent contemplating a final ending. Line 3, *omou koto ari* ("I have had the experience of thinking of . . ."), separates that experience from the present tense of the poem; the seven-syllable length of a normally five-syllable line gives it weight. Line 4, *jogairei naki* ("without exception"), modifies line 5 grammatically, but it also is read with the sense of lines 1 to 3 in mind. The experience of contemplating death, as well as its inevitability, is thus shown to be universal. By omitting a personal pronoun such as the *waga* (my) in the previous poem, the universality of the experience is again indicated. On first reading it seems clear that the poet is thinking of his own death, a reading supported by the poem's inclusion in the posthumously published volume *Tsukikage*. Yet the poem does not indicate whose death is being contemplated, and so it can also be seen to indicate the death of others. By the arrangement of its content, this short tanka is given a breadth that can encompass all of humanity.

The Language

The form and content of Mokichi's tanka were profoundly influenced by his understanding of the *Man'yōshū*. From the beginning of his poetic career, well before he began his scholarly investigations, he "absorbed" the Man'yō style by following Sachio's guidance and Shiki's dictum of reading "from the standpoint of a writer." In his various discussions of technique, poetic viewpoints, shasei, and contemporary tanka, the poems he most often used for illustration were *Man'yōshū* poems.[32] His concern with the details of poetic craft is apparent in the preface to his *Man'yō shūka* (The best poems of the *Man'yō*), in which he emphasized the importance of a careful reading of specific poems:

> In this book, I keep my attention fixed on one poem after another, and do not discuss the so-called *Man'yō* spirit, the Japanese qualities of the *Man'yō,* or the national character of the *Man'yō*. Instead I repeatedly consider such things as how a particle works, or a single verb; or the effect of line 3, or the final line.[33]

As a poet he believed that the source of the tanka "voice" was to be found in the *Man'yōshū* "voice"; to understand it, one had to learn it through the specific examples of the poems.[34] The poems were alive to him, and he did not feel the distance of the thousand years and more between their composition and his reading; he rarely sought a connection between his age and theirs within poems in concrete links with the historic past. His relation was more direct, in what he saw as a shared response to the natural world. The traces of the *Man'yōshū* in his poems were a means of expression he had internalized, and which emerged spontaneously.[35]

His poetic views were established early, and although his style underwent many changes over the length of his career, his adherence to shasei and to his belief in the *Man'yōshū* as the source of tanka expression did not waver. Various aspects of his scholarly research on Kakinomoto Hitomaro have been challenged, notably his views on Hitomaro's death.

Umehara Takeshi, for example, disputes Mokichi's reading of the poems themselves as following a mistaken tradition, begun by Kamo no Mabuchi and continued by Shiki and Sachio, which ignored traditional readings. Mokichi's vision of the tension, honesty, and Dionysian quality of chaos in Hitomaro's work, which he saw in his own poetry as well, is questioned. Umehara finds instead the elegies in *Shakkō*, such as "Hihōrai," "Okuni," and "Shinitamau haha," closest to the true spirit of the *Man'yōshū*, and regrets that Mokichi did not realize and develop that link.[36] However, the question here is how Mokichi's understanding of the *Man'yōshū* influenced his poetry, rather than the accuracy or inaccuracy of his views; if there is a contradiction between Mokichi as a poet and Mokichi as a scholar, it is the poet with whom this discussion is concerned.

Poems are made of words, and the *Man'yōshū* influence is immediately apparent in the words of Mokichi's poems. He made no distinction between the classical and modern languages in terms of their validity as poetic languages: the words had to express the poet's internal rhythms, and for him the language he had absorbed in his reading did so. The blood of his ancestors, he believed, flowed in his veins, and they shared a rhythm that made a shared language appropriate; this would not be true for all poets.[37] It is also not true for all readers, many of whom find Mokichi's archaic diction an obstacle to the enjoyment of his poetry. But it was true for Mokichi, as in the following poem from *Tomoshibi*:

hazama yori	From within the gorge,
sora ni hibikau	resonating through the skies
hisugara ni	(the whole day long
ware wa sabishi e	I have felt such loneliness!)
narusawa no oto	the sound of the resounding rapids—

The word *narusawa* in line 5 was used in the *Man'yōshū*, but rarely thereafter. Mokichi sought words to fit his vision of reality, even, as we have seen, creating new ones if no old one would do, and conducted his search through the whole range of the Japanese language. He wrote, "the word '*narusawa*' means 'the place in which the sound of a mountain stream rises'; but it is better simply to say '*narusawa*.' "[38] That is, he chose here a word that expressed a whole sentence of meaning in four syllables, to achieve as rich an image as possible within the limited

form. The exclamatory particle *e* as well is an "old" one. It intensifies
the interjected sentence composed of lines 3 and 4; the emotional state
that filled a whole day is inserted within the sounds that seem to fill all
of nature.[39] The use of this *e* relates a single day of loneliness to a vast
stretch of time, as though the loneliness itself had its source in antiquity.

Mokichi used *Man'yōshū* words, as he used all words, for both their
meaning and their sounds. This was particularly true of *makurakotoba*
(pillow words), in which the meaning was often only hinted at by the
choice of characters. Their importance in Mokichi's tanka was in large
part the role they played as a musical symbol of meaning.[40] It is apparent in the following poem from the rensaku "Ohiro":

hisakata no	While weeping
hiten no moto ni	far beneath the distant
nakinagara	grieving skies,
hito koinikeri	I was longing for her;
inochi mo hosoku	my very life contracts.
	(*Shakkō*)

The third line of the poem, *nakinagara* (while weeping), balances the
image of a wide, uncaring firmament in lines 1 and 2 against the poet
below, in lines 4 and 5, diminished by a fruitless love. The pillow word
hisakata which opens the poem provides an immediate association of
space and distance, since it is used with celestial images such as sky,
heaven, moon, stars, and clouds. Furthermore, it opens the sequence of
assonance of the *hi* sounds which begin lines 1, 2, and 4, and is tied
euphonically to the pivot line 3 with its three consecutive *a* sounds.

Mokichi took advantage of the implied meanings of pillow words to
indicate subtle changes of situation or perception, as in the sequence
"Shinitamau haha," which narrates the poet's response to the death of
his mother. In the beginning of the sequence, she is referred to simply
as *haha,* mother; as she is closer to death, *haha* is modified by the coined
word *chitaraishi*, then by the pillow word *tarachine no,* both of which
imply by the characters used—breast, sufficiency—nurturance and the
mother-child relationship. After her death, in the intensity of the poet's
grief, *haha* is modified by the pillow word *hahasohano* written in the
kana syllabary to indicate the sounds alone, rather than with the characters to indicate the meaning "oak leaves," so that the main signifi-

cance is the repeated emphasis on the syllables which mean mother, *haha.* In this way the sounds and implied meanings not only heighten the tone but in fact contribute to a sharper depiction of experience.[41]

This use of a single classical word was not the only method Mokichi drew from his absorption of *Man'yōshū* poems: it emerged in his *"kerukamo-chō,"* a tone based on the long verb endings, such as *keri,* and distinctive exclamatory particles, such as *kamo,* characteristic of the Man'yō tone. Again, Mokichi insisted that such a tone was expressive of his own "life," his own responses to experience, and as such were appropriate to his poetry.[42] He believed that tanka as an expression of life was an exclamatory form, and a lyrical one, dealing with matters to be "sung" about rather than spoken of, so that the rhythm of such words was relevant to the completion of the poetic tone, as in the following poem:[43]

yū sareba	As evening drew on,
daikon no ha ni	on radish leaves fell the
furu shigure	early winter rain;
itaku sabishiku	in pain, in loneliness,
furinikeru kamo	how it was raining!
	(*Aratama*)

Line 5 of this poem bears the weight of a homely natural scene of early winter rain falling on the exposed leaves of a *daikon* in a garden, followed by the intense and personal adverbs "painfully, lonelily." It can support the weight of the unexpected contrast because of the tone provided by the *"kerukamo-chō,"* especially as *furinikeru* contrasts with the simple attributive *furu* in line 3. It is the continuing quality of the rain which is emphasized and exclaimed over.

Another Man'yō word Mokichi appreciated for its tone was adapted to fit a particular context.[44] The pillow word *sanitsurau,* implying the color of rosy cheeks, is adapted and used as a verb in this poem from *Shakkō:*

ki no moto ni	When I bit into
ume hameba sushi	a plum beneath the tree, how sour!
osana tsuma	the time has passed
hito ni sanizurau	for my child bride to blush
toki tachinikeri	when she confronts a man.

The juxtaposition of this old word refurbished to apply to the poet's young bride-to-be, herself referred to by a word coined by Mokichi, and the ordinary act of biting into a sour plum, creates a tension which beautifully conveys the complexity of a momentary emotion. An element in this kind of highly successful language was the sensitivity Mokichi had to the way the subjective perception of words and sounds changes over time, and in relation to its context within the structure of a poem and in combination with other words. Mokichi considered the choice of words a complex, subtle, and most important process in the composition of a poem.[45]

The strength of Mokichi's use of language derives not only from the depth provided by classical usages: it comes from the ways in which he created a rich texture in a single tanka by harmonizing classical, modern, colloquial, and even foreign words to communicate emotion.[46] Such a mixture of language is particularly powerful in the following poem from "Ohiro":

> shinshin to   On a night when
> yuki furishi yo ni   silently the snow fell,
> sono yubi no   her fingers—
> ana tsumeta yo to   "how cold they are!"
> iite yorishi ka   I said, drawing near her.
> (*Shakkō*)

The smooth flow of the language in lines 1, 2, 3, and 5 reinforces the image of a cold, silent night; the soft *sh* and *y* sounds are the dominant consonants; *i* and *o* the primary vowels. The two verbs have classical endings, the past attributive *shi* of *furishi,* and the *shi* again with *yoru* followed by the exclamatory *ka*.[47] Within this hushed scene, the conversational, colloquial sound of the sentence *ana tsumeta yo* comes as a shock equal to the physical sensation of suddenly touching cold fingers; the speaker of the words has a solid presence brought about by the immediacy of the language.

The interplay and mutual influence of modern and classical elements is as characteristic of Mokichi's poetry as is the *Man'yōshū* influence, especially in *Shakkō*. The modernity is present in concept as well as in language: here the sensuality of the touch has a modernity. Elsewhere it is apparent in the strong presence of the poetic persona, as seen, for example, in the frequent use Mokichi makes of first-person pronouns. On the whole it is intrinsic to his concept of the tanka as an expression of the life of the poet; a modern sense of ego and of art is fundamental to Mokichi's belief that when one writes a poem, the self is born again in that poem.[48] Mokichi felt that classical language flowed in his blood, but his being existed in the modern world: the effect of his use of language arises from the interplay between these two parts of his consciousness.

Mokichi wrote poetry to order his emotions and responses; from the predominance of autobiographical and diary-like poems, and indeed from the steady, prolific production of poetry over the forty years of his career, writing was clearly an integral means of assimilating experience. He has stated that his poems came from an "internal urgency" (*Drang*) to write. This sense of being unable to exist without writing was a great strength, he believed, but also had its painful aspect: it seemed to him to be a force as inevitable and irresistible as death.[49] Poetry was not only a way to define life; it even became a reason to live:

> ikinokoramu to   I have wanted to live on,
> koinegau   with this entreaty
> kokoro nite   held within my heart:
> uta hitotsu tsukuru   to write a single poem;
> karasu no uta o   a poem about a crow—
>   (*Shirokiyama*)

The poem would be in the tanka form because Mokichi believed that its very limitations were a source of powerful expression. When a free poetic sensibility struggled with a fixed form, he wrote, "light is emitted. Strength lives in colliding with obstacles."[50] In manipulating the syllable count, as in the above poem with both *jiamari* and *jitarazu* lines, the linear structure, the sounds, and the language, Mokichi made the ancient form his own: the struggle suited his poetic voice.

The nature of the experiences traditionally treated in tanka suited his voice as well. The tanka deals primarily with the quality of experience rather than its causes and effects; it is descriptive rather than explanatory. "[T]he objective world is set forth in vivid detail, and the detail harmonizes in such a fashion that it conveys the states of mind and feeling that make up the human experience and awareness of it."[51] When

Mokichi's poetry is weakest, the reader needs to know the specific details, the causes from which the poem emerged. When it is strongest, the form of his individual state of mind and feeling becomes universal, because the quality of experience is so vivid that it rises above its source. At his best, Mokichi was able to express in words those emotions and atmospheres that are impossible to explain, but easy to recognize:

> sayonaka ni   When I awaken
> mezamuru toki ni   in the middle of the night,
> monoto tae   and all sounds cease,
> ware ni namida no   there are times when I feel
> izuru koto ari   my eyes fill with tears.
>   (*Tomoshibi*)

The poem tells us nothing of the cause of his tears, although from context we know it was written while Mokichi was visiting Sawara Ryūō, who was ill. By the distancing effect of *koto ari,* the immediacy of the speaker's experience, emphasized by *ware ni* ("in me"), becomes a universal immediacy.

The tanka form suited Mokichi's voice by structure, tradition, and its inherent struggle with limitations. It also suited his personality, because he was essentially a conservative, unadventurous man. He spent his whole life adapting himself in one way or another to received forms: as an adopted son-in-law, he accepted the family profession with no evidence of resistance, or even overt questioning. When he continued to study, he chose the established field of neuropsychiatry rather than the emerging one of psychoanalysis. He married the wife selected for him, and in the end, rather than flout convention, forced the withdrawal of a woman he had come to love. So although he clearly recognized some of the drawbacks of the form, it is not surprising that he did not choose to invent new forms to replace it, as did many of his contemporaries. His energies were applied to expanding and adapting the received traditional tanka to his modern poetic voice.

CHAPTER FIVE

The Poem Sequence "Ohiro"

The Rensaku Form

SAITŌ MOKICHI believed that the tanka was a lyrical, excla-matory form, deriving strength from the tension between a free po-etic sensibility and the limitations of a fixed form. He also considered its role as a unit of a *rensaku,* or poem sequence, to be an essential characteristic.[1] A rensaku is defined as a poetic form in which two or more tanka by a single poet are used to treat a theme which could not be handled completely within a single poem; the individual poems must combine to form a unified, coherent whole.

The term "rensaku" began to be widely used in poetic circles after it appeared in an article by Mokichi's teacher Itō Sachio in the January 1902 issue of the magazine *Kokoro no hana.* Although Masaoka Shiki had used the term in print earlier, and it was used among his disciples, rensaku was not publicly discussed until Sachio introduced the term.[2] Sachio stated that the form originated with Shiki, and developed natu-rally from a situation in which a single tanka was insufficient to treat a given subject.[3] The article provoked various responses: some poets sup-ported such a form; others denied that Shiki originated it; and still oth-ers dismissed the whole idea as being of nó consequence. One writer Ōtomo Yukie, wrote that a tanka should be like a single oil painting: one should be sufficient. If not, the poet should choose a different form, such as a *chōka,* or a longer free form. In addition, he argued, Shiki had in any case merely copied the poem series originated by such poets as Tachibana Akemi and Sasaki Nobutsuna. Ōtomo's article elicited a response from Shiki, who claimed that he and Akemi had taken different approaches; if they were each to write a series on a garden with ten trees, Akemi would write one poem on each tree, whereas Shiki would look at the whole garden from all directions, and from varied positions, and write ten related poems.[4] Sachio also responded, with "Futatabi uta no rensaku shumi o ronzu" (A second discussion of the nature of a poem sequence), insisting on Shiki's contribution in having unified a series to make it a coherent whole. A rensaku was not simply ten poems on one topic; it was a more highly developed form with its own distinctive characteristics. Sachio's "six conditions" for a rensaku are not clearly thought out, and there is much overlapping, but they repeatedly stress the need for a unifying structure in which several elements, such as time and place, are harmonized into a total, organized whole.[5]

Sachio's definition of the function of a rensaku impressed Mokichi, but, as Sachio's critics had pointed out, the rensaku was not a totally new form. The tendency to combine short poetic forms into longer units appears in various forms throughout Japanese literary history. Sachio referred to a three-poem sequence in the *Man'yōshū* which he considered a rensaku, although he insisted that it was unintentional, whereas a true rensaku was a deliberately structured unit.[6]

The integration of independent poems into larger coherent units is indeed apparent in short sequences from the *Man'yōshū*, as Edwin Cranston has demonstrated, and does seem intentional. Similar methods of integration were later applied to the organization of the imperial anthologies themselves, as Konishi Jin'ichi has shown, as early as the *Kokinshū*, and refined by the time the *Shinkokinshū* was compiled.[7] The techniques used—such as the association of images and the progression through time, space, or event; varying the strength and quality of successive poems; a chronological order based on the date of the poetry included—were applied as well to collections other than imperial anthologies. In shorter private anthologies, similar techniques are apparent. Fujiwara Teika's *Kindai shūka* (Superior poems of our time), for example, was an eighty-seven poem anthology designed as a model of skilled poetic composition. In it, integration was achieved by temporal and spacial progression and the association of poems with similar diction, images, motifs, and rhetorical devices arranged to provide a rhythm that varied in terms of the complexity, distance, and tone of poems in context. In this work, such integrating techniques allowed "Teika to create a beautiful work of art even though he is the author of none of its parts." It can in fact be read as "a poetic whole of 415 lines, in 83 stanzas."[8] Teika, like other twelfth- and thirteenth-century poets, applied similar techniques to long sequences composed of his own poems, as in his "Hundred-Poem Sequence of the Shōji Era."[9] Some of these techniques were then applied to the *renga,* or linked verse, and the descriptive vocabulary developed for renga clarified details of the processes of association and progression.[10]

The brevity of the tanka form is often seen as a shortcoming; however, as Konishi demonstrates, the dual forces apparent in the development of Japanese poetry, for the thousand years before Mokichi's time, were the reduction of the prevailing poetic unit into shorter and shorter forms, "fragmentation" or "disintegration," and the complementary tendency toward recombining these short units into larger wholes, "integration." "The nature of the integration at any given period depended upon the interests of the age,"[11] and for tanka poets in the early twentieth century, a major means of integration was the rensaku. Neither Sachio nor Mokichi, in their discussions of rensaku, mentioned these related forms, nor did they discuss, in their definitions of what a rensaku is, how the poet was to achieve a coherent form. There is no doubt, however, about the structural unity of Mokichi's best rensaku, and many of his techniques are similar to those used to unify imperial anthologies and individually written poem sequences, as well as to order the development of renga.

The major obvious difference is that a rensaku was viewed as an organic form arising out of a specific poetic need: it relied on no externally devised order or required subject matter, such as the imperial anthologies, and owed no allegiance to formal rules of composition, such as those observed in renga. This freedom from restrictions on the one hand gave the poet wide latitude in constructing a sequence; on the other hand, it made the achievements of unity more difficult because the form was defined by internal demands alone.

In the rensaku of Mokichi's early career he demonstrated indisputable mastery of the form; his was the work that most clearly illustrated Sachio's ideal.[12] One of the elements Mokichi added in the interest of providing a structural foundation for the rensaku form was narrative.

He credited the success of the sequence "Shinitamau haha" (My mother is dying) in large part to its narrative base. In much the same manner that Shiki had used to contrast Akemi's sequence, which depicted tree after tree, with his own, which depicted the grove as a whole, Mokichi compared his work to Shiki's:

> This rensaku differs from those such as "Frost on the Pines" by Shiki: rather than looking [at something] while standing, while sitting, from the front, from the back, I wrote the sequence of events from the time I was first informed by telegram of my mother's serious illness, to returning home, to her death and funeral, until, absorbed in my grief, I sought to console myself at the Sugawa hotsprings; as a rensaku form, it was easy to write—that is, it was a simple road [to follow].[13]

The sequence narrates a profound emotional progression as well, manipulating chronological progression and developing techniques of poetic association to portray the psychological process involved in bereavement.[14] The narrative element is the skeletal framework; the flesh and breath of the work are in the emotions. The events and the feelings that accompanied them are unified by temporal and spatial development, contrasting strongly with the quieter and more static rensaku of Shiki.

"Shinitamau haha" and "Ohiro" are the two works most often given credit for the critical acclaim with which *Shakkō* was received. The two share a similar elegiac quality, but the narrative framework is of less importance in the latter. The poet's grief following his separation from the woman he loved is the focus, rather than the event of separation itself, although the intensity of feeling and expression derives from the intersection of memories of past experience with present emotional responses.[15] Since the two sequences are so often associated with each other, however, and since the rensaku that describes the death of Mokichi's mother is so clearly autobiographical, "Ohiro" has occasioned speculation for almost seventy years about the identity of the model for the woman Ohiro. Mokichi refused to help, and even denied the relevance of the matter: "There is no point in delving into the question of whether the woman was an actual person or a poetic creation, or whether I used this or that model." He added that, in any case, she was no longer "of this world."[16] She is, however, very much of the world of the rensaku, as she is seen through the poet's eyes and emotions.

"Ohiro" is widely recognized as a work of unusual power and beauty, and individual poems of the rensaku are often discussed, yet it is rarely considered as a whole; I know of no study which analyzes the structure of the total sequence in detail. The tendency has been to praise and discuss the most powerful poems and pass over the weaker ones. Certainly many of the individual poems are compelling even in isolation, but their power is increased, and the weaker poems gain stature, by their context and function within the sequence. In particular, the weaker poems depict the poet's perception of the world around him with an attention to detail that makes the stronger poems all the more vivid.

Some of the vocabulary developed to discuss the poems in hundred-poem sequences or renga is useful for discussing these variations within a rensaku. The inherent brocade imagery emphasizes the overall unity of the individual poems, and reduces reliance on such value-charged characterizations as "strong" or "weak." The "strong," or most impressive, poems are called *mon* or "pattern" poems—those that are most striking in imagery, concept, language, and effect. Their opposites are *ji,* or "ground" poems—those that weave with more subtlety the context for the sequence. Between these poles are *monji* (or *yaya mon*) poems, that is, primarily pattern poems, although somewhat less striking than strictly *mon* poems; and *jimon* (or *yaya ji*), primarily ground poems, although somewhat brighter than *ji*.[17] Although Mokichi did not use this vocabulary about his own rensaku, it serves as a useful reminder that the whole is composed of all its parts, and the components should be considered accordingly. A good *ji* poem might be weak when torn from its surrounding fabric, but in its proper place it has an important function. The following analysis of the poetic techniques and structural organization of "Ohiro" treats the rensaku as a complete entity; that is, as a forty-four unit work, composed of thirty-one syllable, five-line, tanka "stanzas."*

"Ohiro": Part One

The rensaku "Ohiro" concerns the poet's forced separation from a woman he loves. It is in three parts: the first, poems 1 through 17, is

---

*Since the rensaku was written to be read as an uninterrupted unit, a complete translation of "Ohiro," as it appeared in the first edition of *Shakkō* in 1913, is provided in appendix 1.

set immediately after the separation; the second part, poems 18 through 31, is a return through memory to the past moments of shared love; the concluding section, the final thirteen poems, returns to the present by depicting a gradual easing of the pain of separation.[18] In other words, if the chronological progression is represented by A, B, C, the actual sequence of the poems is B, A, C. The rensaku opens with the following poem:

1.

nagekaeba	Since I keep grieving,
mono mina kurashi	all things are dark—
hingashi ni	even the stars
izuru hoshi sae	that appear in the east
akakaranaku ni	do not shine.

The first line establishes the poet's emotional state as one of continuing grief and as the cause of his perception of a world encased in darkness. The potential source of light, stars rising in the east, fails. The poet's emotions and the appearance of the natural world coincide. The exaggeration of the opening image, "all things are dark," enlarges the scale of the poem, and makes the supporting image in the concluding lines seem appropriate.[19] The poem establishes the tone of part one, which is of an overpowering grief that darkens the whole world, and the imagery, which is of distance and isolation. The flow of the poem is remarkable: from the conditional opening line through the rolling repetitions of assonance and internal rhymes (such as *ae* in lines 1 and 4) to the staccato, and negative, final line, there is a sense of inevitability. The darkness seems the only possible result of the poet's feelings.

2.

tōku tōku	How far, how far
yukinaru naramu	must she have gone now!
dentō o	when I turn out the lamp,
keseba nubatama no	how late the coal-black
yoru no fukenuru	night has grown.

The focus has shifted from the eastern sky to the earthly distance separating the lovers. The darkness is then chosen, as though the poet could not bear the homely light of an electric lamp when the stars were dark. In retrospect it seems that the absent stars in poem 1 are symbolic of the lost Ohiro, in much the same way that the following poem from the *Shinkokinshū* is placed in a context to suggest that the snow is the poet's beloved: [20]

yoso ni nomi	Can it be that I
mite ya yaminamu	Shall never see at closer range
Kazuraki ya	The pure white snow
Takama no yama no	That glimmers in far Kazuraki
mine no shirayuki	On the peak of Mount Takama?

This view is supported by the repetition of imagery from poem 1 in the last poem, 44, in which starlight is overtly associated with Ohiro.

44.	hingashi ni	When the stars
	hoshi izuru toki	appear in the east,
	na ga minaba	should you see them,
	sono me honobono to	let those eyes be
	kanashiki are yo	as gently loving as before.

The prosaic lamplight in poem 2 is unacceptable when starlight is absent because of this association between the stars and Ohiro, and with the return of darkness in poem 2 comes a return to an expanded tone, with the pillow word for darkness, *nubatama*. It prepares the way for poem 3, which is one of the high points of the sequence. Ueda Miyoji says the real subject of the sequence begins in this poem: [21]

3.	yoru kureba	As night falls,
	sayodoko ni neshi	her beloved face,
	kanashikaru	she who lay in my bed,
	omowa mo ima wa	now is no more!
	nashi mo odoko mo	how narrow my bed!

The night brings the sense of loss to an almost unbearable state of tension. The absence of the beloved specifically from the poet's bed makes the sense of loss seem desperate, and the last two lines, with short words punctuated by the repeated exclamatory particle *mo,* express an extremity of feeling. The experience is an outcome of the merging of night and memory. There is a similar juxtaposition in the following old English song:

O westron wind when wilt thou blow
That the small rain down can rain?
Christ that my love were in my arms
And I in my bed again.

Both poems concern a sensual longing set against a change in natural world, one in weather, the other in the cycle of night and day. As Archibald MacLeish writes, "the emotion . . . is held between these two statements in the place where love and time cross each other. . . .[T]he emotion, somehow contained in the poem, is an emotion which words cannot come at directly. . . ."[22] In the sequence "Ohiro" as a whole, specific words of emotion appear in almost half the poems: *kanashi* (sad, grieving or, as in poems 3 and 44, beloved, or loving) twelve times, *sabishi* (lonely) seven, and *aware* (moving, pitiable) three. Yet they are rarely in poems that are most clearly pattern (*mon*) poems, such as 1 and 3. The emotion in the best poems is indirectly stated.

The next three poems in the rensaku are less intense, and describe a random activity undertaken merely to move, to escape the weight of grieving:

4.	furafura to	Distractedly
	tadoki mo shirazu	and at a loss,
	Asakusa no	to the red-lacquered halls
	ninuri no dō ni	of Asakusa
	ware wa kinikeri	have I come.
5.	ana kanashi	The pity of it!
	Kannondō ni	the leper there,
	raisha ite	at Kannon's temple,
	tada hitasura ni	singlemindedly
	zeni horinikeri	beseeching pennies.
6.	Asakusa ni	I came here
	kite udetamago	to Asakusa, bought
	kainikeri	a hard-boiled egg;
	hitasabishikute	in overwhelming loneliness
	waga kaeru naru	I went back home.

These background poems serve several purposes, in addition to relieving for a few moments the tension of poems 1 and 3. They depict the poet moving in a daze through the world, describing his feelings with words such as *kanashi* and *sabishi*.★ The red-lacquered hall is one of only two mentions of color in the seventeen poems of part one; both are reds, a color Mokichi often associated with grief in *Shakkō,* and both heighten the sense of cold darkness elsewhere. The leper in poem 5 is the only animate image in all of part one, except for the poet himself and the memory of Ohiro, and the leper relates to the rest of the world through his disease and poverty. The poet, however, relates to no one among the crowds of Asakusa, a neighborhood he had been familiar with since he first came to Tokyo. Even the trivial act of buying an egg from a street-stall vendor, the least involved way of obtaining food, overwhelms him with a loneliness so great it fills an entire line (*hitasabishikute*). It is, perhaps, the wholeness and simplicity of the egg as a symbol of new life that is so disturbing. Elsewhere, broken eggshells are linked with destruction, as in the later rensaku "Yakeato" (The ruins of the fire) from *Tomoshibi:*

ie idete	When I left the house
ware wa koshi toki	and came here,
Shibuyagawa ni	I saw eggshells
tamago no kara ga	floating, flowing with
nagare inikeri	the Shibuya River.

In "Ohiro," the whole egg evokes loneliness, and the poet leaves the crowded district of Asakusa.

The restless activity that led him to venture forth provided no relief from his own sadness, and the poet "returns" (*kaeru*), not to a place of refuge, but to the image of Ohiro:

7.	hatsuhatsu ni	Because of her,
	fureshi ko nareba	a girl I touched
	waga kokoro	slightly, briefly,
	ima wa hadara ni	now my heart,
	nagekinaru nare	in tatters, grieves.

For the third time in seven poems, the poet's self-awareness is revealed in the use of a personal pronoun (as in poems 4 and 6), and in a sense the development within this poem mirrors that of the whole part one:

★In the revised version, line 1 of poem 4 was changed from *furafura to* to *kanashimite*.

the past event, his contact with Ohiro, is the cause of his grief, but his focus is on himself rather than on the beloved. To escape his own tattered heart, he again flees:

8.   Yoyogino o   I ran desperately
                   hitahashiritari   through the fields
                   sabishisa ni   of Yoyogi, living
                   iki no inochi no   in loneliness, my life
                   kono sabishisa   in this loneliness.

The incomplete sentence fragments of lines 4 and 5, like the breathless, panting exclamations of an exhausted runner, twice juxtapose life with loneliness, as though they were inseparable. The activity is again to no avail, and the brief movement toward memory and life cedes, in the following four poems, to isolation. The four form a sub-sequence that uses a progressive darkening and distancing to lead up to a climactic pattern poem.

9.   sabishi sabishi   Lonely, lonely!
            ima saihō ni   now in the west
            kurukuru to   even the sun setting
            akaku iru hi mo   smoothly, redly,
            koyonaku sabishi   incredibly lonely!

10.   kamikuzu o   From burning wastepaper
           saniwa ni takeba   here in the garden,
           kemuri tatsu   the smoke rises.
           kōshiki hito wa   My beloved one—
           haruka naru kamo   how far removed from me

11.   horohoro to   Wafting softly
           noboru kemuri no   the rising smoke
           ten ni nobori   to the heavens rises,
           kiehatsuru kani   as though to disappear;
           ware mo kenu kani I too would disappear—

12.   hisakata no   While weeping
           hiten no moto ni   far beneath the distant
           nakinagara   grieving skies,
           hito kōinikeri   I was longing for her:
           inochi mo hosoku   my very life contracts.

The repetition within each of the poems is most striking. Poem 9 repeats *sabishi* (lonely) three times, to describe a scene which provides the second, and last, touch of color to the nearly perpetual dusk of part one, and returns attention to the sky, where light is again extinguished. The poet below, in poem 10, lights a fire which is destructive rather than warming; the rising smoke leaves him behind, recalling the beloved one who has also gone away. The smoke, *kemuri,* continues in poem 11, as does the internal repetition. It opens with *horohoro to,* an adverb whose sounds resonate in the repeated verb of rising, *noboru* (lines 2 and 3), while the two forms of the verb *kiyu* (disappear) underscore by their sounds the fading smoke (*kemuri*). As the smoke rises, the skies resume their distant coldness, and the poet is abandoned to his solitary, contracting life. The distance is expressed in words with Buddhist connotations: *hiten,* "grieving skies," is also used to mean Ashura, a combative guardian deity, while the pronunciation *saihō* for "west" implies a region of paradise. Mokichi used them, I believe, for an undertone of mystery which increases the poet's isolation. However, both these words and the constant repetitions in this sub-sequence can also be seen as weaknesses.[23] There is little doubt that none but the last poem can stand alone successfully; the other poems are neither taut nor penetrating. But they are not meant to be; if they were more striking, they could not have fulfilled the function of gradually constructing a gray, hazy world covered by a frighteningly empty expanse. They are background poems which provide the support for the powerful poem 12; they provide evidence of the serious mistake it is to judge individual poems from a rensaku out of context. Mokichi, and the reader, could hardly sustain the great emotional intensity of poems 1, 3, and 8 without longing for relief; the relaxation of tension in poems 9, 10, and 11 are psychologically as well as poetically valid. Following this short period of reduced tension, poem 12 is all the more effective.

    Poems 13 through 16 form another sub-sequence in which the poet returns to a semblance of normal activity in a world of dreary inanimate objects.

13.   hōrinageshi   I pick up and hold
            furoshiki tsutsumi   the cloth-wrapped bundle
            hiroi mochi   thrown down before,
            idakite itari   and hold it to me:
            sabishikute naranu   unbearably lonely.

14.   hittari to   Holding them close
        dakite kanashi mo   to me, so sorrowful—
        hito naranu   they are not she,
        fūtengaku no   these books on lunacy,
        fumi no kanashi mo   themselves so sorrowful.

15.   uzutakaku   Piled high,
        tsumishi shomotsu   the stacks of books
        chiri tamari   have gathered dust,
        mi no kanashi mo yo   painful to look at—
        tadoki shiraneba   since I know not where to turn.

16.   tsutome nareba   Since I must work
        kyō mo densha ni   today as well
        norinikeri   I rode the trolley;
        kanashiki hito wa   my sorrowing beloved—
        haruka naru kamo   so far removed from me.

By picking up the books he had discarded earlier, the poet attempts to resume his ordinary life. His emotions, however, dictate that he "embrace" something (*idakite*), and he has nothing but a lifeless bundle. His loneliness is increased, and expressed with words of emotion, *sabishikute* ("feeling lonely") in poem 13, then the repeated *kanashi* (sorrowful) in poem 14. The futile "embracing" of the books leads to the appearance of Ohiro in memory: his normal life has no substitute for her presence. Poem 14 develops from a close physical contact, *hittari to / dakite . . .* (holding them close / to me . . .), to sorrow (*kanashi mo*), to a mention of Ohiro which can only recall her absence, *hito naranu* (they are not she). The *shimo no ku* contains the weight of his lifeless world in the phrase *fūtengaku no / fumi* (these books on lunacy). Mokichi's use of the old-fashioned *fūten* with its imposing characters in Japanese adds an intimidating sense of strangeness to the objects and seems, like the leper in poem 5, to represent life gone terribly wrong.[24] The life which the poet cannot embrace is replaced at best by life distorted, and therefore sorrowful. In the next poem the quantity of books increases the burden: they stand piled up, mutely increasing their oppressive effect by collecting dust. The dust recalls the smoke of the previous sub-sequence in texture and muted color; the repetition of the word *kanashi* as well as the repeated image of books associates the poem quite closely with the previous two. Also, the poet's inability to act with purpose, *tadoki shiraneba* (since I know not where to turn) is a source of pain; as in poem 4, line 2, *tadoki mo shirazu* (at a loss), he no longer has a point of focus in his world. Action is either random, as was his visit to Asakusa, or externally dictated, such as his ride in the trolley. The two final lines of poem 16 are almost identical to those of poem 10: only the first two syllables of line 4 differ, so that *kōshiki* (beloved) becomes *kanashiki* (sorrowing). She is still "so far removed."

The total atmosphere of part one is dark and colorless; with the loss of the beloved, life itself has fled, leaving behind only inanimate objects—books, for example—or such travesties of a rich life of loving as the leper and the notion of lunacy. Any action involves movement away from the speaker, either in the smoke that rises, Ohiro who has gone away, or light which is extinguished; the exceptions are futile activity, as in the outing to Asakusa, the desperate run through Yoyogi fields, or the obligatory trolley ride. His spirit is diminished before the vast and "grieving skies." The entire section, but especially the blind flight through fields and the emptiness of the distant skies, can be compared with the perception, given modern dress, central to the following *Man'yōshū* poem:[25]

kouro koto	When I went out,
nagusamekanete	in love and yet unable
idete ikeba	to console myself,
yama o kawa o mo	I came back, unaware
shirazu kinikeri	of either mountains, or rivers.

The poet here can see nothing of beauty, as Mokichi, in part one of "Ohiro," sees nothing of the beauty of nature, only darkness or the life-denying or mechanical intrusions of his modern world. His perceptions have been altered by the loss of love: the extent of that alteration is apparent in comparison with parts two and three. The last poem of part one introduces the change:

17.		
	kono asake	At dawn today
	sanshō no ko no	the scent of *sanshō*
	kayoi kite	drifted in
	nageku kokoro ni	penetrated through
	shimitōru nare	this grieving heart.

For the first time there is natural light: the sun is rising, not setting. A living natural image, the fragrant *sanshō* plant, and a natural response appear. There is receptivity rather than constant denial.

"Ohiro": Part Two

Part two opens with a brief return to the night:

18.	honobono to	Since she has left,
	me o hosoku shite	she I embraced,
	itakareshi	enraptured,
	ko wa sarishi yori	my eyes half closed—
	iku yo ka hetaru	how many nights have passed?

The speaker counts the period of loneliness after separation by nights rather than days. The first impression is to recall the sense of overwhelming darkness with which the sequence began. By following a poem at dawn with one at night, Mokichi seems at first glance to be denying the light; the darkness here, however, is not entirely desolate. It had once enabled him to embrace his beloved, and provided the occasion for sensual and emotional pleasure. The transition from darkness is made through sensual perception to the images of light and nature in the next poem, as is a return to a remembered past. The process of remembering, which reaches a peak in poems 24 through 28, progresses through gradually altering nature images, beginning with light and spring flowers:

19.	ureitsutsu	Because despairing
	inishi ko yue ni	she has gone,
	fuji no hana	even the trembling brilliance
	yuru hikari sae	in clusters of wisteria
	kanashiki mono o	has so much sadness—

The word of emotion which opens the poem, *ureitsutsu*, applies to Ohiro, *inishi ko* ("she who has gone"): even in suffering the poet seems less alone. The juxtaposition of despair with beauty makes the beauty sad as well, but it also makes it vivid: poem 19 is a pattern poem. The poet's perception has suddenly widened. Four relatively strong background poems follow. The gentle nature images begin to fill in a brighter picture of the world.

20.
shiratama no
urei no onno
a ni kitari
nagaruru ga goto
ima wa sarinishi

The woman of
pearl–white grief
came to me;
like waters flowing
now she is gone.

21.
kanashimi no
koi ni hitarite
itaru toki
shirafuji no hana
sakitari nikeri

While I have been
immersed in this
grief-laden love,
the white wisteria flowers
have bloomed, have blown.

22.
yūyami ni
kaze tachinureba
honobono to
tsutsuji no hana wa
chirinikeru kamo

In twilight
as the breezes rise,
faintly, faintly
have they fallen,
the azalea flowers!

23.
omoide wa
shimo furu tani ni
nagaretaru
usugumo no goto
kanashiki kanaya

My memories are
filled with a sorrow
like fragile clouds
that flow in valleys
where the frost falls.

Movement is gentle in these poems—waters flow, petals fall, breezes rise, and mist quietly fills cold valleys—rather than desperate or distancing. The introduction of muted color begins with the white of "pearl-white grief," but changes to the living white of wisteria. The wisteria not only recalls the role that flower plays as a major image in "Shini-tamau haha," and the special significance that blossom seems to have for Mokichi; it also is closely associated with the falling blossoms that follow, the azaleas, which suggest pink. The "fragile clouds" are not a blank but a milky white, as the poet's vision is gradually focusing outside himself and the natural world is gaining substance. The word "memory" (*omoide*) in poem 23 prepares for the five poems that follow, the core of part two: they are the intense sensual awareness of the past, and they appear with vivid color and sharp contrast.[26] As the previous short sub-sequence introduced soft light and pale color, these that follow seem to be lit by a dramatic spotlight and painted vividly:

24.   asaborake   I glimpsed her once
                hitome mishi yue   at daybreak, and so
                shibadataku   my heart leapt
                kuroki matsuge o   at the black lashes
                awareminikeri   fluttering.

Ohiro, for the first time, has a striking presence. She is seen in early morning light, and the contrast of her black lashes is emphasized by their movement. She is described in the sequence almost entirely by physical images, rather than, for example, by the comparison of her beauty with natural images, in the manner Mokichi was later to describe Nagai Fusako (see chapter 3). These central poems therefore seem to be about physical love and sensual yearning, as in the following somewhat mysterious poem:

25.   waga areshi   My heart leapt
                hoshi o shitaishi   for the woman with
                kuchibiru no   red lips, who
                akaki onna o   I yearn for as
                awareminikeri   a star I bore.

The red lips, like the black eyelashes earlier, are in sharp focus, and the repetition of the verb *awareminikeri,* which fills the fifth line of both poems 24 and 25, expresses the intensity of the poet's response to Ohiro's physical presence. The mystery is what Mokichi meant by *waga areshi / hoshi* (a star I bore). In one sense, the star is clearly symbolic of Ohiro: it is associated with poem 1, in which the stars not shining symbolized her absence, and poem 44, in which they are a link with her as something that can be shared even across the distance that divides the lovers. In addition the star *hoshi* is being used to mean *hoshimawari,* fortune or luck.[27] Mokichi in this sense is equating his yearning for Ohiro to a yearning for a fate he has controlled, or produced, himself. Such a reading is supported both by the context of the rensaku, in which the lovers are separated unwillingly, and by autobiographical background; in real life, Mokichi was destined for Teruko. The implication seems to be that as the stars symbolize Ohiro, she herself symbolizes a self-determined fate.

From this difficult poem, the sequence progresses to the pinnacle of its depiction of the past brief intimacy the lovers shared:

26.   shinshin to   On a night when
             yuki furishi yo ni   silently the snow fell,
             sono yubi no   her fingers—
             ana tsumeta yo to   "how cold they are!"
             iite yorishika   I said, drawing near her.

The power of the poem as it stands alone, with its internal contrast between the classical language to describe the cold dark night and the conversational tone of line 4, *ana tsumeta yo to,* to make the physical touch of hands immediate and compelling, has been discussed earlier (see chapter 4). In its place in the development of the sequence, however, it works on other levels as well. The snow in its whiteness associates the poem with the "pearl-white grief" and the white wisteria flowers earlier in part two, and the night relates to the question in poem 18 which introduced the section. It also recalls, with a contrast in response, the world of darkness in part one. In addition, and perhaps most important, the regression in season from the spring of the previous poems to winter here completes the backward movement that accompanies memory. The poet began to see the world around him in spring, becoming conscious of fallen flowers, as in poem 21 when the wisteria flowers had fallen. His memories were compared to the spring haze, "like fragile clouds / that flow in valleys." With poem 26 he has returned to the brief meeting that is the central experience of the sequence, and it was winter, "on a night when / silently the snow fell." His memories have reached the source, and as the meeting continues, the sequence moves on to dawn:

27.   kyōin no   While watching
             renga no ue ni   the sun rise red
             asahiko no   above the brick walls
             akaki o mitsutsu   of the asylum,
             kuchi furinikeri   I kissed her lips.

The red sun seems an omen of the suffering to follow, since it usually accompanies grief, and the mention of the mental hospital has an undertone of the life-denying word *fūtengaku* in part one. The dawn brings at least a temporary separation, and hints at a more lasting one. In fact in the revised version of the rensaku, the last line is changed from *kuchi furinikeri* (I kissed her lips) to *nagekikeru kana* (ah, how I was grieving!), which makes explicit this sense of foreboding.

The poet made changes in twelve of the forty-four poems in the revised version of "Ohiro."[28] Most of the changes are relatively minor, however: *onna* to *omina* in poems 20 and 25, for example, or *dakite kanashi mo* to *idakite kanashi* in poem 14. The changes would rarely be reflected in the translations, and in only two cases is the meaning of the poem substantially altered. One is poem 27, as we have just seen, and the other is poem 28:

28. tamakiwaru When we touch,
     inochi hikarite fervent life shining,
     furitareba "no," she says,
     ina to wa iite shrinking back,
     kenugani mo yoru yet drawing nearer.

The poem begins with the pillow word *tamakiwaru,* which was a standard epithet for words such as life or this world; it is used, as always, to broaden the time frame of the poem and to heighten the tone. It is often written with the character for soul, *tama,* and seems to indicate a fundamental sense of being. Their lives have brilliance as they touch. This sense of grandeur adds a poignance to the hesitant yearning of the last two lines *ina to wa iite / kenugani mo yoru* ("no," she says, / shrinking back, / yet drawing nearer). It is not clear whose life is "shining," but since they then touch, it seems that both their lives are. This is changed in the revised version:

     waga inochi When we touched,
     tsui ni hikarite my life at long last shining,
     fureshikaba while saying "no,"
     ina to iitsutsu she was shrinking back,
     kenugani mo yoru yet drawing nearer.

The touch is put in the past tense, although the approach (*yoru*) is so sharp a memory it remains, in the original, in the present. The major change is in lines 1 and 2, although only line 5 is exactly the same in both versions. The poet's own state of feeling is emphasized; with her, he has finally reached a peak of being with *tsui ni,* at long last. It makes the fall from such a height all the darker, yet the reciprocal sense of exaltation in the earlier version reflects poem 26, when their fingers touched, and seems worth keeping.[29]

Mokichi also made a slight alteration in the order of these central poems. Poems 25, 26, and 27 in the original are rearranged to read 26, 27, 25 in the revision. The most dramatically sensual poems, 26 and 28, are thus separated by two poems: the one which refers to Ohiro's red lips and compares her to his own fate; and the sun rising over the red bricks of the asylum. The repetition of the last line *awareminikeri* in poems 24 and 25 is then also divided by two poems. In the order as well as within the poems, the original version seems stronger, if less polished. Mokichi's revision of the sequence demonstrates, in any case, that the order of the poems was as important to the sequence as a whole as the form and content of individual poems, and that Mokichi treated it as a unified work.

The next poem, however, seems foreign to the sequence:

29.   ka no inochi   Were one to say,
                  shiine to iwaba   "may his life end,"
                  nagusamame   it might comfort me;
                  ware no kokoro   yet my own heart
                  iigatenu kamo   cannot so speak.

This is the only mention, except for that of the leper, of a third person in the sequence, and his identity is unclear. It seems probable that since the lovers' separation was forced, this "he" is the one who came between them.[30] There are still unanswered questions: who would suggest his death? What prevents the poet from so wishing it? Is he speaking of his own life in the third person, and suggesting he would rather die than live without Ohiro, had he only the courage? One thing is clear in this unclear poem: the poet feels an anger he is unable to direct outside himself. The anger reappears with a violence of emotion in part three, and so the poem begins the transition from the heightened sense

of the past to the present world without Ohiro. The next two poems
end part two and hint at the tone of part three:

30.   suriorosu   From the rubbing
                      wasabi oroshi yu   of grated *wasabi*
                      shimi idete   the liquid seeps, and
                      taru aomizu no   the green dripping water
                      kanashikarikeri   was heart-rending.

31.   naku koe wa   Although its cries
                      kanashi keredomo   were sorrowful,
                      yūdori wa   the evening bird
                      ki ni nemuri nari   sleeps in its tree;
                      ware wa nenaku ni   I remain sleepless.

By means of two new types of images, these poems prepare the reader
for a change from the intensely vivid sensual memories and high-con-
trast visual images of part two to the more completely filled and relatively tranquil natural world through which the poet wanders in part
three. The image in poem 30 is the common household act of grating
wasabi, a green horseradish. The green dripping water is the first specific mention of a color other than red, which has indicated grief, and
the very commonness of the image is saddening.[31] The poet, instead of
being moved only by extremes of beauty or ugliness, is able again to
focus attention on the ordinary aspects of life. Poem 31 makes use for
the first time of a living natural image, continuing the sense of a wid-
ening perception. It is ironic, in that the poet has perceived sorrow in
the bird's call, but he is the one to lie awake at night, while the bird
sleeps. Irony requires a certain amount of objectivity, or at least, distance; it is a far remove from the darkness hiding the world in part one
and the intensity of most of part two: it prepares for recovery.

"Ohiro": Part Three

There is a similar sense of objective reality in part three as a whole: it
is filled with observations of the world the poet must find his way in
alone. Yet it opens with two poems filled with the sensual longing and
grief characteristic of part two.[32]

32.   ure'etsutsu   Because despairing
           inishi ko no yue   she has gone,
           tōyama ni   ah, my heart!
           moyuru ni hodo   like fires burning
           aga kokoro kana   in distant mountains.

33.   aware naru   Lovingly I stroked
           omina no mabuta   her eyelids, the woman
           koinadete   who so moved me,
           sono yo hotohoto   and that night I felt
           ware wa shinikeri   myself come close to death.

The associations with poems in part two are certainly strong; poem 32
repeats, with minor changes, the first two lines of poem 19:

           ureitsutsu   Because despairing
           inishi ko yue ni   she has gone,
           fuji no hana   even the trembling brilliance
           yuru hikari sae   in clusters of wisteria
           kanashiki mono o   has so much sadness!

However, there is a change in the outcome following the conditional
statement. Earlier, the poet's own misery was seen as an attribute of
the natural world. But the poet has progressed to a certain objectivity;
although the world seems sad, as in the bird's cry of poem 31, the poet
recognizes that it runs its natural course, and he alone is the one to
grieve. The tenor and vehicle of poem 19 are reversed in poem 32:
instead of natural images bearing the burden of his grief, the grief is
described by means of natural images but is centered in the speaker of
the poem. It is his own heart burning like fire; the fires themselves are
not seen to be grieving.

Poem 33 could be a unit of part two without causing any disruption,
having the sensual imagery and the rapture of the central poems. The
majority of poems in part three have a different tone. However, the
transitions from part to part within the rensaku structure are not completed abruptly, any more than alterations of emotion in human life are
always total and sudden. The transitions are more realistic: insight is
unsettled by memory, but not lost, and progress follows. The progression is similar to that in the first fifteen spring poems of the *Shinkokinshū* as analyzed by Konishi: the first signs of spring are interrupted by

brief returns of winter weather, until gradually, in the progression of
the imagery as well as of the natural season, spring dominates.[33]

In part three of "Ohiro," the poet's progress in analyzing and coping
with his own emotions, following the two "regressions," develops in a
sub-sequence of four background poems.

34.   kono kokoro   Trying to lay to rest
            hōran to shite   this heart of mine,
            kitarinure   I came here;
            hatake ni wa mugi wa   in the fields, the wheat
            akaraminikeri   has turned to red.

35.   natsu sareba   Since it is summer
            nōen ni kite   I came here, to farmland,
            kokorogushi   disconsolate,
            mizusumashi oba   and caught water-
            tsukamaenikeri   spiders with my hands.

36.   mugi no ho ni   As light flowed
            hikari nagarete   fluttering among
            tayutaeba   the spears of wheat,
            mukō ni yagi wa   from off in the distance
            nakisomenikere   came the bleating of a goat.

37.   mo no naka ni   I caught sight of
            hisomu imori no   the red belly
            akaki hara   of a water lizard
            hatsuka misomete   hidden amid duckweed—
            utsutsu tomo nashi   was overcome by it.

Poem 34 continues the image of an uneasy heart from poem 32, and
develops it by applying the speaker's will: "trying to lay to rest /
this heart of mine." It is his first goal-directed action since the separation.
He seeks solace in nature, and by doing so depicts the passage of time.
In these poems, the spring, in which he emerged from his most profound grief and could recall the winter night of love, has passed into
summer. The redness of the wheat is ripening rather than grieving.

Succeeding images are of the creatures of nature in their proper world,
and although Mokichi no longer attributes grief to them, he is ill at ease
with such tranquility; the scene is filled with growth and life, yet he
feels "disconsolate," and beside himself. While the world of part one
was in darkness, and part two was flooded with the strong light of

memory which illuminated only the peaks of experience, more detail is visible in part three. Visually it is like a hand-tinted black-and-white photograph: the details are all there, and the highlights are colored. But the poet is estranged, and there is a desperation in his act of catching water-spiders and in the distress he feels when he first sees the lizard. His excursion to farmland "to lay to rest" his pain was unsuccessful. He tries again:

38.	kono kokoro	To lay to rest at last
	hōrihaten to	this heart of mine,
	ho no hikaru	with the glittering
	kiri o tatami ni	point of the awl,
	sashinikeru kamo	I pierced the tatami.

This poem is the culmination of his disordered spirit: it is closely associated with poem 34, expanding its first two lines *kono kokoro / hōran to shite* (Trying to lay to rest / this heart of mine) with "at last" (*haten to*), expressing a rather desperate determination. The anger of the violent action of stabbing the tatami floor recalls the enigmatic poem 29; and the cold light shining on the sharp metal point of the awl recalls the inanimate world of part one. The alternation and repetition of sounds parallel the development of the described action through the five lines: the *kami no ku* is composed of predominantly *k, h,* and *o* sounds, while the *shimo no ku* is more varied; the verb *sashinikeru* (I pierced) dramatically fills almost the entire last line. The poem arrests the reader's attention; it is the only purely "pattern" poem in part three. It functions as a shock for the speaker of the sequence as well: it is the final outburst before the speaker gains control over his emotions.

39.	warajimushi	As the wood-lice
	tatami no ue ni	make their way out
	ide koshi ni	onto the tatami,
	tabako no kemuri	I envelop them
	kakete waga ori	with smoke from cigarettes.

40.	nennen ni	Although unceasingly
	onna o omou	my mind dwells
	ware aredo	on that woman,
	koyoi mo osoku	tonight I am up late
	shu no sumi suru mo	rubbing vermilion ink.

The poet, still seated on the tatami floor, reverts briefly to the sort of random activity of poem 35. The *a* assonance in the first syllables of four of the five lines of poem 39, and the *i* ending of all five lines, have a lax quality.[34] However, the weakness of this poem adds to the strength of the preceding one both by contrast and by its apparent psychological truth: the cathartic action of his anger was exhausting. By poem 40, the poet is ready to move on. For the first time he acts not because of his longing for Ohiro but in spite of it—"although" (-*do*). The return to disciplined activity is purifying, as indicated by the Buddhist word *nennen ni* (ceaselessly), and his use of vermilion, rather than black, ink indicates that he is using the sorrow to some purpose.[35]

The rensaku then concludes with a sense of resignation, but not of total emptiness:

41.   kono ame wa   I wonder if this rain
       samidare naramu   is of the summer rains—
       kinō yori   it has been falling
       waga saniwabe ni   falling in my garden
       furite iru kamo   since yesterday.

42.   tsutsumashiku   Withdrawn and
       hitori shi oreba   all alone, I watch
       kyōin no   the rain fall
       akaki renga ni   on the red brick
       ame no furu miyu   of the asylum.

43.   ruri iro ni   Enclosed in the blue
       komorite maruki   of lapis lazuli, the round seeds
       kusa no mi wa   of the grasses
       waga koibito no   became the eyes
       manako narikeri   of my beloved

44.   hingashi ni   when the stars
       hoshi izuru toki   appear in the east,
       na ga minaba   should you see them,
       sono me honobono to let those eyes be
       kanashiki are yo   as gently loving as before.

The rain falling in the garden has a soothing quality, as in the English song above ("O westron wind when wilt thou blow / that the small rain down can rain?"), compared to part one in which the sky withheld any comfort and all movement was upward or away from the speaker (such as the rising smoke, poems 10 and 11); the rain functions here as a natural support. The poet can even view, without a resurgence of grief, the red brick of the asylum the lovers had watched before at dawn (poem 27). Natural beauty (poem 43) no longer reproaches the poet with his own grief, but seems to welcome the love he has for Ohiro. Finally, she is present to him in beauty and he believes the stars will appear again. He has suffered loss and grief, but something in his vision has been altered and perhaps enriched. The rensaku has transmitted a process, in forty-four poems, that resembles in many ways the pain and healing undergone by George Eliot's Adam Bede:

> It would be a poor result of all our anguish and our wrestling, if we won nothing but our old selves at the end of it. . . . Let us rather be thankful that our sorrow lives in us as an indestructible force, only changing its form, as forces do, and passing from pain into sympathy—the one poor word which includes all our best insight and our best love.[36]

In both cases, the suffering was occasioned by the loss of a beloved, although the cause of loss was a tragic one in Adam's case, and a primarily social one in Mokichi's. There is a sense of the freshness of a first love in both cases, although critics are quick to point out that the depiction, in "Ohiro," of physical desire makes the rensaku a work about sexual passion rather than love. It contains a sense of eagerness and inexperience: the longings are those of a young man.

The sexuality which is so central to the work is sometimes seen as diminishing it. The rush of violent emotion in poem 38, for example, has been seen as inappropriate to mere yearning for a woman; and it has been suggested that Mokichi, denied his parental love in the normal course of his adolescence, deified sex the way most people deify love. The sensuality of the longing in the sequence has probably increased the curiosity about the model for the woman: she is thought to have been, variously, a maid in the Saitō household, Mokichi's sister-in-law, or a prostitute.[37] Although I am inclined to agree with Satō Satarō, and say "the 'model' problem is outside my area of interest,"[38] the distinction so often made between poems of love and poems of sensual desire is an interesting one, and not unrelated to the "model" problem. Kajiki develops the theory that during the period in which Mokichi was writing "Ohiro" and "Shinitamau haha," he was searching for the fundamental "life" (*inochi*) which tanka was to express. In the sequence on his mother's death, he sought that life in the world of nature; in "Ohiro" he sought it in the most fundamental aspect of nature in human beings, that is, in sex. Both were ways for him to permeate the essential spirit of "life," and in the end, sex and nature became equivalent means.[39] The final association, even transformation, of Ohiro with grasses and stars supports this reading, in that the object of the sexual yearning becomes one with the natural world.

The distinction between love and lust in any case is not germane to an understanding of "Ohiro" because the rensaku is fundamentally about loss and grief: loss as an obstacle to the fulfillment of life, and grief as a denial of life.[40] The concern is not whether the lovers had the proper sort of love to enable them to live happily ever after; it is that life had expanded and brightened when they were together, and contracted and darkened when they were separated. In a similar way, the rensaku is not about a single woman, which is perhaps why no one is sure who the woman was, but about the poet's awakening experience with the possibilities of love and sex.[41]

The structure of the rensaku is an indication of its meaning: the B, A, C chronology makes the poet's awareness the central focus. By beginning the sequence after the actual separation, the woman's role is only as a source of grief. The vivid descriptions of the meeting of the lovers are offered only when, by the use of regressing seasonal imagery, the reader knows it to be in an irretrievable past. The whole of part three is a development away from both the despair of part one and the sensual memory of part two. The rensaku is about loss and grief, but above all about the resolution of an emotional crisis; in fact, about a process of maturation. The bold strokes used to depict Ohiro in part two are as foreign to the emerging natural world of part three as they were to the gloom of part one. In the final resolution, the woman—as desirable as she was—is seen as an impediment to self-fulfillment ("Although unceasingly / my mind dwells / on that woman . . .) before she can be integrated into the continuing cycle of life (". . . the round seeds / of the grasses / became the eyes / of my beloved"). While the moments of deepest feeling inspired the most striking poems, the depth of the depiction as a whole results from the progression through the entire rensaku, and from the interplay between the background and the pattern poems.

"Sakashiranami" (White waves churning)

"Ohiro" is so complete a work that it can support a great many speculations and discussions without being diminished by them. As early in his career as 1913, Mokichi had mastered the rensaku form well enough to create a work that continues to speak for itself. It is one of his best; but it is, in subject and treatment, a young man's work, and Mokichi continued to use the rensaku form throughout his career, relying less and less on a narrative framework. The following five-poem rensaku from *Shirokiyama* (White mountains), "Sakashiranami" (White waves churning), written in December 1946, brings into balance the picture of Mokichi's use of the rensaku form.[42]

1.   karigane mo   The wild geese
       sude ni watarazu   no longer cross
       ama no hara   the fields of heaven;
       kagiri mo shirani   unbounded
       yuki furimidaru   the snow falls whirling.

2.   kono haru ni   Oh, my grandson!*
       umare idetaru   who was born
       waga mago yo   last spring—
       hashikeyashi hashikeyashi   how adored, how adored!
       imada minedomo   although still unseen—

3.   Mogamigawa   The snow-filled
       sakashiranami no   twilight has arrived
       tatsu made ni   to where the churning
       fubuku yūbe to   white-capped waves rise up
       narinikeru kamo   on the Mogami River.

4.   kisaragi ni   If the second month
       naraba tsugumi mo   were to arrive, the thrushes
       komu to iu   too will come, they say;
       kuwa no kohara ni   in the grove of mulberries
       yuki wa tsumorinu   the snow accumulates.

*Mokichi's grandson Moichi was born in April 1946, the year the poems were written, which is why Mokichi writes *kono haru,* "this spring"; that is, spring of this year.

5.
hito mina no	I have lived on
nageku tokiyo ni	into these times when
ikinokori	all are grieving;
waga mayu no ke mo	my very eyebrows
shiroku nariniki	have turned white.

The basic unity of this short sequence is achieved by imagery rather than event. Three of the five poems are landscape poems that show the progress of winter. In poem 1, the past is recalled by the negative image of wild geese, who no longer fill the sky; in poem 4, the future is anticipated by the thrushes who are supposed to come in the spring (by the old calendar, the second month was later in the year than February is). Both poems begin with absent birds and end with heavy snow, first whirling through the air, then piling up beneath bare trees. The central poem, often considered a characteristic work of *Shirokiyama,* increases the sense of time passing, with the arriving night. The other two poems are concerned with the progress of human life: poem 2, on the spring of life, is an exclamation in which an old man's joy on the birth of his grandson is mixed with regret that the child, like the geese and thrushes, is absent. The final poem is on the end of a life: the white eyebrows seem to be the snow in the winter of a lifespan. The "times" (*tokiyo*) are the postwar era in Japan, surely a time of much grieving. Since there is an association between the poet's aging and the current winter, the past autumn when wild geese crossed the sky reflects a remembered historical past which had more life. The past spring as well brought life with the birth of the poet's grandson; the anticipated spring, when the thrushes will arrive, suggests a fuller future. In the midst of winter desolation, then, there is hope, as there is beauty in the high white waves. The skillful juxtaposition and association of five poems has intimated a world view—a measure of the possibilities provided by the rensaku form and used to great advantage by Mokichi.

CHAPTER SIX
Subjects and Images

M OKICHI was seriously ill with typhoid fever in 1909; his graduation from medical school was delayed for a year by this illness, but it intensified his awareness of the fundamental pleasures of
experience. A poem he wrote at the time contrasts death and life in a
way that is characteristic of his vision throughout his career.[1]

rinshitsu ni	Although someone was
hito wa shinedomo	dying in the room next to mine,
hitaburu ni	with all my heart
hawakigusa no mi	I wanted nothing but to eat
kuitakarikeri	the berries of the broomweed.

(*Shakkō*)

The simple details of life—such as his craving for a food he had enjoyed
in childhood—are raised in defiance of the bland finality of death. His
appetite is an affirmation of his own continuing experience.

The four periods of his life during which he produced his best poetry
were all marked by crises that concerned either death or destruction.
The first period was treated in *Shakkō* (Crimson light) and *Aratama*
(Uncut gems); the years were marked by the deaths of his mother and
his teacher Itō Sachio, and by his separation from Ohiro. The crisis of
the second period, when he wrote *Tomoshibi* (Lamplight), was the destruction by fire of the Aoyama Hospital, which also marked the end
of his ambitions in medical research. The third period, when he wrote
Shiromomo (White peaches), was associated with the scandal that led to
his separation from his wife and family; and his final poetic flowering,

in *Shirokiyama* (White mountains), occurred amid the desolate postwar era in Japan. The personal tension of these periods was transformed into poetry; the mundane details of life achieved a sense of significance in the context of loss and desolation. Mokichi integrated painful experiences by creating from them a poetic order, and his poetry had the greatest vitality when his existence was most gravely threatened. He confronted the life-denying experiences of death, loss, or destruction with the affirmation of life he believed was inherent in his poetry.

A similar personal tension was produced throughout his poetic career by his work as a doctor; poetry was a means for him to maintain the equilibrium that was constantly being challenged by his experiences as a psychiatrist.

The Poet as Physician, and Other Self-Portraits

The demands of Mokichi's two professions frequently conflicted. When he was training at Sugamo hospital, his absorption in poetry, as we have seen, occasionally interfered with his medical duties. for most of his career, however, his medical responsibilities were primary, and he could rarely forget them:

> nariwai wa   In my calling
> itoma sae nashi   there is not a single
> monogurui no   moment of respite:
> koto o zo omou   I think about insanity
> nete mo samete mo   both waking and sleeping.
>   (*Tomoshibi*)

Mokichi even referred to his literary activities as a hobby or pastime.[2] They were carried out in the time he could spare from his medical duties. This is not to say that he was less than serious about his literature; he was often frustrated by the limited time he had for his poetry and criticism. But he believed that there were benefits as well as drawbacks from his combining two careers. Certainly the world of artistic creativity provided an escape from the stress of his medical responsibilities, but these responsibilities also enriched his art.[3] The two careers were interdependent in Mokichi's life, the medicine providing material for his poetry, and the poetry helping him to withstand the pressures of his medical duties. Katō's neurological simile seems apt: Mokichi's medicine and poetry functioned in his life like the antagonistic equilibrium between the sympathetic and parasympathetic nerves in the body; neither can function properly unless they act in unison.[4] But they interact unconsciously. In a similar way Mokichi's two careers balanced each other without any deliberate attempt at integration. There can be no doubt, though, that there was mutual influence, since they were carried on simultaneously.

In fact, poems concerning his medicine—whether training, research, or clinical practice—appear in all his volumes of poetry: at least 5 percent of the poems in each volume concern his "primary" profession. In *Tsukikage* (Moonlight), written from 1948 to 1952, after he had retired from practice, such topics account for 10 percent of the poems.[5] These poems over the years treated various aspects of his work. As I have indicated (see chapters 1 and 2), he wrote in this manner about research:

kagamarite	While bending over
nō no seppen o	to stain a specimen
somenagara	of brain cells,
akebi no hana o	I found myself thinking
omou narikeri	of akebia blossoms.
	(*Shakkō*)

And he wrote about the pain he experienced following the suicide of a patient in "Kinamida yoroku" (Record of yellow tears):

jisatsu seshi	Behind the coffin
kyōja no kan no	of the madman who has
ushiro yori	killed himself,
memai shite yukeri	I followed, feeling faint;
michi ni irihi akaku	the setting sun red on the road.
	(*Shakkō*)

The suicide of patients was a continuing source of pain from his earliest years as a doctor and throughout his life:

ukemochi no	So many of the
kyōjin mo ikutari ka	lunatics in my charge
shini yukite	have gone to death;

oriori aware   time and again I feel it
o kanzuru kana   to be oh, so pitiable!
                                    (*Shakkō*)

The above poem was written in 1912 after the suicide of a catatonic young girl. Mokichi wrote, "Because mental illness is my profession, my views of the mentally ill are not the popular ones. They are not the unrealistic ones portrayed in poems and novels. Few of my poems describe the mentally ill, but when I do write about them, the world that appears is a real one."[6] Indeed, the relatively few poems that relate to psychiatry open a world that was new to literature, and his experiences influenced his responses in other areas of his life. For example, the suicide in 1927 of Akutagawa Ryūnosuke, whom Mokichi had known since his Nagasaki days, affected him deeply:

yoru fukete   As the night grew late,
nemuri shinamu to   and you thought that you would go
seshi kimi no   to sleep and death,
kokoro wa tsui ni   at the end your spirit
kōri no gotoshi   must have been like ice.

                                    (*Tomoshibi*)

The image here of the suicide's heart being like ice is an indication of Mokichi's response: suicide was the ultimate denial of life. He came to view suicide as abhorrent, even though the act was not considered a sin in Japanese culture as it is in the Judeo-Christian tradition; to Mokichi it was an offense against nature.

jisatsu seshi   As I remember
monoguruira no   all the many lunatics
ikutari o   who have killed themselves,
omoi idashite   I find myself filled
nikumitsutsu ori   with feelings of loathing.

                                    (*Takahara*)

As he wrote in "Jisatsu zōo" (Abhorrence of suicide), the "odium" he felt toward suicide resulted from his repeated discovery of patients after they had hanged themselves or cut their throats; he was obliged to notify their families, and there were legal repercussions, but most repugnant of all was the feeling of failure he experienced. He came to abhor not merely the act of suicide, but the people who took their own lives;

he had to suppress this reaction when he heard that his friend Akutagawa had killed himself, and the abhorrence was stirred even by newspaper reports of the suicides of complete strangers.[7] The ambiguous feelings in these poems—from pain to compassion, then to anger and loathing—depict an emotional complexity that is a direct result of his professional experience.

The practical response to suicides by patients included such devices as the net-covered bed to keep patients safe in their rooms at night (featured in a 1910 advertising pamphlet of Kiichi's); and since so many of Mokichi's patients, such as the one he mourned in "Kinamida yoroku," hanged themselves, Mokichi developed a "safety obi," a short sash which buttoned, to replace the regular seven- or eight-foot-long cloth sash which ties around a kimono. Mokichi himself developed a symptom which he called "phobia telephonica," so great was his fear of being awakened at night to hear of yet another suicide.[8]

Mokichi's responses to suicide produced some very moving poetry, but the simple juxtapositions that arose in the course of his normal daily life as a psychiatrist more clearly evoke the world he experienced and opened to his readers:

kurenai no
sarusuberi wa
sakinuredo
kono kyōjin wa
mono iwazukeri

Crimson
the crape-myrtle
had bloomed,
and yet this madman
said not a word.
(*Shakkō*)

yoru no toko ni
waraikorogete
iru onna
waga tōredomo
kakawari mo nashi

The woman in
her bed at night, rolling
with laughter:
though I pass right by,
there is no connection.
(*Aratama*)

shimo itaku
fureru asake no
niwa koete
nani ka okoreru
kyōjin no koe

Crossing the garden
where the frost falls heavily
as the day breaks,
in a fury over something,
the voice of a madman.
(*Aratama*)

ichigatsu ni nareba	The new year has come,
nabete no hito wa	so that all the people
tanoshikute	now are joyful—
kyōja no mure mo	even the crowd of madmen
shibashi okorazu	is for a while without anger.
	(*Tsukikage*)

The isolation of the mentally ill is the reader's most powerful impression: the "madman" in the first poem cannot respond even to brilliant beauty. The "words" (*kotoba*) which had been considered, since Ki no Tsurayuki's Preface to the *Kokinshū*, the appropriate expression of the "heart" (*kokoro*) in response to beauty, are unspoken; the essential affirmative link between the man and the larger, natural world is missing. In the second poem, the woman's uncontrollable laughter is anything but joyous; the isolation stated in the last line, *kakawari mo nashi* (there is no connection), applies here to the psychiatrist poet as well. The suffering is transmitted as though the emotional isolation were contagious, since no one can form connections alone. The sufferer appears alienated even from himself in the third poem: the disembodied voice, filled with unfocused anger, floats over the cold, frost-filled garden, disconnected from the "madman" and unrelated to the surrounding scene. Even in moments of tranquility, such as the last of the poems above, the reader is moved to compassion because the pleasure (*tanoshikute*) is so fleeting (*shibashi*, for a little while): it is a reminder of what the mentally ill have lost. The poem's success derives in large part from the phrasing: this rare peace is the negative quality of being "without anger." Mokichi wrote that it moved him deeply to see patients with severe symptoms suppress them by a force of will under the influence of customs familiar since childhood.[9] It is a measure of his compassion for his patients that the rare successes, as well as the frequent failures, moved him so deeply:

kiguruishi	A single old man
oibito hitori	who had been mad has gone
waga mon o	from my gate
iete kaeriyuku	cured, to go home:
namidagumashi mo	my eyes fill with tears.
	(*Shiromomo*)

The above poem, Mokichi later wrote, came to him easily and he retained an affection for it, even though he recognized that it was not a major work: "Psychiatry is so often a thankless specialty. An instance like this can only be termed a rare and special case." [10] The isolated and anguished world of the mentally ill reaches the reader so forcefully because Mokichi did not insulate himself against the pain of a compassionate response, and because he transmitted the experiences by means of the poetic juxtaposition of detail that he used so successfully elsewhere. Many of the poems have the lingering sharpness of a dreamed image—in fact, the poem on the patients at the New Year's assembly was written of a remembered experience relived in a dream five years after he had relinquished his practice—but there is no doubt about the sense of reality they possess. As Saitō Shigeta has pointed out, it is of course possible to interpret literary descriptions of behavior in psychiatric terms. For example, the mythical actions of the god Susano'o no Mikoto can be described as symptoms of psychopathic social maladjustment. [11] However, Mokichi's depiction of the real and painful world of his patients in poetic terms has an immediacy that is unique in Japanese literary history

Mokichi's patience and compassion made of him a participant in the world of the mentally ill as well as an observer: his involvement is reflected in his poetic vocabulary. In the above poems, he deliberately used such words as *kyōjin, kyōja, monogurui* (all meaning madman, lunatic, or crazy), well aware of their derogatory connotations. His teacher Kure Shūzō had campaigned to replace them in the medical vocabulary with less highly charged words, such as *seishinbyō* (mental illness). [12] Indeed, Mokichi applauded those efforts. He wrote of them in one of the *bussokusekika* (Buddha's-footprint-stone poems) written to commemorate the twenty-fifth anniversary of Kure's career in medicine:

Rei sū ni	The *Ling shu* * uses
kyō to iu tomo	the term "lunacy," and yet
waga dochi wa	in our profession
kyō to na ii so to	you have instructed us
norashikeru rashi	not to say "lunacy":
yamu hito no tame	for the sake of the sufferers.
	(*Tsuyujimo*)

*The *Ling shu,* or *Huang Ti Nei Ching, Ling Shu,* is a classical Chinese treatise from the former Han period on medical physiology and anatomy.

Mokichi used such words, however, not only to refer to the "sufferers," but to refer to himself as well:

kyōjamori	The guardian of madmen
megane o kakete	puts on his glasses
asaborake	as the dawn breaks;
kyōin e yukazu	goes not to the asylum,
Fuji no yama mi ori	but stands watching Mt. Fuji.

(*Shakkō*)

There is a sporadic quality to the poem in that each line is essentially independent; they are held together by the *k* sounds throughout the first four lines and by the *mori* / *ori* rhyme which is echoed in the *ora* within *asaborake*. The poem contains a sense of self-denigration in the scattered feeling of the linear elements as well as in the inactivity of the "guardian of madmen" himself. The word *kyōjamori* is a denial of his own authority; he is ineffective in that he "guards," he does not cure. This is perhaps an inevitable result of a specialty which was in Mokichi's time still confined for the most part to diagnosis rather than treatment. But the words *kyōja* and *kyōjamori* also put the speaker of the poem closer to the laymen, his readers, in the ordinary world; and so the mystery of his profession is combined with the familiar.[13] Frequently the most he could do was to listen patiently, and he did that well. Kiichi, to appear effective, and at the insistence of his patients, would put his stethoscope to patients' heads, listen, and prescribe a "cure."[14] Mokichi, by referring to himself as *kyōjamori,* was denying the efficacy of both his science and that magic, and was putting himself in a position in which he shared the plight of his patients. His consequent sense of impotence is clear in the next poem:

toshi wakaki	The sadness of
kyōjinmori no	the young guardian
kanashimi wa	of madmen is
akebi no hana no	the sadness of akebia
chirau kanashimi	flowers; falling, scattering.

(*Shakkō*)

By equating his sense of himself to dying flowers, he is placing the world of the "madmen" and their "guardian" beyond the possibility of flowering or fruition. Nonetheless, the sights and sounds of the natural world often appear in counterpoint to the despondent or lifeless worlds of his patients or research, as in the earlier poem on "bending over / to stain a specimen / of brain cells," in which the poet was thinking of akebia blossoms, or in the following:

usagira no	I am starting
nō no shoken to	to write up my findings
keika to o	on development in
kakihajimetari	the cerebra of rabbits,
harusame kikitsutsu	while listening to spring rain—
	(*Henreki*)

Nature is consolation to the poet-researcher and the "guardian of madmen"; in a sense it is the real world, in which there is growth and movement. He sought out that world:

kyōjara o	Forgetting
shibashi wasurete	the madmen for a while,
waga ayumu	I walked:
machi ni wa fuyu no	the streets were filled
moya orinikeri	with wintry mist.
	(*Sekisen*)

In treating his life in medicine, as well as other aspects of his experience, Mokichi used *saji,* trivial details, to characterize a wider experience:

isogashiku	Having finished
yoru no kaishin o	in a rush his night rounds,
owari kite	and come home,
kyōjinmori wa	the guardian of madmen
kaya o tsuru nari	hangs up his mosquito net.
taku no shita ni	While beneath my desk
kayari no kō o	fragrant incense to repel
takinagara	mosquitoes burns,
hito nemurasemu	I am writing out prescriptions
shohō kakitari	to help other people sleep,
	(*Aratama*)

The contrast in the first poem between the hurried business in the *kami no ku* and the simple, quiet preparation for sleep in the *shimo no ku* manages to contain within it some of the tedium and exhaustion of his professional life. In the second, the still night filled with the aroma of the mosquito coils has a sense of timelessness; the poet's own sleep is put off until he has provided for his patients one of the only aids at his disposal. He wrote that he remembered how he had had to struggle to find the phrases *taku no shita ni* (beneath my desk) and *hito nemurasemu* (to help other people sleep). "However, at that time writing even one poem was an unsurpassed pleasure." [15] Writing poetry was a joy that counteracted the tedium, exhaustion, and pain that were part of his working life. As readers who know Mokichi primarily through his poems, it is easy for us to underestimate the extent of his engagement in his psychiatry. Indeed, Mokichi felt this to be true of his audience even during his lifetime, as when he wrote the following poem in 1932:

Mokichi ware	I, Mokichi,
inchō to nari	am called to serve as Director
isoshimu o	of the Hospital:
yo no morobito yo	all you people of the world!
shirite kudasare yo	please learn this about me!
	(Sekisen)

The nature of some of his dreams from 1950—after his retirement—illustrates the quality of his professional involvement; in one, he was making his rounds in wards that seemed to be situated in an air raid shelter:

A certain patient came up to me, and just when he seemed about to say "Happy new year, Doctor," he suddenly flung his arms around me, and I could not extricate myself. With great difficulty I finally calmed him down and struggled loose. In my dreams there were other such scenes. The patient was a middle-aged man who could not help seeing his mother as a fox-spirit, and he had committed the crime of matricide. I also dreamed about things like that. [16]

He was deeply involved with his patients; only with great difficulty did he disengage himself to write poems. But readers of Mokichi's poetry need his scolding reminder that he was often otherwise engaged. With-

out the affirmation of life expressed in his poetry, the denials and im-
pediments to fulfillment that were the constant elements of his practice
would surely have overwhelmed him. Yet he does not seem to have
taken the next step of trying to integrate his disparate worlds by some
coherent overview. He had rejected Freud's theories, which he thought
more applicable to art than to medicine, and he did not consider his
own poetic theories in relation to his other career—although concern
with the act of penetrating reality and becoming one with it would have
been a good place to begin approaching psychotherapy. The pain communicated by his poetry on his psychiatric patients derives in large part
from his own sense of helplessness, a feeling he seems to have exacerbated by a rigorous separation of the worlds of art and science to maintain the state of "antagonistic equilibrium."

Mokichi did not see himself only as the painfully ineffective "guardian of madmen," however; especially in his later years, when that heavy
burden was lifted, he could see himself with a lighter sense of perspective:

> akagane no   The color of copper
> iro ni naritaru   it has turned,
> hageatama   my bald head—
> kaku no gotoku ni   to become like this
> ikinokorikeri   have I lived on.
>   (*Shōen*)

The irony of having persevered through life to end with only a cop-
per-colored head to show for it is also self-deprecating, but with good-
humored resignation rather than self-condemnation. Mokichi was serious about this kind of irony, which led his sons to consider him
humorless.[17] Nonetheless there are many poems that are clearly amusing,
although they are never frivolous: Mokichi used humor for serious purposes. His humorous poems are almost all self-portraits:

> kōmori o   Don Quixote,
> moteru Don Kihōte wa   holding on to his umbrella,
> Asakusa no   comes to the Edo
> Edokan ni kite   Theater in Asakusa,
> namida o otosu   to let his tears flow.

kan no yo wa	In the cold night
imada asaki ni	a continuing slight
hanamizu wa	snivel
Uinkeruman no	falls on the pages
ue ni ochitari	of the Winkelmann.★
	(*Kan'un*)

hito shirezu	Unnoticed,
oitaru kanaya	how I have aged!
yo o komete	in the dark night
waga isarai mo	even my buttocks
hiyuru kono goro	freeze, these days—
	(*Shōen*)

In the first of these self-portraits, Mokichi is referring to his own habit of always carrying an umbrella, rain or shine: he ventures forth with this mock spear not to challenge and conquer, but to laugh until he cries at a popular theater.[18] In the second, he was certainly reading earnestly in the collected works of Johann Winkelmann, an archaeologist and classical scholar whom Mokichi admired and compared to Kamo no Mabuchi. Mokichi's affection for the poem was because it portrayed "a fragment of life," a fragment in which an earnest scholar's perception of his own importance is qualified by a runny nose.[19] The solitary realization of aging in the third poem, lamented in the first two lines and punctuated by the grouped exclamatory particles *kanaya,* is supported by the hard fact of a cold bottom, but the lament is serious. (The poem was apparently written during a predawn air raid in 1944.)[20] As with the previous poem, it is a "fragment of life"; the humor is used to present a full view of a whole experience, and much of experience is at best mundane, and occasionally ridiculous. Mokichi once wrote of the paintings of Pieter Brueghel that they contained "the lonely humor hidden in human life," and the humor in his own poetry is similar in containing within it loneliness and sadness. There is sadness in an old man feeling his body grow cold, but a lightness in the choice of the details to describe it. Satō compares Mokichi's old-age poems with the self-portraits Rembrandt painted late in life, for a gentleness in the vi-

---

★Mokichi is referring to the writings of Johann Joachim Winkelmann (1717–1768), a German scholar of classical antiquity. See Mokichi's "Mabuchi to Uinkeruman" and "Uinkeruman hoi," nos 226 and 227 of *Doba sanbō yawa* (*SMZ* 8:410–18).

sion; they have the same good humor.[21] Life in its normal progress could be viewed with good humor, but it was always a serious business to Mokichi because of its great value. The absence of life was intolerable, and he sought ways to fill the void. As in the first poem cited in this chapter, he responded to the death around him with an intense appetite, a craving for sustenance and satisfaction.

Exterior Views

Mokichi turned to nature as a rest from the world of the mentally ill, but more often simply for the affirmations of life and growth which it contains. His poetry on events in his life, on the deaths of people he loved, on daily activities, indeed on all subjects, is filled with natural imagery, but he wrote most often on nature alone. His childhood was spent in the countryside of rural Japan, and he retained throughout his life an awareness of the intricate patterns of natural cycles that was based on a detailed knowledge of the natural world. The immediacy of Mokichi's response to nature is a result of his childhood experience, and also of his constant search for affirmations of life. It is apparent even in his sorrow at the absence of life:

taema naki	There is a stone
tagichi no koyuru	the torrents flow over
ishi arite	ceaselessly,
shōnaki mono o	and I grieve for
ware wa kanashimu	all lifeless things.
	(*Shiromomo*)

He felt more in sympathy with movement and activity; passive objects which were merely acted upon were to be pitied. The exhilaration of natural movement flows through the following poem:

mukō yori	I was standing there
se no shiranami no	by the Tenryū River
tagichikuru	where white-capped waves
Tenryūgawa ni	of the river rapids
oritachinikeri	came cascading from beyond.
	(*Tomoshibi*)

The continuing rush of water is expressed in the poem's structure: the five lines form a single, flowing sentence. The scene opens in the distance in line 1 (*mukō yori,* from beyond), and travels down the white waves of the river to the poet in line 5 (*oritachinikeri,* "[I] was standing"), thus encompassing a whole landscape, which is given scale by the human figure although it contains meaning in itself. Movement was to Mokichi a symbol of the beauty of life—that which is unsuppressible:

taema naki	As the waves
mizuumi no nami	of the lake incessantly
yosuru toki	approach the shore,
nami o kaburite	crowning the waves
yuki kenokoreri	the snow remains, unmelted.
	(*Shirokiyama*)

In this poem, the movement is conveyed by sound, especially the undulating repetitions and alterations of the component sounds of *nami* (wave), itself repeated. Through the sounds the scene "moves like a movie": the nature Mokichi depicted was rarely static.[22]

Mokichi even found "quietude" (*shizukesa*) not in silence but in sounds, as active signs of life:

shizukesa wa	Is this what
kaku no gotoki ka	quietude is like?
fuyu no yo no	on a winter night
ware o megureru	the sounds of the air
kūki no oto su	which surrounds me
	(*Shirokiyama*)

In the following poem, sound and sight are related:

amazutau	Amid the snowbanks
hi no terukaesu	reflecting the sunlight
yuki no be wa	which fills the heavens,
misosazai naku	the wrens sing out
aiyobu rashi mo	as if calling to each other.
	(*Shirokiyama*)

The scene again opens in the distance (*amazutau / hi,* the sunlight / which fills the heavens), and moves, this time on light, to the snow-covered earth. The dazzling light is related not to human scale but to natural sound (*misosazai naku,* the wrens sing out), which heightens the impression of crystal clear air given in the *kami no ku.*

The context of the movement and sound in nature poems such as these is often visual imagery. Mokichi's depiction of changes in perspective as his focus shifts from distance to foreground, as well as an Impressionistic concern with the effects on color of changing light, gives his visual imagery a "painterly" quality:

amatsuhi no	At the time when
katamuku goro no	the sun is sinking,
Mogamigawa	the Mogami River
watatsumi no iro ni	turns the color of the sea
narite nagaruru	and runs its course.

(Shirokiyama)

When Mokichi began to paint from nature, late in life, he was unsuccessful in his attempts to portray stones; he found his subjects in plants, fruits and vegetables, and flowers. His most beautiful and skillful paintings, those of peonies, seem to be visual versions of the following poem from the rensaku "Haru yori natsu" (From spring into summer):

chikayorite	I draw near
ware wa mamoramu	to fix my gaze on it,
shiratama no	the pearl-white
botan no hana no	peony blossom,
sono jizaishin	its center of being.

(Shirokiyama)

In the first two lines, the poet is actively approaching an object to examine it closely; in the next three lines, the object is given the attribute of color in line 3, the form of a particular flower in line 4, and its essential quality in the final word of the last line, *jizaishin.* The word *jizaishin,* "free spirit," or "the spirit of one's own heart," and translated here as "center of being," was coined by Mokichi for this poem. There is general agreement that the poem is a fine one, but there are various interpretations of the definition of *jizaishin.* Satō Satarō insists that it means the "heart" of the flower, and therefore the stamen and pistils (*shibe*). Motobayashi Katsuo contends that it is the life of the flower in its intrinsic beauty, its "soul." Various Buddhist words, such as *ji-zainin,* the Buddha, whose virtue is free and unrestrained, are offered as indications of its meaning; and the appearance of the compound in Chinese poems is cited in discussions of the word's meaning. Itagaki Kaneo reported asking Mokichi directly what he meant by it, and was told that it meant many things: "its meaning is one with unrestricted boundaries." [23] The word is an attempt, I believe, to name the indefinable essence of a living thing, as all poetry is an attempt to find a form for meanings which can be transmitted in no other way. Its definition derives from its position within the poem; a perfect translation would perhaps have a newly coined word to represent it. In the poem on the peony, it symbolizes the goal of the art of "penetrating reality": it is to arrive at an essential quality of being. For the peony this essence is its emergence into beauty: the flower is the fulfillment of the plant's growth.

In another, simpler poem from the same sequence, the essence is a similar, indomitable fulfillment of a natural impulse:

> mizusumashi   The water-spider
> nagare ni mukai   confronts the current
> sakanoboru   and swims upstream:
> na ga ikioi yo   you have such spirit!
> kasukanaredomo   (although so delicate—)
> *(Shirokiyama)*

Mokichi's poetry, in this view, can be seen as the fruit of his continuing search for affirmations of life in the face of currents of grief, loneliness, and discouragement.

Conclusion

The two previous sections, on Mokichi's poetic views of himself and of the natural world around him, represent two of the most successful aspects of his work. It was through such works that his readers have felt they learned to know Mokichi intimately. The literary critic Kubota Masafumi, for example, recalls the time during his middle-school years when he first heard a friend read aloud the following poem from "Ohiro":

omoide wa	My memories are
shimo furu tani ni	filled with a sorrow
nagaretaru	like fragile clouds
usugumo no goto	that flow in valleys
kanashiki kanaya	where the frost falls—
	(*Shakkō*)

Later, he felt he fully appreciated the depth of poems from the sequence "Shigure" (Early winter rains), such as the following, while looking out a train window as he rode through Shinano:

yū sareba	As evening drew on,
daikon no ha ni	on radish leaves fell the
furu shigure	early winter rain;
itaku sabishiku	in pain, in loneliness,
furinikeru kamo	how it was raining!
	(*Aratama*)

Kubota writes that "they have the feeling that [Mokichi] touched upon the basis of human existence, without trying to explain it; rather, as though he touched upon a brief flash of life which he seemed to be able to grasp intuitively."[24]

We have seen how Kajiki was moved to tears by the impact of a poem he could not yet even understand; he also wrote of his own discussions of the poet that "Mokichi, for better or worse, lives inside me, and I want to satisfy myself clearly about what sort of thing it is [within me]." In other words, " 'Mokichi' is definitely not the name of some other person" outside himself, but an integral part of his own conscious being.[25] Akutagawa felt the same way: he wrote that he found it difficult to write about Mokichi because "Mokichi, at some point, put down roots in a corner of my heart." He felt it as impossible to be objective about Mokichi as about himself, having learned from him to see the world in a new way. The reasons for this depth of feeling were elusive: it was as if one were to ask "Jihei the paper merchant why he loved Koharu of Sonezaki" in Chikamatsu's *Shinjū ten no Amijima* (The love suicides at Amijima). To list the special qualities does not answer the question; the reason resides in the whole person behind the list.[26]

That whole person is accessible through his poems: "Mokichi the man lives in his tanka, and it is impossible to think of Mokichi separated from tanka."[27] The tanka form, traditionally concerned with the quality of experience, was particularly well suited to Mokichi's vision. The juxtaposition of his detailed perceptions of the world around him with his specific responses to particular moments or events, that is, the interaction between a self and the world, enables a reader to share the poet's experience. The impact of the best of these tanka has been a profound one for many readers. All of Mokichi's poetry is not, of course, equally good; the excellence of *Shakkō, Tomoshibi, Shiromomo,* or *Shirokiyama* is only occasionally apparent in, for example, *Henreki* or *Takahara.* Yet in all his work, the man who "lives in the tanka" is present, and the reader achieves an unusual intimacy with him.

The body of Mokichi's poetry contains the perceptions and responses to the whole of his experience, throughtout an eventful lifetime. The work has a unity of form because of Mokichi's almost exclusive use of the tanka as a medium of expression; and it has a unity of purpose in that he always tried to write poems that were "an expression of life," an affirmation of being. He tried to do this with a constant reliance on the practice of shasei, a process of permeating nature and becoming one with it, and found himself "born" in each new poem he wrote.

In a sense, Mokichi's poetry as a whole can be considered a 14,200-verse rensaku on the life of one man. Most discussions of his rensaku focus primarily on the strongest, most vibrant poems, the pattern poems, as most criticism has been focused on his strongest collections, such as *Shakkō, Aratama, Shiromomo,* and *Shirokiyama.* Readers like Akutagawa, Kajiki, and Kubota have been induced by these pattern poems to make a more extensive examination of his poetry, and find that in so doing they have discovered an identity of vision. The lesser works function in much the same way as the ground poems do in a rensaku: they enhance the better poems by providing a context which enlarges their significance. In the end we are able to share experience profoundly because so many aspects of that experience have been communicated. We have the full vision of a total being, thanks in part to the variations in quality within a lifetime's body of work.

This intimacy could not possibly emerge from the ground poems if the pattern poems were less brilliant. In them, Mokichi was able to transmit a segment of his experience in a form that seemed inevitable and with a sense of completeness, by personalizing the external world even as he made his own experiences in it universal:

yoiyami no	In the fleeting
hakanakarikeru	darkness of evening,
tōku yori	from the distance,
rai todorokite	thunder rumbling;
umi ni furu ame	on the sea, falling rain.

(*Sekisen*)

yowa ni shite	Although I have
namida nagaruru	at midnight felt
koto aredo	my tears flow,
junan no namida	they are not tears
to iu wa arazu	that spring from suffering.

(*Shirokiyama*)

In tanka such as these, the brightest facets of a multifaceted body of work, Mokichi opened worlds to his readers, enabling us by his poetic skill to perceive them as he wrote of them, "by following the impetus of poetic feeling, freely, directly, profoundly, and with certainty."[28]

APPENDIX ONE

Ohiro

Part I

1. nagekaeba
   mono mina kurashi
   hingashi ni
   izuru hoshi sae
   akakaranaku ni

   Since I keep grieving
   all things are dark—
   even the stars
   that appear in the east
   do not shine.

2. tōku tōku
   yukinaru narame
   dentō o
   keseba nubatama no
   yoru mo fukenuru

   How far, how far
   must she have gone now!
   when I turn out the lamp,
   how late the coal-black
   night has grown.

3. yoru kureba
   sayodoko ni neshi
   kanashikaru
   omowa mo ima wa
   nashi mo odoko mo

   As night falls,
   her beloved face,
   she who lay in my bed,
   now is no more!
   how narrow my bed!

4. furafura to
   tadoki mo shirazu
   Asakusa no
   ninuri no dō ni
   ware wa kinikeri

   Distractedly
   and at a loss,
   to the red-lacquered hall
   of Asakusa
   have I come.

NOTE: I have numbered the poems for ease of reference. In making the translations I relied on the commentaries in Motobayashi Katsuo and Shibōta Minoru, *Saitō Mokichi shū,* pp. 68–74, and Motobayashi, *Saitō Mokichi,* pp. 113–20.

5. ana kanashi   The pity of it!
    Kannondō ni   the leper there,
    raisha ite   at Kannon's temple,
    tada hitasura ni   singlemindedly
    zeni horinikeri   beseeching pennies.

6. Asakusa ni   I came here
    kite udetamago   to Asakusa, bought
    kainikeri   a hard-boiled egg;
    hitasabishikute   in overwhelming loneliness
    waga kaeru naru   I went back home.

7. hatsuhatsu ni   Because of her,
    fureshi ko nareba   a girl I touched
    waga kokoro   slightly, briefly,
    ima wa hadara ni   now my heart,
    nagekinaru nare   in tatters, grieves.

8. Yoyogino o   I ran desperately
    hitahashiritari   through the fields
    sabishisa ni   of Yoyogi, living
    iki no inochi no   in loneliness, my life
    kono sabishisa ni   in this loneliness—

9. sabishi sabishi   Lonely, lonely!
    ima saihō ni   now in the west
    kurukuru to   even the sun setting
    akaku iru hi mo   smoothly, redly,
    koyonaku sabishi   incredibly lonely.

10. kamikuzu o   From burning wastepaper
    saniwa ni takeba   here in the garden
    kemuri tatsu   the smoke rises.
    kōshiki hito wa   My beloved one—
    haruka naru kamo   how far removed from me!

11. horohoro to   Wafting softly
    noboru kemuri no   the rising smoke
    ten ni nobori   to the heavens rises
    kihatsuru kani   as though to disappear;
    ware mo kenu kani   I too would disappear—

12. hisakata no   While weeping
    hiten no moto ni   far beneath the distant
    nakinagara   grieving skies,

hito koinikeri
inochi mo hosoku

I was longing for her;
my very life contracts.

13. hōrinageshi
     furoshiki tsutsumi
     hiroimochi
     idakite itari
     sabishikute naranu

I pick up and hold
the cloth-wrapped bundle
thrown down before,
and hold it to me;
unbearably lonely.

14. hittari to
     dakite kanashi mo
     hito naranu
     fūtengaku no
     fumi no kanashi mo

Holding them close
to me, so sorrowful—
they are not she,
these books on lunacy,
themselves so sorrowful.

15. uzutakaku
     tsumishi shomotsu
     chiri tamari
     mi no kanashi mo yo
     tadoki shiraneba

Piled high,
the stacks of books
have gathered dust,
painful to look at—
since I know not where to turn.

16. tsutome nareba
     kyō mo densha ni
     norinikeri
     kanashiki hito wa
     haruka naru kamo

Since I must work,
today as well
I rode the trolley;
my sorrowing beloved—
so far removed from me!

17. kono asake
     sanshō no ka no
     kayoikite
     nageku kokoro ni
     shimitōru nare

At dawn today
the scent of *sanshō* ★
drifted in,
penetrated through
this grieving heart.

Part II

18. honobono to
     me o hosoku shite
     itakareshi
     ko wa sarishi yori
     iku yo ka hetaru

Since she has left,
she I embraced,
enraptured,
my eyes half-closed—
how many nights have passed?

★ *Sanshō:* Japanese pepper.

19. ureitsutsu
    inishi ko yue ni
    fuji no hana
    yuru hikari sae
    kanashiki mono o

    Because despairing
    she has gone,
    even the trembling brilliance
    in clusters of wisteria
    has so much sadness—

20. shiratama no
    urei no onna
    a ni kitari
    nagaruru ga goto
    ima wa sarinishi

    The woman of
    pearl-white grief
    came to me;
    like waters flowing
    now she has gone.

21. kanashimi no
    koi ni hitarite
    itaru toki
    shirafuji no hana
    sakitarinikeri

    While I have been
    immersed in this
    grief-laden love,
    the white wisteria flowers
    have bloomed, have blown.

22. yūyami ni
    kaze tachinureba
    honobono to
    tsutsuji no hana wa
    chirinikeru kamo

    In twilight
    as the breezes rise,
    faintly, faintly
    have they fallen,
    the azalea flowers.

23. omoide wa
    shimo furu tani ni
    nagaretaru
    usugumo no goto
    kanashiki kanaya

    My memories are
    filled with a sorrow
    like fragile clouds
    that flow in valleys
    where the frost falls—

24. asaborake
    hitome mishi yue
    shibadataku
    kuroki matsuge o
    awareminikeri

    I glimpsed her once
    at daybreak, and so
    my heart leapt
    at the black lashes
    fluttering.

25. waga areshi
    hoshi o shitaishi
    kuchibiru no
    akaki onna o
    awareminikeri

    my heart leapt
    for the woman with
    red lips, who
    I yearn for as
    a star I bore.

26. shinshin to
    yuki furishi yo ni
    sono yubi no

    On a night when
    silently the snow fell,
    her fingers—

ana tsumeta yo to — "how cold they are!"
iite yorishika — I said, drawing near her.

27. kyōin no — While watching
    renga no ue ni — the sun rise red
    asahiko no — above the brick walls
    akaki o mitsutsu — of the asylum,
    kuchi furinikeri — I kissed her lips.

28. tamakiwaru — When we touch,
    inochi hikarite — fervent life shining,
    furitareba — "no," she says,
    ina to wa iite — shrinking back,
    kenugani mo yoru — yet drawing nearer.

29. ka no inochi — Were one to say,
    shiine to iwaba — "may his life end,"
    nagusamame — it might comfort me;
    ware no kokoro wa — yet my own heart
    iigatenu kamo — could not so speak.

30. suriorosu — From the rubbing
    wasabi oroshi yu — of grated *wasabi* ★
    shimi idete — the liquid seeps, and
    taru aomizu no — the green dripping water
    kanashikarikeri — was heart-rending.

31. naku koe wa — Although its cries
    kanashi keredomo — were sorrowful,
    yūdori wa — the evening bird
    ki ni nemuri nari — sleeps in its tree;
    ware wa nenaku ni — I remain sleepless.

Part III

32. ure'etsutsu — Because despairing
    inishi ko no yue — she has gone,
    tōyama ni — ah my heart!
    moyuru hi hodo no — like fires burning
    aga kokoro kana — in distant mountains.

★ *Wasabi:* a kind of horseradish.

33. aware naru
    omina no mabuta
    koinadete
    sono yo hotohoto
    ware wa shinikeri

Lovingly I stroked
her eyelids, the woman
who so moved me,
and that night I felt
myself come close to death.

34. kono kokoro
    hōran to shite
    kitarinure
    hatake ni wa mugi wa
    akaraminikeri

Trying to lay to rest
this heart of mine,
I came here:
in the fields, the wheat
has turned to red.

35. natsu sareba
    nōen ni kite
    kokorogushi
    mizusumashi oba
    tsukamaenikeri

Since it is summer,
I came here, to farmland,
disconsolate,
and caught water-
spiders with my hands.

36. mugi no ho ni
    hikari nagarete
    tayutaeba
    mukō ni yagi wa
    nakisomenikere

As light flowed
fluttering among
the spears of wheat,
from off in the distance
came the bleating of a goat.

37. mo no naka ni
    hisomu imori no
    akaki hara
    hatsuka misomete
    utsutsu tomo nashi

I caught sight of
the red belly
of a water lizard
hidden amid duckweed—
was overcome by it.

38. kono kokoro
    hōrihaten to
    ho no hikaru
    kiri o tatami ni
    sashinikeru kamo

To lay to rest at last
this heart of mine,
with the glittering
point of the awl
I pierced the tatami.

39. warajimushi
    tatami no ue ni
    ide koshi ni
    tabako no kemuri
    kakete waga ori

As the wood-lice
make their way out
onto the tatami,
I envelop them
with smoke from cigarettes.

40. nennen ni
    onna o omou
    ware aredo

Although unceasingly
my mind dwells
on that woman,

koyoi mo osoku   tonight I am up late
shu no sumi suru mo   rubbing vermilion ink.

41. kono ame wa   I wonder if this rain
     samidare naramu   is of the summer rains—
     kinō yori   it has been falling
     waga saniwabe ni   falling in my garden
     furite iru kamo   since yesterday.

42. tsutsumashiku   Withdrawn and
     hitori shi oreba   all alone, I watch
     kyōin no   the rain fall
     akaki renga ni   on the red brick
     ame no furu miyu   of the asylum.

43. ruri iro ni   Enclosed in the blue
     komorite maruki   of lapis lazuli, the round seeds
     kusa no mi wa   of the grasses
     waga koibito no   became the eyes
     manako narikeri   of my beloved.

44. hingashi ni   When the stars
     hoshi izuru toki   appear in the east,
     na ga minaba   should you see them,
     sono me honobono to   let those eyes be
     kanashiku are yo   as gently loving as before.

APPENDIX TWO

Shinitamau Haha
(My Mother Is Dying)

Part I

1. hiroki ha wa
   ki ni hirugaeri
   hikaritsutsu
   kakuroinitsutsu
   shizugokoro nakere

   As the wide leaves
   flutter on the tree,
   now gleaming,
   now darkening,
   my heart is uneasy.

2. shirafuji no
   tarihana chireba
   shimijimi to
   ima wa sono mi no
   miesomeshi kamo

   Since the hanging flowers
   of the white wisteria scattered,
   how it wounds me
   now that its seed pods
   have started to appear.

3. Michinoku no
   haha no inochi o
   hitome min
   hitome min to zo
   isogu narikere

   Oh that I might see her,
   my mother, in life,
   at Michinoku,
   thinking, oh that I might see her,
   how I hurried.

4. uchihisasu
   miyako no yoru ni
   hi wa tomori
   akakarikereba
   isogu narikeri

   When the lamps
   were lit
   and shining bright
   in the glittering capital,
   how I hurried.

NOTE: The translation of this sequence first appeared in " 'My Mother is Dying': Saitō Mokichi's *'Shinitamau Haha'*," in *Monumenta Nipponica* (Winter 1978) 33(4):413–23, and is reprinted with permission.

5. haha ga me o
   hitome o min to
   isogitaru
   waga nuka no he ni
   ase idenikeri

   As I hurried thinking,
   oh that I might see
   my mother's eyes,
   the sweat stood out
   on my forehead.

6. tomoshi akaki
   miyako o idete
   yuku sugata
   karisome tabi to
   hito miru ran ka

   As I leave the capital
   where the lamps
   are shining bright,
   will the others see me
   as a carefree traveler?

7. tamayura ni
   nemurishi kana ya
   hashiritaru
   kisha nuchi ni shite
   nemurishi kana ya

   Even for a little while
   can I have slept?
   while in this
   rushing train,
   can I have slept?

8. Azumayama ni
   yuki kagayakeba
   Michinoku no
   waga haha no kuni ni
   kisha irinikeri

   As the snow glistened
   on the Azuma mountains,
   the train entered
   Michinoku,
   my mother's home.

9. asa samumi
   kuwa no ki no ha ni
   shimo furedo
   haha ni chikazuku
   kisha hashiru nari

   In the morning cold,
   while the frost settles
   on the leaves of mulberry,
   the train rushes on,
   closer to my mother.

10. numa no ue ni
    kagirou aoki
    hikari yori
    ware no ure'e no
    komu to iu kaya

    I wonder can it be
    that my own grief
    arises from
    the pale blue light
    that shimmers on the marsh?

11. Kaminoyama no
    teishaba ni ori
    wakaku shite
    ima wa yamo'o no
    otōto mitari

    I got off at the station
    at Kaminoyama
    and saw him—
    my still young
    yet now widowed brother.

Part II

12. harubaru to
    kusuri o mochite
    koshi ware o
    mamori tamaeri
    ware wa ko nareba

    I, who come from afar,
    bring medicine to her,
    she who follows me
    with her eyes,
    since I am her child.

13. yorisoeru
    ware o mamorite
    iitamau
    nani ka iitamau
    ware wa ko nareba

    She gazes at me
    as I draw near her
    and speaks,
    says something,
    since I am her child.

14. nageshi naru
    ninuri no yari ni
    chiri wa miyu
    haha no be no waga
    asame ni wa miyu

    On the red-lacquered spear
    hanging from the crossbeam
    there is dust;
    lying by my mother, as I
    open my eyes, I see dust.

15. yama izuru
    taiyōkō o
    ogamitaru
    odamaki no hana
    sakitsuzukitari

    Bowing before the sunlight
    coming out of the mountains,
    the columbines
    are blossoming
    abundantly.

16. shi ni chikaki
    haha ni soine no
    shinshin to
    tōta no kawazu
    ten ni kikoyuru

    As I lie beside my mother
    who is close to death,
    piercingly the call
    of frogs in distant fields
    echoes in the heavens.

17. kuwa no ka no
    aoku tadayou
    asaake ni
    taegatakereba
    haha yobinikeri

    At dawn when
    the scent of mulberry
    greenly hovered,
    it was so hard to bear,
    I cried out to my mother.

18. shi ni chikaki
    haha ga me ni yori
    odamaki no
    hana sakitari to
    iinikeru kana

    Drawing near before the gaze
    of my mother
    who is close to death,
    the columbines are
    flowering, I said.

19.   haru nareba
       hikari nagarete
       uraganashi
       ima wa nu no be ni
       buto mo areshika

       Since it is spring
       the sunlight streams—
       heartbreaking—
       now even the gnats
       emerge in the fields.

20.   shi ni chikaki
       haha ga hitai o
       sasuritsutsu
       namida nagarete
       itarikeru kana

       I keep stroking the brow
       of my mother
       who is close to death
       and find my tears
       keep flowing.

21.   haha ga me o
       shimashi karekite
       mamoritaru
       ana kanashimo yo
       kōko no nemuri

       Leaving for a moment
       my watchful vigil
       over my mother's eyes—
       oh, the grief of it!
       the sleep of the silkworm.

22.   waga haha yo
       shi ni tamaiyuku
       waga haha yo
       wa o umashi
       chitaraishi haha yo

       Oh my mother!
       she draws close to death.
       Oh my mother!
       she who bore me,
       my mother who nurtured me!

23.   nodo akaki
       tsubakurame futatsu
       hari ni ite
       tarachine no haha wa
       shinitamau nari

       Two red-throated swallows
       are perched
       on a crossbeam;
       my cherishing mother
       is dying.

24.   inochi aru
       hito atsumarite
       waga haha no
       inochi shiyuku o
       mitari shiyuku o

       The living ones
       gather to watch
       as my mother's life
       approaches death,
       moves on to death.

25.   hitori kite
       kōko no heya ni
       tachitareba
       waga sabishisa wa
       kiwamarinikeri

       I came out alone
       and stood
       in the silkworm room
       and my loneliness
       was complete.

Part III

26.   nara wakaba
        terihirugaeru
        utsutsunani
        yamako wa aoku
        arenu yamako wa

In the new oak leaves
run riot,
gleaming and fluttering,
the wild silkworms are green,
the newborn wild silkworms.

27.   hi no hikari
        hadara ni morite
        uraganashi
        yamako wa imada
        chiisakarikeri

The sunlight, dappled,
filters through
and I grieve—
the wild silkworms
still are small.

28.   hōri michi
        sukanbo no hana
        hohoketsutsu
        hōri michibe ni
        chirinikerazu ya

The sorrel flowers
along the funeral road
are past their prime—
weren't they scattered
along the funeral road?

29.   okinagusa
        kuchi akaku saku
        no no michi ni
        hikari nagarete
        warera yukitsu mo

By the country road
where anemones flower
red-throated,
the light streams forth
and we walk on.

30.   waga haha o
        yakaneba naranu
        hi o moteri
        amatsusora ni wa
        miru mono mo nashi

We have brought the flame
which must burn
my mother;
in the heavens there is
nothing to be seen.

31.   hoshi no iru
        yozora no moto ni
        akaaka to
        hahasoha no haha wa
        moeyukinikeri

Brightly, brightly
beneath the starlit
evening sky,
my lamented mother
then began to burn.

32.   sayo fukaku
        haha o hōri no
        hi o mireba
        tada akaku mo zo
        moenikeru kamo

As night deepened
while we watched
her funeral pyre,
how brightly
did it blaze!

33. hōribi no
     mamori koyoi wa
     fukenikeri
     koyoi no ten no
     itsukushiki kamo

     We watched over
     the funeral pyre
     and the night grew late,
     oh, the stern grandeur
     of the sky tonight.

34. hi o morite
     sayo fukenureba
     otōto wa
     utsushimi no uta
     utau kanashiku

     Watching the fire
     as the night grew late
     my brother sang
     a song of the living
     lamentingly.

35. hitagokoro
     mamoran mono ka
     honoakaku
     noboru kemuri no
     sono kemuri haya

     Will I so intently
     keep watch over it?
     faintly red,
     the rising smoke,
     oh, the smoke.

36. hai no naka ni
     haha o hiroeri
     asahiko no
     noboru ga naka ni
     haha o hiroeri

     We gathered up my mother
     from amid the ashes;
     as the morning sun
     was rising,
     we gathered up my mother.

37. fuki no ha ni
     teinei ni atsumeshi
     honekuzu mo
     mina kotsugame ni
     ireshimaikeri

     Reverently we collected them
     in leaves of bittersweet
     and put them all,
     the bits of bone,
     in an ossuary urn.

38. uraura to
     ten ni hibari wa
     nakinobori
     yuki hadara naru
     yama ni kumo izu

     The skylark rose
     brightly singing
     to the heavens
     and no clouds lay
     above the snow-streaked hills.

39. dokudami mo
     azami no hana mo
     yake itari
     hitohōrido no
     ame akenureba

     The lizard's-tails
     and thistle flowers
     had also burned
     when the dawn broke
     at the cremation ground.

Part IV

40. kagiroi no
    haru narikereba
    ko no me mina
    fukiizuru yamabe
    yukiyuku ware yo

    Into the mountains
    where in shimmering spring
    the buds on all the trees
    burst forth,
    I go on alone.

41. honoka ni mo
    akebi no hana no
    chirinureba
    yamabato no koe
    utsutsu naru kana

    While the akebia blossoms
    silently scatter,
    I am spellbound
    by the voices
    of the turtledoves.

42. yamakage ni
    kiji ga nakitari
    yamakage no
    suppaki yu koso
    kanashikarikere

    In the mountain shadows
    the pheasants call;
    at the sulphur springs
    in the mountain shadows,
    how sad they are.

43. san no yu ni
    mi wa suppori to
    hitari ite
    sora ni kagayaku
    hikari o mitari

    Immersing myself
    entirely
    in the sulphur springs,
    I watch the starlight
    sparkle in the sky.

44. furusato no
    wagie no sato ni
    kaeri kite
    shirafuji no hana
    hidete kuikeri

    Returning to my village,
    to my old home
    in my home town,
    I ate white wisteria
    steeped in broth.

45. yamakage ni
    kenokoru yuki no
    kanashisa ni
    sasa kakiwakete
    isogu narikeri

    Through the sadness of
    the still unmelted snow
    in the mountain shadows,
    pushing aside the bamboo grass
    how I hurried.

46. sasahara o
    tada kakiwakete
    yukiyukedo
    haha o tazunen
    ware naranaku ni

    I just kept on
    pushing my way through
    thickets of bamboo grass—
    not that I was
    searching for my mother.

47. hi no yama no
     fumoto ni izuru
     san no yu ni
     hitoyo hitarite
     kanashiminikeri

Bathing at night
in the sulphur springs
flowing from the base
of the fiery mountain,
how sorrowful I was.

48. honoka naru
     hana no chirinishi
     yama no be o
     kasumi nagarete
     yukinikeru hamo

Through the mountains
where the faint blossoms
have scattered,
how the mist
keeps flowing.

49. harukeku mo
     hazama no yama ni
     moyuru hi no
     kurenai to a ga
     haha to kanashiki

Far in the distance
I see the crimson of a fire
burning in a mountain gorge:
recalling my mother,
how sad I am.

50. yamahara ni
     moyuru hi nareba
     akaaka to
     kemuri wa ugoku
     kanashikaredomo

As the fire burns
on the mountainside
brightly, brightly,
the smoke wafts—
oh, but it is sad.

51. tara no me o
     tsumitsutsu yukeri
     sabishisa wa
     ware yori hoka no
     mono to kawa shiru

As I go gathering
aralia shoots—
does anyone else know
a loneliness
such as mine?

52. sabishisa ni
     taete wakeiru
     waga me ni wa
     kuroguro to akebi
     no hana chirinikeri

As I make my way through,
enduring my loneliness,
night-black
before my eyes
the akebia flowers fall.

53. miharukasu
     yamahara nadari
     sakite iru
     kobushi no hana wa
     honoka naru kamo

The magnolia blossoms
seen from afar
open cascading
down the mountainside—
how pale they are!

54. Zaōsan ni
     hadara yuki kamo
     kagayaku to

There are patches of snow
on Zaō mountain;
as evening came

yū sarikureba
sowa yukinikeri

in brilliance
I walked the steep paths.

55.   shimijimi to
      ame furi itari
      yama no be no
      tsuchi akaku shite
      aware naru kamo

The rain fell
relentlessly,
turning red
the mountain soil—
how it moved me!

56.   onten o
      nagarau kumo ni
      tamakiwaru
      inochi wa nashi to
      ieba kanashiki

To think there is
no vital life
among those clouds afloat
in the distant sky
calls forth sorrow.

57.   yamakai ni
      hi wa toppuri to
      kuretareba
      ima wa yu no ka no
      fukakarishi kamo

Now that the sun
has set completely
in the mountain gorge,
the scent of the hot spring—
how intense it is!

58.   yudokoro ni
      futayo neburite
      junsai o
      kueba sarasara ni
      kanashiminikere

I slept two nights
at the hot springs;
at the taste of *junsai* ★
I felt anew
the stab of grief.

59.   yama yue
      sasatake no ko o
      kuinikeri
      hahasoha no haha yo
      hahasoha no haha yo

Here in the mountains
I ate the young shoots
of the bamboo grass
oh, my lamented mother!
oh, my lamented mother!

★*Junsai:* watershield.

APPENDIX THREE
The Poetry Books

Publishing History

MOKICHI'S first two volumes of poetry, *Shakkō* and *Aratama*, were published shortly after their composition. Then there was a hiatus of nearly twenty years during which Mokichi published his poems in periodicals but did not prepare manuscripts for book publication. The reasons Mokichi did not publish books of poetry during these years are not clear, but in the late 1930s he began to assemble his earlier work for publication by working backwards. *Kan'un, Gyōkō,* and *Shiromomo,* published in the early forties, contain work from the mid- to late thirties. *Noboriji,* which includes the work from 1939 and 1940, was the next volume to be published shortly after it was written.

When Mokichi resumed preparing manuscripts of earlier work, he started by working chronologically from where he had left off following *Aratama,* and *Tsuyujimo, En'yū,* and *Henreki* were published in order. There was a break again when recent work in *Shōen* and *Shirokiyama* was published in 1949. Mokichi returned to the sequential publication of his older work with *Tomoshibi, Takahara, Renzan, Sekisen,* and finally, *Shimo.* Thus sixteen volumes were published during Mokichi's lifetime, although for a long period of his career his poetic reputation rested on his two earliest works, *Shakkō* and *Aratama,* and periodical publications.

The seventeenth volume, *Tsukikage,* was published a year after his death by his colleagues and disciples, although Mokichi had revised most of the manuscript himself. The table sets out the composition and publication history.

Table. Order of Composition

Title	Period of Composition	Date and Order of Publication	
(1) *Shakkō* (Crimson light)	1905–13	Oct. 1913	(1)
(2) *Aratama* (Uncut gems)	1913–17	Jan. 1921	(2)
(3) *Tsuyujimo* (Dew and frost)	1917–22	Aug. 1946	(7)
(4) *En'yū* (Distant travels)	1922–23	Aug. 1947	(8)
(5) *Henreki* (Pilgrimage)	1923–25	Apr. 1948	(9)
(6) *Tomoshibi* (Lamplight)	1925–28	Jan. 1950	(12)
(7) *Takahara* (High fields)	1929–30	June 1950	(13)
(8) *Renzan* (Mountain range)	1930	Nov. 1950	(14)
(9) *Sekisen* (Stone spring)	1931–32	June 1951	(15)
(10) *Shiromomo* (White peaches)	1933–34	Feb. 1942	(5)
(11) *Gyōkō* (Crimson dawn)	1935–36	June 1940	(4)
(12) *Kan'un* (Cold clouds)	1937–39	Mar. 1940	(3)
(13) *Noboriji* (Rising road)	1939–40	Nov. 1943	(6)
(14) *Shimo* (Frost)	1941–42	Dec. 1951	(16)
(15) *Shōen* (Small gardens)	1943–46	Apr. 1949	(10)
(16) *Shirokiyama* (White mountains)	1946–47	Aug. 1949	(11)
(17) *Tsukikage* (Moonlight)	1948–52	Feb. 1954	(17)

Glossary

bussokuseki (-ka) (-tai) 仏足石（歌）（体）
A thirty-eight syllable poem divided into six lines of 5–7–5–7–7–7 syllables.

chitaraishi 乳足らひし
A pillow word (*makurakotoba*) coined by Mokichi to use in addition to *tarachine no*.

chōka 長歌
A "long poem" form, found especially in the *Man'yōshū*, composed of alternating lines of five and seven syllables, and ending with two seven-syllable lines; often followed by tanka.

dokuei (-ka) 独詠（歌）
A poem "recited alone"; addressed to oneself.

fūten 瘋癲
Lunacy, insanity.

hachō 破調
"Broken meter"; lines in a fixed-form poem such as a tanka which are either longer or shorter than the usual number of syllables.

inochi no araware 命のあらはれ
"An expression of life"; in Mokichi's view, the essential characteristic of the tanka.

ji 地
"Ground": used to describe poems that are not especially striking or impressive, but serve in a poetic sequence as the context for *mon* ("pattern") poems.

jiamari 字余り
"Excessive words": a greater number of syllables in a line than the standard number in a fixed poetic form such as the tanka.

jimon 地文; *yaya ji* やや地
Poems that are somewhat more striking than simple *ji* poems.

jissai 実際
Reality.

jissō 実相
> Reality; a Buddhist word.

jissō kannyū 実相観入
> "To penetrate reality": the goal of the tanka poet in Mokichi's theory of shasei as a poetic technique.

jitarazu 字足らず
> "Insufficient words": fewer syllables than the standard number required for a line in a fixed poetic form such as a tanka.

kami no ku 上の句
> "The upper lines": the first three lines of the five-line tanka form.

kannyū 観入
> "To penetrate": a word coined by Mokichi for use in his definition of shasei.

kerukamo-chō けるかも調
> A poetic tone, based on the use of archaic diction characterized by verb endings such as *-keru* and exclamations such as *kamo*; used by Mokichi to describe his own poetry.

kyō 狂
> "Lunacy": Kure Shūzō sought to replace this character in words used to describe the mentally ill.

makurakotoba 枕詞
> "Pillow word": a poetic epithet often now undefinable, usually of five syllables, used to modify a specific class of words.

mon 文
> "Pattern": used to describe especially striking or impressive poems in a poetic sequence.

monji 文地; *yaya mon* やや文
> Poems that are less impressive and so moving closer to "ground" (*ji*) poems.

renga 連歌
> A form of linked poetry, most often a standard number of verses written by more than one poet according to specific requirements. Renga flourished especially in the fifteen and sixteen centuries.

rensaku 連作
> A poetic sequence of varying length with a coherent internal structure, written by a single poet on a unified theme.

saji 瑣事
> "Trivia": intrinsically insignificant details used by Mokichi in his poetry to express deeper meaning.

seishinbyō 精神病
> "Mental illness": the modern replacement for derogatory words such as *kyō* (lunacy); the adoption of this usage was urged by Kure Shūzō.

shasei 写生
> "The depiction of life": a theory of poetic expression, derived from a term in the visual arts, first propounded by Masaoka Shiki and expanded and refined by Mokichi.

shimo no ku 下の句
> "The lower lines": the final two seven-syllable lines of the five-line tanka form.

taiei(-ka) 対詠（歌）
> "Recited to another": in contrast to *dokueika*, "poems recited alone," a poem addressed to another person.

tanka 短歌
> "Short poem": the thirty-one syllable, five-line form divided into lines of 5–7–5–7–7 syllables; until modern times frequently called *waka*.

tarachine no 足乳ねの
> A pillow word (*makurakotoba*) used to modify mother or parent.

waka 和歌
> "Japanese poetry": used most often to mean a tanka ("short poem") of thirty-one syllables in five lines.

Notes

PREFACE

1. Satō Satarō, *Mokichi kaisetsu*, p. 59.
2. Katagiri Akinori, *Saitō Mokichi: hito to sakuhin*, p. 43.
3. Satō, *Kaisetsu*, p. 97.

1. CHILDHOOD, MARRIAGE, AND MEDICINE, 1882–1917

1. Katagiri Akinori, *Saitō Mokichi: hito to sakuhin*, pp. 8–10; I visited Kanakame in September 1979.
2. Makabe Jin, *Teihon ningen Mokichi*, pp. 16, 44; Shibōta Minoru, *Saitō Mokichi den*, pp. 8–9, 21.
3. Saitō Mokichi, "Misujimachi kaiwai," in *Saitō Mokichi zenshū*, 6:432 (hereafter referred to as *SMZ*); Shibōta, *Mokichi den*, p. 13.
4. *Nenjushū*, *SMZ* 5:195.
5. *Ibid.*, pp. 202–3.
6. Makabe, *Ningen Mokichi*, pp. 9, 23; Shibōta, *Mokichi den*, p. 19.
7. *Shakkō*, *SMZ* 1:112–13.
8. Amy Vladeck Heinrich, " 'My Mother is Dying': Saitō Mokichi's 'Shinitamau haha'," pp. 435–36.
9. Satō Satarō, *Mokichi shūka*, 1:4–5; Fujioka Takeo, *Saitō Mokichi to sono shūhen*, p. 25.
10. Makabe, *Ningen Mokichi*, p. 8; Shibōta, *Mokichi den*, p. 20.
11. *Nenjushū*, *SMZ* 5:220–22.
12. Mokichi read some of his grandfather's tanka as an adult, and was not impressed. Saitō Shigeta and Kita Morio, *Kono chichi ni shite*, p. 89; Fujioka, *Shūhen*, p. 12; Shibōta, *Mokichi den*, p. 16.
13. Takahashi Shirōhē, "Ani no shōnen jidai sono hoka," p. 13.
14. "Yamako," *SMZ* 5:681.
15. Fujioka Takeo, *Saitō Mokichi: hito to bungaku*, pp. 12–13.
16. See, for example, the fictionalized life of the Saitō family by Mokichi's son Kita Morio, in which this custom is described. *Nireke no hitobito*, p. 47.

17. Shibōta, *Mokichi den,* p. 25.
18. "Misujimachi kaiwai," *SMZ* 6:432–34.
19. *Ibid.,* p. 431.
20. *Ibid.,* p. 170.
21. Shibōta, *Mokichi den,* pp. 33, 36, 38–40; Motobayashi Katsuo, *Saitō Mokichi: kindai tanka—hito to sakuhin,* 8:30.
22. "Watakushi no komatta gakka," *SMZ* 7:256–59; see also Suida Junsuke, "Chūgaku jidai no Mokichi-kun, sono hoka," pp. 17–21, and Uchida Yōji, "Chūgaku jidai no Mokichi-san," p. 17; Shibōta, *Mokichi den,* pp. 40–43.
23. Katō Yoshiko, *Saitō Mokichi to igaku,* p. 35; Shibōta, *Mokichi den,* p. 47; Motobayashi, *Hito to sakuhin,* p. 39; Fujioka, *Saitō Mokichi,* pp. 15–16.
24. Takano Rokurō, "Ichikōsai jidai no Mokichi," and Maeda Tamon, "Ichikō jidai no Mokichi," pp. 21–23; Saitō Mokichi, "Daiichi Kōtō Gakkō omoide danpen," *SMZ* 5:246–57.
25. "Omoidasu kotodomo," *SMZ* 5:27–28; cited by Fujioka, *Shūhen,* p. 10; Motobayashi, *Hito to sakuhin,* pp. 44–45; and others.
26. Fujioka, *Shūhen,* p. 13.
27. Janine Beichman, "Masaoka Shiki: His Life and Works," pp. 141–61; see also Robert H. Brower, "Masaoka Shiki and Tanka Reform," pp. 379–418.
28. "Bungaku no shi—igaku no shi," *SMZ* 7:316–17.
29. Fujioka, *Shūhen,* pp. 17–18; Saitō Mokichi, "Sakka keiko no omoide," *SMZ* 11:679.
30. *Sakka yonjūnen, SMZ* 10:381–82.
31. Fujioka, *Shūhen,* pp. 20–23.
32. "Omoidasu kotodomo," *SMZ* 5:29; "Bungaku no shi," *SMZ* 7:317–18.
33. "Omoidasu kotodomo," *SMZ* 5:30–31.
34. *Ibid.,* p. 31.
35. "Bungaku no shi," *SMZ* 7:320.
36. *Ibid.,* pp. 320–21.
37. Kajiki Gō, *Zōho Saitō Mokichi,* pp. 40–42.
38. Shibōta, *Mokichi den,* pp. 26–27, 30–31.
39. Saitō Shigeta, *Seishinkai sandai,* pp. 9, 34–37.
40. *Ibid.,* pp. 20–31, 35–36; Katō, *Igaku,* pp. 34–35.
41. Saitō Shigeta, *Sandai,* pp. 9–10, 38–40.
42. *Ibid.,* pp. 46, 51.
43. *Ibid.,* pp. 47, 58–62; Shibōta, *Mokichi den,* p. 32; Motobayashi, *Hito to sakuhin,* pp. 41–42.
44. "Bungaku no shi," *SMZ* 7:322.
45. "Omoidasu kotodomo," *SMZ* 5:36–38.
46. *Ibid.,* p. 39.
47. Saitō Shigeta, *Sandai,* pp. 71–72; Katō, *Igaku,* pp. 3, 14–17.
48. Shimoda Kōzō, "Sugamo ikyoku jidai," p. 27.
49. *Ibid.*
50. A full translation of the sequence appears in appendix 2; there is also a translation by Hiroaki Sato, entitled "Mother Dies," in Sato and Burton Watson, *From the Country of Eight Islands: An Anthology of Japanese Poetry,* pp. 456–61.
51. "Omoidasu kotodomo," *SMZ* 5:36–37.
52. "Inochi no araware," *Doba mango, SMZ* 9:10–11.
53. Kajiki, *Saitō Mokichi,* p. 49.

54. W. H. Auden, *Collected Poems*, ed. Edward Mendelson (New York: Random House, 1976), p. 146.

55. Kobori Keiichirō, meeting of Honyaku Kenkyūkai, Tokyo, January 8, 1979.

56. Fujioka, *Hito to sakuhin*, p. 176.

57. Katō, *Igaku*, pp. 6–10; Saitō Shigeta, *Sandai*, pp. 76–82; Shimoda, *Sugamo ikyoku jidai*, p. 27.

58. Fujioka, *Hito to sakuhin*, pp. 165, 167–72, 174–75.

59. Takahashi, "Ani," p. 15; Saitō and Kita, *Kono chichi*, p. 93.

60. Saitō Shigeta, *Sandai*, pp. 83–84.

2. NAGASAKI, EUROPE, AND RECONSTRUCTION, 1918–1927

1. Katō Yoshiko, *Saitō Mokichi to igaku*, pp. 20, 24.

2. Katagiri Akinori, *Saitō Mokichi: hito to sakuhin*, p. 62; Katō, *Igaku*, pp. 32–33.

3. Yamagami Jirō, *Saitō Mokichi no shōgai*, pp. 214–15.

4. *SMZ* 33:334, letter dated September 20, 1918; cited by Katō, *Igaku*, p. 21.

5. Saitō Shigeta, *Sandai*, p. 86; Katō, *Igaku*, pp. 22–23.

6. Katō, *Igaku*, p. 32.

7. Saitō Shigeta, *Sandai*, p. 86; Yamagami, *Shōgai*, pp. 216–22.

8. Yamagami Jirō, *Saitō Mokichi no koi to uta*, p. 155; Saitō Shigeta and Kita Morio, *Kono chichi ni shite*, p. 24.

9. Kita, *Nireke no hitobito*, p. 76.

10. "Tanka ni okeru shasei no setsu," *SMZ* 9:828; Yamagami, *Shōgai*, p. 230.

11. "Shasei no setsu," *SMZ* 9:802.

12. Cited in *ibid.*, pp. 779–81.

13. *Ibid.*, p. 804.

14. *Doba mango*, *SMZ* 9:212–14.

15. "Shasei no setsu," *SMZ* 9:822.

16. *Ibid.*, pp. 819–21. See Janine Beichman, "Masaoka Shiki: His Life and Works," pp. 163–72, for a fuller analysis of this poem and the context in which it appears.

17. "Shasei no setsu," *SMZ* 9:822.

18. *Ibid.*, p. 814.

19. *Ibid.*, p. 815. Mokichi does not give the source for his quotation from Rodin; however, similar views on sketching from life can be found in Anthony M. Ludovici, *Personal Reminiscences of Auguste Rodin*, pp. 138–39, and Paul Gsell, *Rodin on Art*, pp. 33–34.

20. "Shasei no setsu," *SMZ* 9:818.

21. Emily Dickinson, *The Complete Poems*, ed. Thomas H. Johnson, poem no. 448, p. 215.

22. Satō Satarō, *Mokichi shūka*, 1:65.

23. Yamagami, *Shōgai*, p. 239. See appendix 3 for the dates of composition and publication of Mokichi's seventeen volumes of poetry.

24. *Ibid.*, pp. 233–37.

25. "Hakushū-kun," *SMZ* 5:18; cited in Yamagami, *Shōgai*, pp. 337–38.

26. Saitō Shigeta, *Sandai*, p. 98.

27. Katō, *Igaku*, pp. 64–65.

28. Yamagami, *Shōgai*, pp. 246–47, 267.

29. *SMZ* 33:462.
30. *SMZ* 24:3–184 (German text).
31. Saitō Shigeta, *Mokichi no taishū*, p. 288; Uchimura Sukeyuki, "Kagakusha to shite no Mokichi," pp. 43–45; Katō, *Igaku*, pp. 49–63.
32. See *SMZ* 24:185–252 for these papers.
33. Katō, *Igaku*, pp. 40–46.
34. "Obersteiner sensei," *SMZ* 5:579.
35. *Ibid.*, pp. 577–78.
36. *SMZ* 1:559.
37. Nakamura Minoru, "Zai-Ō zuihitsu no miroku," pp. 1–4.
38. Katō, *Igaku*, pp. 50, 74, 88; "Obersteiner sensei," *SMZ* 5:568.
39. Franz G. Alexander and Sheldon T. Selesnick, *The History of Psychiatry: An Evaluation of Psychiatric Thought and Practice from Prehistoric Times to the Present*, p. 164.
40. "Sigmund Freud," *SMZ* 6:863–64.
41. Saitō Shigeta, *Sandai*, p. 101.
42. "Nankinmushi nikki," *SMZ* 5:790.
43. Yamagami, *Shōgai*, pp. 269–79; Katō, *Igaku*, p. 56; *SMZ* 33:520.
44. *SMZ* 5:195–96.
45. "Nihon daijishin," *SMZ* 5:797.
46. *Ibid.*, p. 800.
47. *Ibid.*, p. 801.
48. Saitō Shigeta, *Sandai*, pp. 106–7.
49. Yamagami, *Shōgai*, pp. 263–64.
50. Saitō Shigeta, *Sandai*, pp. 103–4; Katō, *Igaku*, pp. 103–4.
51. "Emil Kraepelin," *SMZ* 5:331–32.
52. *Ibid.*, pp. 332–37.
53. Katō, *Igaku*, pp. 105–8; Yamagami, *Shōgai*, p. 256.
54. "Uma," *SMZ* 5:868–70.
55. Uchimura, "Kagakusha," pp. 45–46; Saitō Shigeta, *Taishū*, p. 289.
56. "Araragi hyōshiga kaisetsu," *SMZ* 24:369, 385.
57. Katagiri, *Hito to sakuhin*, p. 80; Saitō and Kita, *Kono chichi*, pp. 34–35.
58. Saitō Shigeta, *Sandai*, pp. 118–22.
59. *SMZ* 29:67.
60. Saitō and Kita, *Kono chichi*, pp. 51–53, 56.
61. *SMZ* 29:248–49.
62. "Obersteiner sensei," *SMZ* 5:601.
63. Saitō Shigeta, *Taishū*, p. 299.
64. *SMZ* 11:754.
65. *Ibid.*; Satō, *Kaisetsu*, pp. 51–52.
66. *SMZ* 2:148, 143.
67. Fujioka, *Hito to bungaku*, p. 187.
68. Satō, *Shūka*, 1:197.
69. *Ibid.*, pp. 108–9.
70. Katō, *Igaku*, pp. 146–47.
71. Katō, *Igaku*, pp. 156–68; Saitō Shigeta, *Sandai*, pp. 130–31.

3. SEPARATION, THE WAR YEARS, AND THE FINAL YEARS, 1928–1953

1. Katagiri Akinori, *Saitō Mokichi: hito to sakuhin*, pp. 87–88, 92; Yamagami Jirō, *Saitō Mokichi no shōgai*, pp. 337–45, 347–48.
2. *SMZ* 10:567.
3. Okai Takashi, *Mokichi no uta: shiki*, pp. 19–20.
4. Satō Satarō, *Mokichi shūka*, 1:183.
5. Kenneth Burke, "On Musicality in Verse," p. 12.
6. *Sakka yonjūnen*, *SMZ* 10:673.
7. "Goki" to *Shiromomo*, *SMZ* 2:645.
8. Fujioka Takeo, *Saitō Mokichi: hito to bungaku*, pp. 65–69; Yamagami Jirō, *Saitō Mokichi no koi to uta*, pp. 213–32.
9. Satō, *Shūka*, 2:39.
10. John Berryman, "Snow Line," no. 28, *Dream Songs*, p. 32.
11. Fujioka, *Hito to bungaku*, pp. 78–82; Yamagami, *Shōgai*, pp. 399–404.
12. Fujioka, *Hito to bungaku*, pp. 69–72.
13. Makabe Jin, *Teihon ningen Mokichi*, p. 293.
14. *Ibid.*, pp. 233, 266–67.
15. Yamagami, *Koi*, pp. 339–47.
16. Nagai Fusako, "Saitō Mokichi: ai no shokan," pp. 180–91.
17. Makabe, *Ningen Mokichi*, p. 234.
18. Saitō Shigeta and Kita Morio, *Kono chichi ni shite*, pp. 127, 102–3, 144.
19. Fujioka, *Hito to bungaku*, pp. 209–10.
20. Kajiki Gō, *Zōho Saitō Mokichi*, p. 30.
21. "Yunifōmuteki uta," *Doba sanbō yawa*, *SMZ* 8:744.
22. Yamagami, *Shōgai*, pp. 445–57.
23. Donald Keene, "Japanese Writers and the Greater East Asian War," in *Landscapes and Portraits: Appreciations of Japanese Culture*, p. 302.
24. Margaret Benton Fukasawa, "Kitahara Hakushū: His Life and Poetry," pp. 263–64.
25. Saitō and Kita, *Kono chichi*, p. 102.
26. Yamagami, *Shōgai*, pp. 450–55; Ueda Miyoji, *Saitō Mokichi*, pp. 271, 279–81.
27. *Man'yōshū*, 3:235 (hereafter cited as *MYS*); translation from Ian Hideo Levy, *The Ten Thousand Leaves: A Translation of the Man'yōshū, Japan's Premier Anthology of Classical Poetry*, 1:151. The Japanese text reads: "ōkimi wa / kami nishi maseba / amakumo no / Ikazuchi no ue ni / iori seru kamo."
28. The connection between the poems is made by Yamagami, *Shōgai*, pp. 454–55.
29. Ueda, *Saitō Mokichi*, pp. 260–61, 268, 283–84.
30. Yamagami, *Shōgai*, p. 451.
31. *Sakka yonjūnen*, *SMZ* 10:756.
32. *Doba mango*, *SMZ* 9:5.
33. Ueda, *Saitō Mokichi*, p. 288.
34. Saitō Shigeta, *Seishinkai sandai*, pp. 147–54.
35. *Ibid.*, pp. 163–64.
36. Saitō Nao, "Shōjidai no ani; Kanakame sokai tōji no koto," p. 16.
37. Satō, *Shūka*, 2:113; Katagiri, *Hito to sakuhin*, pp. 124–25.
38. Ueda Miyoji, "Shirokiyama no Mokichi," pp. 200, 207.

39. Satō, *Shūka*, 2:125.
40. *Ibid.*, p. 122.
41. Ueda, *"Shirokiyama,"* p. 202.
42. Itagaki Kaneo, "Mokichi gagyō yowa," p. 13.
43. Saitō and Kita, *Kono chichi*, p. 130; Satō Satarō, *Mokichi kaisetsu*, p. 75. See also chapters 1 and 2 above.
44. Katō Tōryō, "Mokichi sensei no e ni tsuite," pp. 7–9; Saitō Shigeta, "Chichi no e," p. 18.
45. Itagaki, pp. 11–12.
46. Katō Tōryō, "Mokichi no e," p. 10; Itagaki, "Gagyō yowa," p. 11. A limited edition of the book contains the same text as the general edition, but full-color, rather than monochromatic, reproductions of all the paintings.
47. See especially plates 58–67, *Saitō Mokichi zengashū*. Excerpts from Mokichi's diaries (pp. 20–23) aid in dating the works.
48. Ueda, *"Shirokiyama,"* pp. 204–7.
49. Saitō Shigeta, *Sandai*, pp. 170–71; Saitō and Kita, *Kono chichi*, pp. 64–65.
50. Saitō and Kita, *Kono chichi*, pp. 171–72.
51. Saitō Shitega, *Mokichi no taishū*, pp. 120–22.
52. Saitō and Kita, *Kono chichi*, p. 165.

4. TANKA

1. "Shi sono hoka" and "Haiku," *SMZ* 24:451–74, 437–38.
2. "Bussokusekitai," *Doba mango*, *SMZ* 9:109–10.
3. Kajiki Gō, *Zōho Saitō Mokichi*, pp. 22–23.
4. Margaret Benton Fukasawa, "Kitahara Hakushū: His Life and Poetry," p. 97. Fukasawa is citing Hakushū's *Kiri no hana to kasutera*.
5. Okai Takashi, *Mokichi no uta: shiki*, p. 273.
6. *Man'yō tanka seichō ron*, *SMZ* 13:302; *Tanka seichō ron*, *SMZ* 13:123–38.
7. Okai, *Uta*, p. 273.
8. Satō Satarō, *Mokichi shūka*, 2:59.
9. This analysis is based on the much more detailed study of this poem in Okai, *Uta*, pp. 174–90.
10. "Tanka seichō ron," *SMZ* 13:149.
11. Tsukamoto Kunio, *Mokichi shūka: "Shakkō" hyakushu*, p. 161.
12. See *SMZ* 1:72, 151.
13. *SMZ* 10:459.
14. *SMZ* 2:162–70.
15. *SMZ* 2:225.
16. "Tanka no keishiki. Hachō no setsu," *Doba mango*, *SMZ* 9:74–75: Satō, *Shūka*, 1:149–52.
17. Johann Wolfgang Goethe, *Faust: Part Two*, Philip Wayne, trans., pp. 140, 128–29.
18. Mori Rintarō [Ōgai], *Fausto dainibu*, p. 469; the translation was first published in 1912.
19. Akutagawa Ryūnosuke, "Hekiken," pp. 254–55.
20. Kajiki, *Saitō Mokichi*, p. 18.
21. "Tanka seichō ron," *SMZ* 13:183.

22. Kajiki, *Saitō Mokichi*, pp. 19–20.
23. Donald Keene, *Anthology of Japanese Literature*, p. 196.
24. " 'Inochi narikeri' to iu kekku," *Doba mango, SMZ* 9:79.
25. See also "Sachio-sensei no koto," *SMZ* 5:4–5; Akutagawa, "Hekiken," p. 260.
26. Kajiki, *Saitō Mokichi*, pp. 13, 24.
27. Satō, *Shūka*, 2:49.
28. *Sakka yonjūnen, SMZ* 10:725.
29. Sasaki Yukitsuna, "Kajin Saitō Mokichi no kanjō," pp. 30–33.
30. Satō, *Shūka*, 2:11.
31. "Tanka seichō ron," *SMZ* 13:155.
32. Satō Satarō, *Saitō Mokichi kenkyū*, p. 198; Gomi Yasuyoshi, "Saitō Mokichi to *Man'yōshū*," pp. 8–11.
33. *SMZ* 22:40.
34. "Tanka seichō ron," *SMZ* 13:185.
35. Satō, *Kenkyū*, pp. 199–202; Hirano Jinkei, *Shiki to Mokichi*, pp. 243–48; Saitō Mokichi, "Kogo no mondai," *Doba mango, SMZ* 9:65.
36. Umehara Takeshi, "Saitō Mokichi ni okeru dentō," pp. 15–20.
37. "Uta kotoba," *Doba mango, SMZ* 9:29–30.
38. *Tanka shōgakumon, SMZ* 10:243.
39. Satō, *Shūka*, 1:134–35.
40. *Tanka shōgakumon, SMZ* 10:239; "Tanka seichō ron," *SMZ* 13:239.
41. For a more detailed discussion of "Shinitamau haha" see Amy Vladeck Heinrich, " 'My Mother is Dying': Saitō Mokichi's *'Shinitamau haha'*," pp. 424–39.
42. "Kogo no mondai," *Doba mango, SMZ* 9:65.
43. "Tanka no keishiki," *Doba mango, SMZ* 9:12.
44. *Tanka shōgakumon, SMZ* 10:239.
45. "Tanka seichō ron," *SMZ* 13:151–52.
46. Satō, *Kaisetsu*, p. 38.
47. I am following the commentary of Motobayashi Katsuo and Shibōta Minoru, *Saitō Mokichi shū*, p. 72.
48. Hirano, *Shiki to Mokichi*, pp. 249–50; Kajiki, *Saitō Mokichi*, p. 48.
49. "Sakka no taido," *Doba mango, SMZ* 9:27–28.
50. "Uta no keishiki to kaidan," *ibid.*, p. 53.
51. Robert H. Brower and Earl Miner, *Japanese Court Poetry*, p. 460.

5. THE POEM SEQUENCE "OHIRO"

1. "Tanka shōgen," *SMZ* 14:1000.
2. "Tanka rensaku ron no yurai," *SMZ* 11:189–297, relates the early development of the term. Hereafter the article will be referred to as "Rensaku ron."
3. See Janine Beichman, "Masaoka Shiki: His Life and Works," pp. 163–73, 200–2 for analyses of several of Shiki's rensaku.
4. "Rensaku ron," *SMZ* 11:197–98. Masaoka Shiki's article, "Byōshō kawa," appeared in *Kokoro no hana*, 5(7).
5. Itō Sachio's article also appeared in *Kokoro no hana*, 5(7), and is reprinted in *Itō Sachio zenshū*, 5:142–51. The important points are summarized in Mokichi, "Rensaku ron," *SMZ* 11:199–201.

6. Itō Sachio, "Futatabi uta no rensaku o ronzu," *Itō Sachio zenshū*, 5:144, 150. The three poems, *MYS* 3:446–48, were written in 730 by Ōtomo Tabito, and have been translated by Ian Hideo Levy in *The Ten Thousand Leaves*, 1:225–26.

7. See Edwin A. Cranston, "Five Poetic Sequences from the *Man'yōshū*," pp. 5–40; Roy Andrew Miller, *The Footprints of the Buddha*; and Konishi Jin'ichi, "Association and Progression: Principles of Integration in Anthologies and Sequences of Japanese Court Poetry, A.D. 900–1350," especially pp. 67–70, 110–11.

8. Robert H. Brower and Earl Miner, *Fujiwara Teika's Superior Poems of Our Time*, p. 30.

9. For a complete translation and discussion, see Robert H. Brower, *Fujiwara Teika's Hundred-Poem Sequence of the Shōji Era, 1200*.

10. See Konishi Jin'ichi, "The Art of Renga," pp. 27–61; and Earl Miner, *Japanese Linked Poetry*.

11. Konishi, "Association and Progression," p. 125.

12. Tsuchiya Bunmei, "Itō Sachio: rensaku ron o chūshin to shite," p. 18.

13. *Sakka yonjūnen*, *SMZ* 10:401–2.

14. For a full analysis, see Amy Vladeck Heinrich, " 'My Mother is Dying': Saitō Mokichi's *'Shinitamau haha'*," pp. 407–39.

15. Motobayashi Katsuo, *Saitō Mokichi ron*, pp. 120–21.

16. *Sakka yonjūnen*, *SMZ* 10:400.

17. For more detailed descriptions and applications of these terms, see Konishi, "Renga," pp. 51–52; Miner, *Japanese Linked Poetry*, pp. 72, 76; and Brower, *Teika's Hundred-Poem Sequence*, pp. 26–27.

18. Motobayashi, *Mokichi ron*, p. 121.

19. Tsukamoto Kunio, *Mokichi shūka: "Shakkō" hyakushu*, p. 100.

20. *Shinkokinshū*, 9:990. The interpretation is offered in Konishi, "Association and Progression," pp. 88–89, from which the translation is drawn.

21. Ueda Miyoji, *Saitō Mokichi*, p. 232.

22. Archibald MacLeish, *Poetry and Experience*, p. 62.

23. Tsukamoto, *"Shakkō" hyakushu*, p. 101.

24. *Ibid.*, p. 102; Motobayashi, *Mokichi ron*, p. 122.

25. *MYS* 9:2414, from the "Hitomaro Collection"; Motobayashi, *Mokichi ron*, p. 122.

26. Tsukamoto, *"Shakkō" hyakushu*, pp. 105, 109.

27. *Ibid.*, p. 108; Motobayashi Katsuo, *Saitō Mokichi*, p. 177n637.

28. To compare the two versions of "Ohiro," see Motobayashi Katsuo and Shibōta Minoru, *Saitō Mokichi shū*, pp. 68–74 or *SMZ* 1:134–38 for the original version, and Motobayashi, *Saitō Mokichi*, pp. 113–20 or *SMZ* 1:89–95 for the revision.

29. Most critics, in fact, use the original version, in spite of Mokichi's stated preference for the revised version. See the Afterword to the revised edition of *Shakkō*, in *SMZ* 1:115–16.

30. Motobayashi and Shibōta, *Mokichi shū*, p. 72n4, and p. 433n60.

31. The only other mention is the blue of lapis lazuli in poem 43. Tsukamoto, *"Shakkō" hyakushu*, p. 116.

32. Tsukamoto thinks they are misplaced, and should have been in part two; *"Shakkō" hyakushu*, pp. 111–12.

33. Konishi, "Association and Progression," pp. 74–77.

34. Okai Takashi, *Mokichi no uta: shiki*, p. 69.

35. Tsukamoto, *"Shakkō" hyakushu*, pp. 114–15.

36. George Eliot, *Adam Bede*, book 4, chapter 50, p. 460.

37. For reviews of various theories about the identity of Ohiro, see, for example, Ueda, *Saitō Mokichi*, pp. 229–34; and Fujioka Takeo, "Mokichi to joseitachi," 10:73–74; and Fujioka, *Hito to bungaku*, p. 129.

38. Satō Satarō, *Mokichi shūka*, 1:23.

39. Kajiki Gō, *Zōho Saitō Mokichi*, pp. 56–70.

40. Motobayashi, *Mokichi ron*, pp. 121–22.

41. Ueda, *Saitō Mokichi*, pp. 231–32.

42. These translations follow the commentary in Motobayashi, *Saitō Mokichi*, pp. 256–57.

6. SUBJECTS AND IMAGES

1. Satō Satorō, *Mokichi shūka*, 1:7–8; see also Kajiki Gō, *Zōho Saitō Mokichi*, pp. 29–40, for an analysis of this poem.

2. *Doba sanbō yawa*, *SMZ* 8:149; see also Furukawa Tetsushi, *Saitō Mokichi*, p. 187.

3. See, for example, diary entries in *SMZ* 29:385, 440, 565.

4. Katō Yoshiko, *Saitō Mokichi to igaku*, p. 25.

5. Shibusawa Kimio, "Sensei no hongyō," p. 3.

6. *Sakka yonjūnen*, *SMZ* 10:395.

7. *Chijin no zuihitsu*, *SMZ* 6:471–75.

8. Saitō Shigeta, *Seishinkai sandai*, p. 66; Katō, *Igaku*, pp. 13, 159; Saitō Mokichi, "Fōbia terefonika," in *Chijin no zuihitsu*, *SMZ* 6:475–77.

9. "Shinnen," *SMZ* 7:775.

10. *Sakka yonjūnen*, *SMZ* 10:649.

11. Saitō Shigeta, *Sandai*, pp. 10–16.

12. Kure's "Seishinbyō no meigi ni tsukite" (Concerning the names of mental illnesses), appeared in *Shinkeigaku zasshi* (January 1909) 7(10). Katō, *Igaku*, p. 35. See also chapter 2, above.

13. Okai Takishi, *Mokichi no uta: shiki*, pp. 66–68.

14. Saitō Shigeta, *Sandai*, pp. 70–71, 141; Shibusawa, "Sensei no hongyō," pp. 2–3.

15. *Sakka yonjūnen*, *SMZ* 10:434.

16. "Shinnen," *SMZ* 7:776–77.

17. Saitō Shitega and Kita Morio, *Kono chichi ni shite*, pp. 133–34.

18. Satō, *Shūka*, 2:77; Motobayashi Katsuo, *Saitō Mokichi: kindai tanka—hito to sakuhin*, p. 283.

19. *Sakka yonjūnen*, *SMZ* 10:778.

20. Satō, *Shūka*, 2:102.

21. Satō Satarō, *Mokichi kaisetsu*, pp. 57–58, 70–74.

22. Satō, *Shūka*, 2:9.

23. Satō, *Shūka*, 2:116, and *Kaisetsu*, p. 29; Motobayashi Katsuo, *Saitō Mokichi: kindai tanka—hito to sakuhin*, p. 299 and *Saitō Mokichi*, p. 212n104; pp. 360–61n94, and p. 368n4, citing Itagaki, "Ōishida no Mokichi-sensei," *Gunzan*, September 1969.

24. Kubota Masafumi, *Gendai tanka no sekai*, pp. 130–34.

25. See chapter 4, above, and Kajiki, *Saitō Mokichi* pp. 10–11.

26. Akutagawa Ryūnosuke, "Hekiken," pp. 253–57.

27. Satō, *Kaisetsu*, p. 59.

28. "Shasei no setsu," *SMZ* 9:818.

Bibliography

Works by Saitō Mokichi cited in text

NOTE: The year in parentheses following the title indicates the year of original publication. *SMZ* refers to *Saitō Mokichi zenshū*.

Araragi hyōshiga kaisetsu アララギ表紙画解説. *SMZ* 24:369–435.
Aratama あらたま (1921). *SMZ* 1:209–328.
"Bungaku no shi—igaku no shi" 文学の師・医学の師 (1942). *SMZ* 6: 456–82.
"Chijin no zuihitsu" 癡人の随筆 (1937). *SMZ* 6:456–82.
"Daiichi Kōtō Gakkō omoide danpen" 第一高等学校思出断片. *SMZ* 5:246–57.
"Die Hirnkarte des Paralytikers: Studien uben das Wesen und die Ausbreitung des paralytischen Prozesses in der Hirnrunde" (1923). *SMZ* 24:3–184.
"Donau genryū yuki" ドナウ原流行 (1927). *SMZ* 5:260–96.
Doba mango 童馬漫語 (1919). *SMZ* 9:1–229.
  77 "Bussokusekitai" 佛足石体 (1919): 109–10.
   1 "Dokuei to taieika" 独詠と対詠歌 (1918): 5–7.
 135 "Hirafuku Hyakusui-shi" 平福百穂氏 (1918): 212–24.
  58 "'Inochi narikeri' to iu kekku" 『命なりけり』といふ結句 (1914): 78–81.
   4 "Inochi no araware" いのちのあらはれ (1911): 10–12.
  46 "Kogo no mondai" 古語の問題 (1915): 66.
  15 "Sakka no taido" 作歌の態度 (1912): 27–28.
   5 "Tanka no keishiki" 短歌の形式 (1911): 12.
  53 "Tanka no keishiki. Hachō no setsu" 短歌の形式.破調の説 (1914): 74–75.
  16 "Uta kotoba" 歌ことば (1912): 29–30.
  35 "Uta no keishiki to kadan" 歌の形式と歌壇 (1913): 52–54.
Doba sanbō yawa 童馬山房夜話 (1935–46). *SMZ* 8.
"Emil Kraepelin" エミール・クレペリン (1926). *SMZ* 5:331–42.
En'yū 遠遊 (1947). *SMZ* 1:455–560.

Gyōkō 暁紅 (1940). *SMZ* 2:649–795.

"Haiku" 俳句. *SMZ* 24:437–38.

"Hakushū-kun" 白秋君 (1919). *SMZ* 5:16–19.

Henreki 遍歴 (1948). *SMZ* 1:561–704.

Kan'un 寒雲 (1940). *SMZ* 3:1–174.

Man'yō tanka seichō ron 万葉短歌声調論 (1933). *SMZ* 13:301–75.

"Misujimachi kaiwai" 三筋町界隈 (1937). *SMZ* 6:430–55.

"Nagasaki tsuioku" 長崎追憶 (1928). *SMZ* 5:729–34.

Nenjushū 念珠集 (1925–26). *SMZ* 5:195–234.

"Nihon daijishin" 日本大地震 (1929). *SMZ* 5:796–807.

"Nihon ōna" 日本媼 (1929). *SMZ* 5:778–83.

Noboriji のぼり路 (1943). *SMZ* 3:175–290.

"Obersteiner sensei" オウベルシュタイネル先生 (1927). *SMZ* 5:565–601.

"Omoidasu kotodomo" 思出す事ども (1919). *SMZ* 5:20–44.

Renzan 連山 (1950). *SMZ* 2:231–334.

"Sachio-sensei no koto" 佐千夫先生のこと (1913). *SMZ* 5:2–5.

Saitō Mokichi zenshū 斎藤茂吉全集. 36 vols. Tokyo:Iwanami shoten, 1973–75.

"Sakka keiko no omoide" 作歌けい古の思出 (1920). *SMZ* 11:678–84.

Sakka yonjūnen 作歌四十年 (1942–44). *SMZ* 10:377–861.

Sekisen 石泉 (1950). *SMZ* 2:335–491.

"Seppun" 接吻 (1925). *SMZ* 5:130–43.

Shakkō 赤光 (1913. Rev. ed., 1921). *SMZ* 1:121–208; 1–120.

"Shi sono hoka" 詩その他. *SMZ* 24:451–74.

Shimo 霜 (1951). *SMZ* 3:291–424.

Shirokiyama 白き山 (1949). *SMZ* 3:547–672.

Shiromomo 白桃 (1942). *SMZ* 2:493–648.

Shōen 小園 (1949). *SMZ* 3:424–545.

"Sigmund Freud" シグムンド・フロイド. *SMZ* 6:863–64.

"Tanka ni okeru shasei no setsu" 短歌に於ける写生の説 (1920). *SMZ* 9:763–885.

"Tanka rensaku ron no yurai" 短歌連作論の由来 (1912; 1919). *SMZ* 11:189–207.

Tanka seichō ron 短歌声調論 (1932). *SMZ* 13:116–87.

Tanka shōgakumon 短歌初学門. *SMZ* 10:171–376.

"Tanka shōgen" 短歌小言 (1913). *SMZ* 14:998–1002.

Takahara 高原 (1950). *SMZ* 2:149–230.

Tomoshibi ともしび (1950). *SMZ* 2:1–148.

Tsukikage つきかげ (1954). *SMZ* 3:673–820.

Tsuyujimo つゆじも (1946). *SMZ* 1:329–454.

"Uma" 馬. *SMZ* 5:867–71.

"Watakushi no komatta gakka" 私の困つた学科 (1941). *SMZ* 7:256–59.
"Yamako" 山蚕 (1928). *SMZ* 5:678–82.

Japanese Sources

Akutagawa Ryūnosuke 芥川龍之介. "Hekiken" 僻見. *Akutagawa Ryūnosuke zenshū*. Vol. 6. Tokyo: Iwanami shoten, 1935. Pp. 251–302.

Araragi: Shakkō hihyōgo アララギ『赤光』批評号, (March–April 1915), 8 (3 and 4).

Araragi: Saitō Mokichi tsuioku gō アララギ斎藤茂吉追悼号. (October 1953).

Fujioka Takeo 藤岡武雄. *Hyōden Saitō Mokichi* 評伝斎藤茂吉. Tokyo: Ōfusha, 1972.

—— "Mokichi to joseitachi" 茂吉と女性たち, *Kokubungaku* (October 1972), 17(10):69–76.

—— *Saitō Mokichi: hito to bungaku* 斎藤茂吉人と文学. Tokyo: Ōfusha, 1976.

—— *Saitō Mokichi to sono shūhen* 斎藤茂吉とその週辺. Tokyo: Kiyomizu Kōbundō, 1975.

Furukawa Tetsushi 古川哲史. *Saitō Mokichi* 斎藤茂吉. Tokyo: Yūshindō, 1961.

Gendai tanka jiten 現代短歌辞典. *Tanka* magazine (September 1978).

Gomi Yasuyoshi 五味保義. "Saitō Mokichi to *Man'yōshū*" 斎藤茂吉と万葉集. *Saitō Mokichi zenshū geppo* (1975) 29:8–12.

Hirano Jinkei 平野仁啓. *Shiki to Mokichi* 子規と茂吉. Tokyo: Kyoiku shuppan sentā, 1976.

Itagaki Kaneo 板垣家子夫. "Mokichi gagyō yowa" 茂吉画業余話. In *Saitō Mokichi zengashū*. Tokyo: Chūō kōron bijutsu shuppan, 1969. Pp. 11–14.

Itō Sachio 伊藤左千夫. "Rensaku shumi ron" 連作趣味論. *Kokoro no hana*, 5(1).

—— "Futatabi uta no rensaku shumi o ronzu" 再び歌の連作趣味を論ず. In *Itō Sachio zenshū*. Tokyo: Iwanami shoten, 1929. 5:142–51.

Kajiki Gō 梶木剛. *Zōho Saitō Mokichi* 増補斎藤茂吉. Tokyo: Kinzan shuppan, 1977.

Katagiri Akinori 片桐顕智. *Saitō Mokichi: hito to sakuhin* 斎藤茂吉人と作品. Tokyo: Shimizu shoin, Century Books, 1967.

Katō Tōryō 加藤淘綾. "Mokichi sensei no e ni tsuite" 茂吉先生の画について. In *Saitō Mokichi zengashū*. Tokyo: Chūō kōron bijutsu shuppan, 1969. Pp. 7–10.

Katō Yoshiko 加藤淑子. *Saitō Mokichi to igaku* 斎藤茂吉と医学. Tokyo: Misuzu shōbō, 1978.

Keene, Donald. "Saitō Mokichi" 斎藤茂吉. *Nihon bungaku o yomu* 日本文学を読む. Tokyo: Shinchōsha, Shinchō sensho, 1977. Pp. 114–17.

Kimata Osamu 木俣修. *Man'yōshū: jidai to sakuhin* 万葉集―時代と作品. NHK Books, no. 49. Tokyo: Nihon Hōsō shuppan kyōkai, 1966.

Kita Morio 北杜夫. *Nireke no hitobito* 楡家の人びと. Tokyo: Shinchōsha, 1964.

Kokubungaku: kaishaku to kyōzai no kenkyū 国文学―解釈と教材の研究. *Tokushū: Saitō Mokichi* (August 1972), 17:10.

Kubota Masafumi 久保田正文. *Gendai tanka no sekai* 現代短歌の世界. Tokyo: Shinchōsha, Shinchō sensho, 1972.

Maeda Tamon 前田多門. "Ichikō jidai no Mokichi" 一高時代の茂吉. *Araragi* (October 1953), pp. 22–23.

Makabe Jin 真壁仁. *Teihon ningen Mokichi* 定本人間茂吉. Tokyo: Sanseidō, 1976.

Man'yōshū 万葉集. Kojima Noriyuki 小島憲之, Kinoshita Masatoshi 木下正俊, and Satake Akihiro 佐竹昭広, eds. Nihon koten bungaku zenshū, vols. 2–5. Tokyo: Shogakkan, 1971–1975.

Masaoka Shiki 正岡子規. "Byōshō kawa" 病床歌話. *Kokoro no hana* 5(7).

Matsui Toshihiko 松井利彦. *Masaoka Shiki shū* 正岡子規集. Nihon kindai bungaku gaikei, vol. 16. Tokyo: Kadokawa shoten, 1972.

Mori Rintarō [Ōgai] 森林太郎 [鴎外], trans. *Fausuto dainibu* ファウスト第二部. Tokyo: Iwanami bunkobun, Iwanami shoten, 1928.

Motobayashi Katsuo 本林勝夫. "Nimen no Mokichi: Saitō Mokichi ron e no ikkanten" 二面の茂吉：斎藤茂吉論への一視点. *Kokubungaku* 17(10):10–14.

—— *Saitō Mokichi* 斎藤茂吉. Kindai bungaku chūshaku taikei. Tokyo: Yūseidō, 1974.

—— *Saitō Mokichi: kindai tanka—hito to sakuhin* 斎藤茂吉：近代短歌人と作品. Tokyo: Ōfūsha, 1963.

—— *Saitō Mokichi ron* 斎藤茂吉論. Tokyo: Kadokawa shoten, 1971.

Motobayashi Katsuo 本林勝夫 and Shibōta Minoru 柴生田稔, eds. *Saitō Mokichi shū* 斎藤茂吉集. Nihon kindai bungaku taikei, vol. 46. Tokyo: Kadokawa shoten, 1970.

Nagai Fusako 永井ふさ子. "Saitō Mokichi: ai no shokan" 斎藤茂吉愛の書簡. *Shōsetsu chūō kōron* (November 1963), pp. 180–91.

Nakamura Minoru 中村稔. "Zai-Ō zuihitsu no miroku" 滞欧随筆の魅力. *Saitō Mokichi zenshū geppō* (1973), 6:1–4.

Nakano Shigeharu 中野重治. *Saitō Mokichi nōto* 斎藤茂吉ノート. Tokyo: Chikuma shobō, 1964.

Nihon Bungaku Kenkyū Shiryō Kankōkai 日本文学研究資料刊行会, eds.

Kindai tanka: Masaoka Shiki, Yosano Akiko, Saitō Mokichi, Kitahara Hakushū 近代短歌：正岡子規・与謝野晶子・斎藤茂吉・北原白秋 . Tokyo: Yūseidō, 1972.

Odagiri Hideo 小田切秀雄 . *Man'yō no dentō* 万葉の伝統 . Tokyo: Kōzōsha, 1968.

Okai Takashi 岡井隆 . *Mokichi no uta: shiki* 茂吉の歌私記 . Tokyo: Sōbokusha, 1973.

Saitō Nao 斎藤なを . "Shōnenji no ani; Kanakame sokai tōji no koto" 少年時の兄・金瓶疎開当時のこと . *Araragi* (October 1953), pp. 16–17.

Saitō Shigeta 斎藤茂太 . "Chichi no e" 父の絵 . *Saitō Mokichi zengashū*. Tokyo: Chūō kōron bijutsu shuppan, 1969.

—— *Mokichi no shūhen* 茂吉の周辺 . Tokyo: Mainichi shinbunsha, 1973.

—— *Mokichi no taishū* 茂吉の体臭 . Tokyo: Iwanami shoten, 1964.

—— *Seishinkai sandai* 精神科医三代 . Tokyo: Chūō kōron, Chūkō shinsho, 1971.

——, ed. *Saitō Mokichi zengashū* 斎藤茂吉全画集 . Tokyo: Chūō kōron bijutsu shuppan, 1969.

Saitō Shigeta 斎藤茂太 and Kita Morio 北杜夫 . *Kono chichi ni shite* この父にして . Kuwabara Ryūjiro 桑原隆次郎 , ed. Tokyo: Mainichi shinbunsha, 1975.

—— "Chichi Mokichi o kataru" 父茂吉を語る . Edited by Yamashita Hidenosuke 山下秀之助 . *Kokubungaku*, 17(10):78–94.

Sasaki Yukitsuna 佐佐木幸綱 . "Kajin Saitō Mokichi no kanjō" 歌人斎藤茂吉の感性 . *Kokubungaku*, 17(10):27–33.

Sato Sataro 佐藤佐太郎 . *Mokichi kaisetsu* 茂吉解説 . Tokyo: Yayoi shobō, 1977.

—— "Mokichi-sensei to e" 茂吉先生の絵 . *Saitō Mokichi zengashū*. Tokyo: Chūō kōron bijutsu shuppan, 1969. Pp. 15–17.

—— *Mokichi shūka* 茂吉秀歌 . 2 vols. Tokyo: Iwanami shinsho, Iwanami shoten, 1978.

—— *Saitō Mokichi kenkyū* 斎藤茂吉研究 . Tokyo: Saginomiya shobō, 1967.

Shibōta Minoru 柴生田稔 . *Saitō Mokichi den* 斎藤茂吉伝 . Tokyo: Shinchōsha, 1979.

Shibusawa Kimio 澁澤喜守雄 . "Sensei no hongyō" 先生の本業 . *Saitō Mokichi zenshū geppō* (1975), 28:1–4.

Shigematsu Yasuo 重松泰雄 . "Mokichi to kyōki" 茂吉と狂気 . *Kokubungaku*, 17(10):64–68.

Shimoda Kōzō 下田光造 . "Sugamo ikyoku jidai" 巣鴨医局時代 . *Araragi* (October 1953), pp. 26–28.

Suida Junsuke 吹田順助 . "Chūgaku jidai no Mokichi-kun, sono hoka"

中学時代の茂吉君、その他. *Araragi* (October 1953), pp. 17–21.

Suzuki Keizō 鈴木啓蔵. *Mokichi no ashiato* 茂吉の足あと. Tokyo: Tanka shinbunsha, 1974.

Takahashi Shirōhē 高橋四郎兵衛. "Ani no shōnen jidai sono hoka" 兄の少年時代其他. *Araragi* (October 1953), pp. 12–15.

Takano Rokurō 高原六郎. "Ichikōsei jidai no Mokichi" 一高生時代の茂吉. *Araragi* (October 1953), pp. 21–22.

Tanaka Takahisa 田中隆尚, Ōta Ichirō 太田一郎, and Nakamura Minoru 中村稔. *Saitō Mokichi no sekai* 斎藤茂吉の世界. Tokyo: Seidosha, 1981.

Tsuchiya Bunmei 土屋文明. "*Itō Sachio*: rensaku ron o chūshin to shite" 『伊藤佐千夫』連作論を中心として. *Tanka* (April 1958), pp. 8–19.

Tsukamoto Kunio 塚本邦雄. *Mokichi shūka: "Shakkō" hyakushu* 茂吉秀哥: 『赤光』百首. Tokyo: Bungei shūnju, 1977.

Uchida Yōji 内田祥三. "Chūgaku jidai no Mokichi-san" 中学時代の茂吉さん. *Araragi* (October 1953), p. 17.

Uchimura Sukeyuki 内村祐之. "Kagakusha to shite no Mokichi" 科学者としての茂吉. *Araragi* (October 1953), pp. 41–47.

Ueda Miyoji 上田三四二. *Saitō Mokichi* 斎藤茂吉. Tokyo: Chikuma shobō, 1964.

—— "*Shirokiyama* no Mokichi" 『白き山』の茂吉. In *Kindai tanka*. Edited by Nihon Bungaku Kenkyū Shiryō Kankōkai.

Umehara Takeshi 梅原猛. "Saitō Mokichi ni okeru dentō" 斎藤茂吉における伝統. *Kokubungaku*, 17(10):15–20.

Yamagami Jirō 山上次郎. *Saitō Mokichi no koi to uta* 斎藤茂吉の愛と歌. Tokyo: Shinkigensha, 1966.

—— *Saitō Mokichi no shōgai* 斎藤茂吉の生涯. Tokyo: Bungei shunjū, 1974.

Yokoto Seichi 横田正知. *Saitō Mokichi: Nihon bungaku arubamu* 斎藤茂吉: 日本文学アルバム. Tokyo: Chikuma shobō, 1961.

Yoshida Seiichi 吉田精一. "Saitō Mokichi no bungakushiteki igi" 斎藤茂吉の文学史的意義. In *Kindai tanka*. Edited by Nihon Bungaku Kenkyū Shiryō Kankōkai. Tokyo: Yūseidō, 1972. Pp. 134–39.

English Sources

Alexander, Franz G., and Sheldon T. Selesnick. *The History of Psychiatry: An Evaluation of Psychiatric Thought and Practice from Prehistoric Times to the Present*. New York: Harper & Row, 1966.

Beichman, Janine. "Masaoka Shiki: His Life and Works." Ph.D. dissertation, Columbia University, 1974.

Berryman, John. *Dream Songs*. New York: Farrar, Straus, 1964.

Borton, Hugh. *Japan's Modern Century: From Perry to 1970*. 2d ed. New York: Ronald Press, 1970.

Bownas, Geoffrey, and Anthony Thwaite. *The Penguin Book of Japanese Verse*. Middlesex, England: Penguin Books, 1964.

Brower, Robert H. *Fujiwara Teika's Hundred-Poem Sequence of the Shōji Era, 1200*. Monumenta Nipponica Monographs, no. 55. Tokyo: Sophia University Press, 1978.

—— "Masaoka Shiki and Tanka Reform." In *Tradition and Modernization in Japanese Culture*, edited by Donald H. Shively. Princeton, N.J.: Princeton University Press, 1971. Pp. 379–418.

Brower, Robert H. and Earl Miner. *Fujiwara Teika's Superior Poems of Our Time*. Stanford, Calif.: Stanford University Press, 1967.

—— *Japanese Court Poetry*. Stanford, Calif.: Stanford University Press, 1961.

Burke, Kenneth. "On Musicality in Verse." In *The Philosophy of Literary Form*. 1941. Reprint. Berkeley: University of California Press, 1973. Pp. 369–78.

Cranston, Edwin A. "Five Poetic Sequences from the *Man'yōshū*." *Journal of the Association of Teachers of Japanese* (April 1978) 13(1):5–40.

Dickinson, Emily. *The Complete Poems of Emily Dickinson*. Edited by Thomas H. Johnson. Boston: Little, Brown, 1960.

Eliot, George. *Adam Bede*. New York: Signet Classics, New American Library, 1981.

Fukasawa, Margaret Benton. "Kitahara Hakushū: His Life and Poetry." Ph.D. dissertation, Columbia University, 1977.

Goethe, Johann Wolfgang. *Faust: Part Two*. Translated by Philip Wayne. Middlesex, England: Penguin Books, 1959.

Goldstein, Sanford and Shinoda Seishi, trans. *Tangled Hair: Selected Tanka from "Midaregami" by Akiko Yosano*. Lafayette, Ind.: Purdue University Press, 1971.

Gsell, Paul. *Rodin on Art*. Translated by Romilly Fedden. Introduction by Richard Howard. 1912. Reprint. New York: Horizon Press, 1971.

Heinrich, Amy Vladeck. "'My Mother is Dying': Saitō Mokichi's '*Shinitamau haha*'," *Monumenta Nipponica* (Winter 1978) 33(4):407–39.

Keene, Donald. *Anthology of Japanese Literature*. New York: Grove Press, 1955.

—— *Modern Japanese Literature*. New York: Grove Press, 1956.

—— *The Japanese Discovery of Europe, 1720–1830*, 1952. Rev. ed. Stanford, Calif.: Stanford University Press, 1969.

—— *Landscapes and Portraits: Appreciations of Japanese Culture*. Tokyo and Palo Alto, Calif.: Kodansha International, 1971.

—— *World Within Walls: Japanese Literature of the Pre-Modern Era, 1600–1867*.

New York: Holt, Rinehart & Winston, 1976.

—— "The Barren Years: Japanese War Literature," *Monumenta Nipponica* (Spring 1978) 33(1):67–112.

Konishi Jin'ichi. "The Art of Renga." Translated by Karen Brazell and Lewis Cook. *The Journal of Japanese Studies* (Autumn 1975) 2(1):29–61.

—— "Association and Progression: Principles of Integration in Anthologies and Sequences of Japanese Court Poetry, A.D. 900–1350." Translated and adapted by Robert H. Brower and Earl Miner. *Harvard Journal of Asian Studies* (December 1958) 21:67–127.

Levy, Ian Hideo. *The Ten Thousand Leaves: A Translation of the Man'yōshū, Japan's Premier Anthology of Classical Poetry*. Vol. 1. Princeton, N.J.: Princeton University Press, 1981.

Lucorici, Anthony M. *Personal Reminiscences of Auguste Rodin*. Philadelphia: J. B. Lippincot, 1926.

MacLeish, Archibald. *Poetry and Experience*. Boston: Houghton Mifflin, Riverside Press, 1961.

Matsunaga Daigan and Alicia Matsunaga. *Foundations of Japanese Buddhism, Vol. II: The Mass Movement*. Los Angeles & Tokyo: Buddhist Books International, 1976.

Miller, Roy Andrew. *The Footprints of the Buddha: An Eighth-Century Old Japanese Poetic Sequence*. New Haven, Conn.: American Oriental Society, 1975.

Miner, Earl. "The Techniques of Japanese Poetry," *Hudson Review* (August 1955) 8:350–66.

—— *Japanese Linked Poetry: An Account with Translations of Renga and Haikai Sequences*. Princeton, N.J.: Princeton University Press, 1979.

—— *An Introduction to Japanese Court Poetry*. Stanford, Calif.: Stanford University Press, 1968.

Nippon Gakujutsu Shinkōkai, trans. and eds. *The Man'yōshū*. New York: Columbia University Press, 1965.

Rewald, John. *The History of Impressionism*. New York: Museum of Modern Art, 1961.

Sanders, Gerald DeWitt, John H. Nelson, M.L. Rosenthal, eds. *Chief Modern Poets of England and America, Vol. I: The British Poets*. New York: Macmillan, 1962.

Sato, Hiroaki and Burton Watson, trans. and eds. *From the Country of Eight Islands: An Anthology of Japanese Poetry*. Seattle: University of Washington Press, 1981.

Sesar, Carl, trans. *Takuboku: Poems to Eat*. Tokyo and Palo Alto, Calif.: Kodansha International, 1966.

Shiffert, Edith Marcombe and Sawa Yūki, trans. and comps. *Anthology of Japanese Poetry*. Tokyo: Charles E. Tuttle, 1972.

Smith, Barbara Herrnstein. *Poetic Closure: A Study of How Poems End*. Chicago & London: University of Chicago Press, 1968.

Index of First Lines

Index

Studies of the East Asian Institute

THE LADDER OF SUCCESS IN IMPERIAL CHINA, by Ping-ti Ho. New York: Columbia University Press, 1962.

THE CHINESE INFLATION, 1937–1949, by Shun-hsin Chou. New York: Columbia University Press, 1963.

REFORMER IN MODERN CHINA: CHANG CHIEN, 1853–1926, by Samuel Chu. New York: Columbia University Press, 1965.

RESEARCH IN JAPANESE SOURCES: A GUIDE, by Herschel Webb with the assistance of Marleigh Ryan. New York: Columbia University Press, 1965.

SOCIETY AND EDUCATION IN JAPAN, by Herbert Passin. New York: Teachers College Press, Columbia University, 1965.

AGRICULTURAL PRODUCTION AND ECONOMIC DEVELOPMENT IN JAPAN, 1873–1922, by James I. Nakamura. Princeton: Princeton University Press, 1966.

JAPAN'S FIRST MODERN NOVEL: UKIGUMO OF FUTABATEI SHIMEI, by Marleigh Ryan. New York: Columbia University Press, 1967. Also in paperback.

THE KOREAN COMMUNIST MOVEMENT, 1918–1948, by Dae-Sook Suh. Princeton: Princeton University Press, 1967.

THE FIRST VIETNAM CRISIS, by Melvin Gurtov. New York: Columbia University Press, 1967. Also in paperback.

CADRES, BUREAUCRACY, AND POLITICAL POWER IN COMMUNIST CHINA, by A. Doak Barnett. New York: Columbia University Press, 1967.

THE JAPANESE IMPERIAL INSTITUTION IN THE TOKUGAWA PERIOD, by Herschel Webb. New York, Columbia University Press, 1968.

HIGHER EDUCATION AND BUSINESS RECRUITMENT IN JAPAN, by Koya Azumi. New York: Teachers College Press, Columbia University, 1969.

THE COMMUNISTS AND CHINESE PEASANT REBELLIONS: A

STUDY IN THE REWRITING OF CHINESE HISTORY, by James P. Harrison, Jr. New York: Atheneum, 1969.

HOW THE CONSERVATIVES RULE JAPAN, by Nathaniel B. Thayer. Princeton: Princeton University Press, 1969.

ASPECTS OF CHINESE EDUCATION, edited by C. T. Hu. New York: Teachers College Press, Columbia University, 1969.

DOCUMENTS OF KOREAN COMMUNISM, 1918–1948, by Dae-Sook Suh. Princeton: Princeton University Press, 1970.

JAPANESE EDUCATION: A BIBLIOGRAPHY OF MATERIALS IN THE ENGLISH LANGUAGE, by Herbert Passin. New York: Teachers College Press, Columbia University, 1970.

ECONOMIC DEVELOPMENT AND THE LABOR MARKET IN JAPAN, by Kōji Taira. New York: Columbia University Press, 1970.

THE JAPANESE OLIGARCHY AND THE RUSSO-JAPANESE WAR, by Shumpei Okamoto. New York: Columbia University Press, 1970.

IMPERIAL RESTORATION IN MEDIEVAL JAPAN, by H. Paul Varley. New York: Columbia University Press, 1971.

JAPAN'S POSTWAR DEFENSE POLICY, 1947–1968, by Martin E. Weinstein. New York: Columbia University Press, 1971.

ELECTION CAMPAIGNING JAPANESE STYLE, by Gerald L. Curtis. New York: Columbia University Press, 1971.

CHINA AND RUSSIA: THE "GREAT GAME," by O. Edmund Clubb. New York: Columbia University Press, 1971. Also in paperback.

MONEY AND MONETARY POLICY IN COMMUNIST CHINA, by Katherine Huang Hsiao. New York: Columbia University Press, 1971.

THE DISTRICT MAGISTRATE IN LATE IMPERIAL CHINA, by John R. Watt. New York: Columbia University Press, 1972.

LAW AND POLICY IN CHINA'S FOREIGN RELATIONS: A STUDY OF ATTITUDES AND PRACTICE, by James C. Hsiung. New York: Columbia University Press, 1972.

PEARL HARBOR AS HISTORY: JAPANESE-AMERICAN RELATIONS, 1931–1941, edited by Dorothy Borg and Shumpei Okamoto, with the assistance of Dale K. A. Finlayson. New York: Columbia University Press, 1973.

JAPANESE CULTURE: A SHORT HISTORY, by H. Paul Varley. New York: Praeger, 1973.

DOCTORS IN POLITICS: THE POLITICAL LIFE OF THE JAPAN MEDICAL ASSOCIATION, by William E. Steslicke. New York: Praeger, 1973.

JAPAN'S FOREIGN POLICY, 1868–1941: A RESEARCH GUIDE, edited by James William Morley. New York: Columbia University Press, 1973.

THE JAPAN TEACHERS UNION: A RADICAL INTEREST GROUP IN JAPANESE POLITICS, by Donald Ray Thurston. Princeton University Press, 1973.

PALACE AND POLITICS IN PREWAR JAPAN, by David Anson Titus. New York: Columbia University Press, 1974.

THE IDEA OF CHINA: ESSAYS IN GEOGRAPHIC MYTH AND THE-
ORY, by Andrew March. Devon, England: David and Charles, 1974.

ORIGINS OF THE CULTURAL REVOLUTION, by Roderick Mac-
Farquhar. New York: Columbia University Press, 1974.

SHIBA KŌKAN: ARTIST, INNOVATOR, AND PIONEER IN THE
WESTERNIZATION OF JAPAN, by Calvin L. French. Tokyo: Weather-
hill, 1974.

EMBASSY AT WAR, by Harold Joyce Noble. Edited with an introduction by
Frank Baldwin, Jr. Seattle: University of Washington Press, 1975.

REBELS AND BUREAUCRATS: CHINA'S DECEMBER 9ERS, by John
Israel and Donald W. Klein. Berkeley: University of California Press, 1975.

HOUSE UNITED, HOUSE DIVIDED: THE CHINESE FAMILY IN TAI-
WAN, by Myron L. Cohen. New York: Columbia University Press, 1976.

INSEI: ABDICATED SOVEREIGNS IN THE POLITICS OF LATE HEIAN
JAPAN, by G. Cameron Hurst. New York: Columbia University Press, 1976.

DETERRENT DIPLOMACY, edited by James William Morley. New York:
Columbia University Press, 1976.

CADRES, COMMANDERS AND COMMISSARS: THE TRAINING OF
THE CHINESE COMMUNIST LEADERSHIP, 1920–45, by Jane L. Price.
Boulder, Colo.: Westview Press, 1976.

SUN YAT-SEN: FRUSTRATED PATRIOT, by C. Martin Wilbur. New
York: Columbia University Press, 1976.

JAPANESE INTERNATIONAL NEGOTIATING STYLE, by Michael Blaker.
New York: Columbia University Press, 1977.

CONTEMPORARY JAPANESE BUDGET POLITICS, by John Creighton
Campbell. Berkeley: University of California Press, 1977.

THE MEDIEVAL CHINESE OLIGARCHY, by David Johnson. Boulder,
Colo.: Westview Press, 1977.

ESCAPE FROM PREDICAMENT: NEO-CONFUCIANISM AND CHI-
NA'S EVOLVING POLITICAL CULTURE, by Thomas A. Metzger.
New York: Columbia University Press, 1977.

THE ARMS OF KIANGNAN: MODERNIZATION IN THE CHINESE
ORDNANCE INDUSTRY, 1860–1895, by Thomas L. Kennedy. Boulder,
Colo.: Westview Press, 1978.

PATTERNS OF JAPANESE POLICYMAKING: EXPERIENCES FROM
HIGHER EDUCATION, by T. J. Pempel. Boulder, Colo.: Westview Press,
1978.

THE CHINESE CONNECTION, by Warren Cohen. New York: Columbia
University Press, 1978.

MILITARISM IN MODERN CHINA: THE CAREER OF WU P'EIFU, 1916–
1939, by Odoric Y. K. Wou. Folkestone, England: Wm. Dawson & Sons,
1978.

A CHINESE PIONEER FAMILY, by Johanna Meskill. Princeton: Princeton
University Press, 1979.

PERSPECTIVES ON A CHANGING CHINA: ESSAYS IN HONOR OF PROFESSOR C. MARTIN WILBUR, edited by Joshua A. Fogel and William T. Rowe. Boulder, Colo.: Westview Press, 1979.

THE MEMOIRS OF LI TSUNG-JEN, by T. K. Tong and Li Tsu-ngjen. Boulder, Colo.: Westview Press, 1979.

UNWELCOME MUSE: CHINESE LITERATURE IN SHANGHAI AND PEKING, 1937–1945, by Edward Gunn. New York: Columbia University Press, 1979.

YENAN AND THE GREAT POWERS: THE ORIGINS OF CHINESE COMMUNIST FOREIGN POLICY, 1944–1946, by James Reardon-Anderson. New York: Columbia University Press, 1980.

UNCERTAIN YEARS: CHINESE-AMERICAN RELATIONS, 1947–1950, edited by Dorothy Borg and Waldo Heinrichs. New York: Columbia University Press, 1980.

THE FATEFUL CHOICE: JAPAN'S ADVANCE INTO SOUTHEAST ASIA, 1939–1941, edited by James W. Morley. New York: Columbia University Press, 1980.

TANAKA GIICHI AND JAPAN'S CHINA POLICY, by William F. Morton. Folkestone, England: Wm. Dawson & Sons, 1980.

THE ORIGINS OF THE KOREAN WAR: LIBERATION AND THE EMERGENCE OF SEPARATE REGIMES, 1945–1947, by Bruce Cumings. Princeton: Princeton University Press, 1981.

CLASS CONFLICT IN CHINESE SOCIALISM, by Richard Kurt Kraus. New York: Columbia University Press, 1981.

EDUCATION UNDER MAO: CLASS AND COMPETITION IN CANTON SCHOOLS, 1960–1980, by Jonathan Unger. New York: Columbia University Press, 1982.

THE CHINA QUAGMIRE, edited by James William Morley. New York: Columbia University Press, 1983.

FRAGMENTS OF RAINBOWS: THE LIFE AND POETRY OF SAITŌ MOKICHI, 1882–1953, by Amy Vladeck Heinrich. New York: Columbia University Press, 1983.